RISK AND THE STATE

RISK AND THE STATE

How Economics and Neuroscience Shape
Political Legitimacy to Address Geopolitical,
Environmental, and Health Risks
for Sustainable Governance

Phillip G. LeBel, Ph.D.

Universal-Publishers
Irvine • Boca Raton

Risk and the State:
How Economics and Neuroscience Shape Political Legitimacy to Address Geopolitical,
Environmental, and Health Risks for Sustainable Governance

BrownWalker Press / Universal Publishers, Inc.
Irvine • Boca Raton
USA • 2021
www.BrownWalkerPress.com

ISBN: 978-1-59942-610-5 (pbk.)
ISBN: 978-1-59942-611-2 (ebk.)

Typeset by Medlar Publishing Solutions Pvt Ltd, India
Cover design by Ivan Popov

Library of Congress Cataloging-in-Publication Data

Names: LeBel, Phillip G., author.
Title: Risk and the state : how economics and neuroscience shape political legitimacy
    to address geopolitical, environmental, and health risks for sustainable governance /
    Phillip G. LeBel, Ph.D.
Description: Irvine : Brown Walker Press, 2021. | Includes bibliographical references and
    index.
Identifiers: LCCN 2020056301 (print) | LCCN 2020056302 (ebook) |
    ISBN 9781599426105 (paperback) | ISBN 9781599426112 (ebook)
Subjects: LCSH: Economics--Political aspects. | Political science--Economic aspects. |
    Risk perception. | Social choice.
Classification: LCC HB74.P65 L43 2021 (print) | LCC HB74.P65 (ebook) |
    DDC 338.5--dc23
LC record available at https://lccn.loc.gov/2020056301
LC ebook record available at https://lccn.loc.gov/2020056302

For
Natasha, Melissa, Ethan, Aurelia,
and
Laurence

TABLE OF CONTENTS

LIST OF TABLES

LIST OF FIGURES

ACKNOWLEDGMENTS

The January 6, 2021 insurrectionist attack on the Capitol in Washington, D.C. by extremists seeking to overturn the results of the November 3, 2020 Presidential election serves as a reminder that democracy cannot be taken for granted. To maintain a durable democracy, we need not just transparent and inclusive institutions, but also a clear foundation on which principles of state and market relations can be sustained. Inasmuch as the U.S. Constitution set forth remarkable checks and balances, maintaining a democratic rule of law resides on a common understanding of the values by which we choose to live.

The ideas expressed here represent a distillation of a career in teaching, research, and consulting. With an initial focus on economics, my horizon expanded with the insights afforded by neuroscience as I tackled some classic questions in political economy. How we view and respond to various types of risk, and the mechanisms that drive our responses is how I have come to revisit the notion of political legitimacy.

I owe a debt of gratitude to students who in the first instance were engaged in these ideas. In addition, I have had numerous conversations with colleagues and friends over the years and whose ideas have helped me to refine how the various themes are interrelated. Among those who have either read or shared ideas as this project has evolved, I am pleased to acknowledge insights from: Dula Abdu, Tekie Alemu, Hubert Basehart, François Boye, Daniel Caraco, Magatte Diop, Harold Flint, Lawrence

Goldhirsch, Robert Hocutt, Chinappa Jayachandran, David B. Levine, Seddik Meziani, Paul Mifsud, Franck Schulders, Abdourahmane Thiam, Richard Vengroff, and the late Norman J. Singer, and Suresh Desai, among others. Needless to say, they are not responsible for any errors or views expressed here.

PREFACE

The theme of political legitimacy today is a subject of increasing interest by specialists in many countries. Research points to a number of unresolved issues that are evolving in a world in constant evolution for which the future is difficult to discern in an unequivocal and clear pattern.

Geopolitical analysis, which encompasses the question of political legitimacy, is drawing interest not just of economists, but also specialists in public international law and those involved in international business. We all face decisions that to varying degrees must be made on the basis of accurate and realistic forecasts, and in the presence of risk and uncertainty. Such forecasts must take into account the status of international relations involving both home-based norms as well as those of their international partners with whom trade and investment decisions are based.

As globalization expands the importance of international trade and investment, not only is there the need for local legislative conformity, but also whether such agreements reinforce or undermine domestic standards of governance. China's experience is instructive. Once an essentially closed communist regime, it began to open its borders to trade under Deng Xiaoping, and set in motion a path of rapid economic growth. While many thought economic prosperity would bring forth a genuinely open trading system and democratic reforms, this has not been the case. China's current mercantile practices seek to limit imports while promoting exports and imposing technology sharing agreements for those wishing to do business in the country.

In this context, the topic of political legitimacy, well formulated by Professor LeBel, can henceforth best be understood in reference to international economic relations. It is relevant, when in a world that sometimes remains mute, decisions by one country to address economic, social, political, and recently health crises inevitably affects the governance of other economies, whether they be client or exporting partners.

The evolution of global trading blocs today affects more countries than those making key governance decisions. Another example is the UK decision to pursue a Brexit strategy of withdrawing from the European Union. It affects not just the UK but the whole of the EU, and in which trade and investment may revert to historically more closed patterns of the past. It also is pertinent when one contemplates the outcome of the U.S. presidential election in terms of its relations with other major trading partners, with attendant consequences on Sino-global, East European, Latin American, and African relations as well.

Professor LeBel's approach to political legitimacy proceeds in the first instance on the basis of rationality in decision-making. He does so first in a world of perfect information, and then in the presence of risk and uncertainty. As such, he examines the key economic functions of the public sector as they pertain to the allocation and distribution of resources. These functions are equally relevant not just to satisfy a domestic norm but also at an international level.

The historical approach that the author uses clarifies across different time periods the extent to which the economic development of a country is linked to a particular conception of progress. Whether looking at Christopher Columbus or a post-colonial regime, differing notions of legitimacy are seen through differences in historical experience over time. The evolution of differing conceptions of international relations has affected the nature of enterprise organization as well as the various economic functions of the state. What provides continuity is the underlying notion of how to achieve both good political and economic governance.

In examining varying notions of political legitimacy, the author looks at contemporary relations as to whether a more, or less, intrusive form of government best serves the economic and social needs of society. Thus, in a world of increasing socio-economic interdependence, to what extent does a Chinese authoritarian, or a mixed European, or free market American system provides the optimal path of sustainable growth and governance. This is particularly relevant when taking into consideration income inequality, global warming, or the current COVID-19 pandemic.

As to whether one system of governance or another provides the best answer depends on the institutional legacy of a region as well as to whether a measure of global convergence and cooperation can best serve the world community. Professor LeBel's book is an important contribution in addressing the enduring question of political legitimacy as we look to the future.

Guy Schulders
Professor at Large
University of Paris I
Panthéon-Sorbonne

CHAPTER ONE

POLITICAL LEGITIMACY ON TRIAL

Why Political Legitimacy

Political legitimacy is a set of rules and conventions by which a population chooses or accepts to be governed. It differs from military conflicts where the setting of geographic boundaries is often decided. In the West, by which we can think of Western European nations and those in North America for the most part, political legitimacy has come to mean the emergence of democratically elected governments in which sovereignty vested in the population determines who shall govern. This said, it also in the West that political legitimacy is now on trial.

Democracy is often thought to be the logical successor to oligarchies and dictatorships. That notion, a product of the 18th century European Enlightenment, runs counter to historical experience. Ancient Greece and Rome each went through a period of republican government, only to fall to civil unrest and the emergence of dictatorships. France toppled its absolutist monarchy in 1789, and then went through a wave of regimes before settling on a more democratic system in the 20th century. The Weimar Republic, founded after the end of World War I, eventually succumbed to the rise of Nazi Germany under Adolf Hitler. What numerous examples point to is a simple observation: Democracy cannot be taken for granted, nor is it universally recognized as a superior form of government. The question is why should this be so and is it the foreordained path to the future?

The Enigma of Economic Prosperity and Political Nationalism

We live in an age of economic prosperity amidst rising protectionist nationalism. How can we explain the contradiction of growing economic prosperity alongside nationalist movements? Four considerations may helpful in understanding the nationalist reaction to globalization, even if they do not provide a ready justification nor a solution. They are: 1. The geographical and structural contours of states; 2. Rising economic inequality in an age of prosperity; 3. The gathering and dissemination of information relevant to decision-making; and 4. Perceptions of risk that shape the economic functions of the public sector. These considerations can be understood by looking first at the current state of governance in various regions.

It is paradoxical that authoritarian nationalist regimes should arise at a time when globalization has produced unparalleled increases in income and wealth. Real per capita incomes have grown substantially over the past 70 years with global life expectancy reaching never before attained levels.[1] Much of this wealth creation is a result of pro-growth and market-based policies through which international trade and investment have played a key role. Why, then, should we see the rise of nationalist authoritarian regimes at a time of economic prosperity?

One key to understanding the paradox of authoritarian nationalism amidst economic prosperity is in terms of how national identity and geographic frontiers are redefined through globalization. Borders of traditional nation-states coalesced historically along lines of ethnic, religious, or language and cultural traditions. In many cases, they emerged from empires founded in previous centuries in which conformity with narrow lines of identity often were less important that the commercial prosperity that an imperial regime used to justify its existence. In Europe, the British, French, Russian, and Ottoman empires were carved out of the conquest of trading routes, and then fell apart following the destruction wrought by World Wars I and II. What can be said is that the stronger the geographic border, the narrower is the definition of sovereignty, and thus, the narrower will be the range of civil and political rights for residents within such a country.

In the West, it was long thought that rising economic prosperity through multilateral trade and investment agreements would lead to the emergence of electoral democracy in authoritarian countries. This was clearly the case that emerged from the Second World War in which democratic governments took on and won against authoritarian regimes in Germany, Japan, and Italy. Those same democratic governments also embarked on a reconstruction of the global economy through a series of international agreements in support of international trade and investment, along with the creation of international security institutions to promote such cooperation. It was a remarkable transformation that, with some exceptions, produced both economic prosperity and the expansion of more inclusive democratic institutions.

Following the end of the Second World War, reconstruction in Europe first placed emphasis on the building of institutions that could provide a basis for sustained economic prosperity. On April 3, 1948, U.S. President Harry S. Truman signed the Economic Recovery Act, and which became known as the Marshall Plan, after the then U.S. Secretary of State George C. Marshall. It was a signal event that helped shape the future of Europe.

Under the Marshall Plan, the United States provided over U.S. $12 billion dollars in low cost loans and grants to West European countries, equivalent to almost $100 billion in 2018 dollars. This initiative was driven in part by the unfolding Cold War, which was first characterized by former British Prime Minister Winston Churchill as an Iron Curtain between Stalin's Soviet Russian occupation of Eastern Europe and the Allied countries in the West.[2]

George F. Kennan, Deputy Chief of the United States to the USSR from 1944 to 1946, wrote an article in *Foreign Affairs* in 1947 under the pseudonym "X", that would shape a U.S. Cold War strategy of containment of the Soviet Union rather than engage in a further direct military confrontation with an erstwhile World War II ally.[3] As a Cold War policy, containment largely succeeded, culminating with the fall of the Berlin Wall in 1989 and the formal dissolution of the Soviet Union in 1991.

Containment and the Marshall Plan reflected a key consequence of the Second World War. West European countries were essentially bankrupt, and could not rebuild quickly to restore confidence in their governments. In contrast, the United States emerged with the bulk of international financial reserves and a surplus balance of payments. Through bilateral policies of foreign aid and multilateral policies driven under the auspices of the newly created World Bank and the International Monetary Fund, the U.S. demonstrated considerable leverage in not just international economic growth, but also in how other countries might be amenable to adopting Western style models of governance. Democratic political legitimacy thus would be affirmed through a mix of economic and political reforms from which enduring prosperity could be realized. What were the aims that drove these decisions?

A major objective of every government is stability. In the first instance, this may mean simply political stability over time.[4] At the same time, it also may encompass economic stability, and, through time, economic growth in per capita income. What is not clear is what form of government best leads to economic stability and growth, especially in an age of globalization where national boundaries become increasingly fluid. If stability is a fundamental goal of governments, is it a single responsibility for one country such as the United States, or a global responsibility of one or more countries through such collective political institutions as NATO, the EU, or the UN? Political legitimacy thus depends on setting boundaries and jurisdictions of designated governmental authority.

Borders notwithstanding, achieving stability depends in part on how the exercise of governmental authority affects the level of individual political and economic rights. Put simply, when states exercise expansive authority over its citizens in the pursuit of political stability, individual freedom is reduced.[5] At some point this leads to rebellion and the overthrow of the state in search of a new political and social order. At the other extreme, where states exercise too little authority, anarchy could arise to a point where individual political and economic rights also are undermined. We thus face the challenge of how stability can be achieved while at the same time preserving individual liberty.

Visions of an Enlarged Political Union in Europe

Within Western Europe, while nation-states were still considered to be politically legitimate organizations, efforts were made in the postwar era to create a larger economic and political union. This was driven as much by a determination to avoid another war in Europe as it was in responding to Soviet expansion in Europe. It also was driven by the goal of creating an integrated economic region that could better compete in global markets.

In 1950, French Foreign Minister Robert Schuman proposed a regulatory mechanism to oversee coal and steel production in several European countries, notably, France, West Germany, Italy, the Netherlands, Luxembourg and Belgium. It was formally established by the Treaty of Paris signed in 1951. By establishing a multinational governing institution, the European Coal and Steel Community represented a first step in building a United States of Europe. While that has yet to be realized, European countries would go on to create intermediate building blocks, starting with the creation of the Common Market in 1957.

The Treaty of Rome in 1957 created the European Economic Community, or Common Market, across six European countries, namely, France, Germany, Italy, Belgium, Luxembourg, and the Netherlands. Building on the European Coal and Steel Community, it incorporated the European Atomic Energy Agency (EURATOM) and pledged to see a reduction of external tariffs among member states reduced to zero over a ten-year period.

Over the next several decades, the European Economic Community expanded from six countries to thirteen in 1993 when the European Union was created. At first, Great Britain and a number of Scandinavian countries resisted the idea of a supranational organization that could establish regulations over individual nation states. In 1957, the British sponsored the creation of the European Free Trade Association (EFTA), a looser confederation of countries devoted to expanding free trade while preserving greater sovereignty with individual states over matters of fiscal and monetary policy.

As the EEC began to expand, the British changed their position and applied for admission to the EEC in 1967. It first was rejected by French President Charles De Gaulle, but was later admitted in 1973. The agreement of 1973 allowed for England to retain control over its currency, as was the case with Scandinavian countries that had been part of EFTA, even as it accepted such rules as the Common Agricultural Policy that involved extensive agricultural subsidies.

A pivotal moment in the evolution of the Common Market came in 1992 with the Maastricht Treaty, which established the European Union as a successor institution to the EEC. A 1999 Treaty of Amsterdam, a Treaty of Nice in 2003, and the Treaty of Lisbon in 2009, the European Union looked to greater economic and political unification in Europe. Adoption of the euro in 1993 greatly facilitated international trade. The Schengen agreement of 1985 allowed for not just greater trade and investment, but also a freer movement of labor across borders, effectively removing a key dimension of national borders within the Union.

Several treaties noted above elaborated the contours of the emerging European Union. The Treaty of Amsterdam establish European parliamentary control across national borders on immigration, civil and criminal laws, and enacting foreign and security policy. The Treaty of Nice established the foundations of a European Union Constitution, as well as measures for an orderly expansion of the Union. Finally, the Treaty of Lisbon established the principle of qualified voting majority that would provide for a stronger European Parliament with a bicameral legislature. It also established a long-term President of the European Council and a High Representative of the Union for Foreign Affairs and Security Policy. And, critically, it established through Article 50 a procedural mechanism for member states that may choose to withdraw.

What the amended form of the European Union did not do was to move toward greater fiscal union, leaving the burden of economic decisions to monetary policy as implemented by the European Central Bank. This has resulted in some countries experiencing both balance of payments and growth burdens while others could enjoy the fruits of an enlarged economic market. The PIGS, that is, Portugal, Italy, Greece, and Spain, which had weaker economic growth, would experience financial crises through periodic defaults on international debt. Greece in particular went through financial crises in 2008, 2015, and again in 2019, resulting in periodic refinancing negotiations, and changes in government.

Some have argued that while the euro provides greater ease of financial transactions, the imposition of university standards threatens the unity of the Union. A key issue is whether EU members are prepared to cede greater sovereignty through greater fiscal union to address such issues as common defense, climate change, and regional inequality. Agreements on such issues as climate change through the adoption of the Paris Agreement of 2016 within the United Nations Framework Convention on Climate Change (UNFCCC). The Paris Agreement, which sets climate control goals for 2050, does not have an enforcement mechanism and, as with other international agreements, relies on voluntary compliance. That the United States withdrew its agreement in 2019 represents a setback to achievement of the EU climate goals, as does the decision to withdraw from a nuclear accord with Iran which has been upheld by the EU.

Brexit and the Future of the EU

The shift away from the EU has been most dramatically illustrated by the United Kingdom 2016 referendum on membership. At the time,

Great Britain was experienced an influx of undocumented migrants coming mostly across the English Channel, and for which EU legislation provides for financial support in settlement and citizenship normalization. England already experienced a backlash on immigration well before its accession to EEC membership in 1973, but as a member of the EU, tensions increased when EU liberalization on labor migration laws expanded.[6] Having kept the British pound sterling while a member of the EU, Great Britain held an ambiguous relationship to the continent, even as its own economy thrived in terms of global finance transactions in London. Therein stood Great Britain, faced with a crisis of identity—a post-imperial, European, or trans-Atlantic power in a "special relationship" with the United States, its erstwhile colonial appendage on whose power it had now come to depend.

In 2016, British Prime Minister David Cameron decided to ask Parliament to hold a referendum on membership in the EU. Given concerns over rising immigration, citizens voted to withdraw from the EU. Later, Theresa May's government foundered on the deep divisions in the country as to whether to pursue an exit from the EU. Opposition, and indecision on the terms of exit, ensued until Boris Johnson won an overwhelming majority in 2019 with the objective of withdrawing from the EU early in 2020. "Brexit", the move to withdraw has raised uncertainty as to how the UK can prosper outside of the EU rather than within.

Brexit poses the risk that other EU members may choose to leave, thereby posing the possibility that the EU itself may come apart. Whether in England, or elsewhere in the EU, those who are proposing to withdraw are without exception, nationalists who consider that membership in the EU dilutes English identity, and thus the future of an individual population within the greater Union. Now that the UK has withdrawn from the EU, questions remain as to whether the EU can continue to function in its present form. It thus raises the question whether Great Britain will itself dissolve into England, Scotland, and Wales, for example.

Outside the EU, the question is whether Great Britain can hold together politically and produce sufficient economic prosperity to justify Brexit.

Following a protracted period of conflict between Ireland and Northern Ireland, a Good Friday, or Belfast, Agreement was signed between the Provisional Irish Republican Army (IRA) and the British government Representative in Northern Ireland.

With Brexit, the truce that was agreed may now come apart, given the it had established a relatively free movement of goods and services while both governments were under EU rules. A sticking point in Brexit negotiations has been whether a soft or hard border would be established once Great Britain withdrew while Ireland remains an EU member. Northern Ireland could thus face a choice between complete absorption within England, or complete absorption within the Republic of Ireland, which in the meantime may result in renewed violence by pro-Ireland IRA and Northern Ireland Protestants.

Another point of contention is the relationship of Scotland to Great Britain. In the referendum of 2016, Scots voted overwhelmingly to remain in the EU by 62 percent to 38 percent. Nicola Sturgeon, First Minister of Scotland and leader of the Scottish National Party (SNP), has declared intent to hold a second referendum on the EU, which if a remain majority is reaffirmed, would set the stage for a process of Scottish independence from Great Britain. The end result of Brexit thus could mean the end of Great Britain as it has been for centuries, and thus a much-diminished country in world affairs. Were Scotland to secede from the 1707 union that had established Great Britain, England would be going it alone once again, save for whatever agreements it could negotiate with the EU, the United States, or with other countries of the British Commonwealth.

The Geography of Authoritarian Nationalism

As Brexit illustrates, greater political unions and global governance institutions are now viewed with increasing skepticism by populations expressing fear over the loss of national identity from globalization. Transparency and social inclusion, central to democratic political legitimacy, are now threatened by the politics of grievance and narrow self-interest. Nationalist leaders seek to redefine political legitimacy along more narrow lines of ethnicity, religion, and race. They look to limiting opposition through intimidation of journalists, the jailing of political opponents, as well as undermining the rule of law.

Nationalist impulses point to a narrowing of the definition of who is a citizen, who has political and civil rights, and what borders define the scope of governance. In the United States, this has come to mean tighter immigration restrictions and the erection of a wall along the border with Mexico where President Trump has accused Mexico as the source of "drug dealers, rapists, and criminals" seeking to illegally enter the United States.[7] That such restrictions carry racist overtones is obvious to anyone who reads beyond the headlines. They make a mockery of U.S. claims to global leadership based on political and economic freedom.

Nationalist policies put narrow economic protection first and foremost over international institutions and the benefits of globalization. NATO, the European Union, the North America Free Trade Agreement, the Paris Global Climate Accords, and the World Trade Organization all are viewed as suspect and preventing a country from realizing its nationalist ambitions. Taken together, it is a recipe for failure, as any careful reading of history can attest. The question is how, whether, and when will nationalist policies be replaced by a re-engagement with international globalization.

Thus far, the globalization model faces a backlash. Faced with uneven outcomes, leaders in various countries are resorting to mercantile policies in which governments manipulate trade and investment. Domestic economic policies often favor the concentration of power in the hands of elites rather than in the majority of the population, even as leaders proclaim that they are serving the needs of the least advantaged members of society.

Where do we see today the expansion of authoritarian nationalist governments? Kim Jong Un in North Korea, Recep Tayyip Erdogan of Turkey, Viktor Orbán of Hungary, Vladimir Putin of Russia, Jair Bolsonaro of

Brazil, and Xi Jinping of China each epitomize variants of authoritarian governance. In the United States, Donald Trump has displayed a similar approach to governing, as his campaign slogan—"Make America Great Again"—attests. Such slogans are mirrored across the political landscape in any number of countries embracing a similar nationalistic chant. They also reflect questions of individual and collective identity, answers to which are tied to psychology and neuroscience from which emerge government policies that frame economic decisions.

China is a notable case in point. Following the death of Mao Tse Tung in 1976, Deng Xiao Ping began a policy of economic liberalization that led to a dramatic increase in per capita income in the decades that followed. At the same time, Deng and his successors operated on the basis that as long as wealth was being created, the Chinese Communist Party would retain its monopoly on government control. Those that viewed the Tiananmen demonstrations in 1989 as a hopeful sign for democratic reforms would soon learn that no such change was about to take place. Since then, Chinese leaders have pursued mercantile policies with great success, lifting millions out of poverty, and making the country the second largest economy in the world after the United States.

Growth accelerated with the accession of China to WTO membership in 2011, even as China pursued its mercantile economic policies through export-led growth. In 2018, the Chinese Communist Party voted in 2018 to remove term limits to the Chinese Constitution, thus enabling Xi Jinping to remain as President for Life should the Party so choose.[8] Political legitimacy in China thus is seen as one in which a political monopoly by the Communist Party is justified in exchange for rising economic prosperity.

China is far from alone in the embrace of authoritarian rule. Following the collapse of the Soviet Union in 1991, Russian President Boris Yeltsin embarked on what many thought would be a dramatic opening of markets and democratic change in Russia. His rule was marked by a surge in economic growth but operated under deeply embedded corruption. When Yeltsin resigned in 1999, it was clear that the transition from a state-owned economy to a market one could not succeed in the absence of institutions that could guarantee both individual liberties and property rights.

Vladimir Putin, a former KGB agent from St. Petersburg, took over the Presidency of Russia in 2000, serving two terms before stepping down to his designated successor Dimitry Medvedev, who served from 2008 until 2012. Vladimir Putin was again elected President in 2012 and was re-elected for yet another term in 2018. In 2019, the Russian Parliament has approved a change in the Constitution that opens the way for an extended presidency without term limits.[9] Putin's regime resembles the Romanov dynasty that ruled over Russia for centuries until the Russian Revolution of 1917. One key difference is that political absolutism now is reinforced by the secret police traditions and practices under the former Soviet Union. No substantive challenges to Putin's authority can be found today.

In a 2005 speech, Putin openly stated that the greatest tragedy to befall Russia was the collapse of the Soviet Union and the border arrangements that had prevailed since the Second World War.[10] More recently, he declared that he would undertake steps to restore the Soviet Union.[11] The absorption of the Crimea by Russian-supported forces in February–March 2014 was one step to redraw borders, followed by military support of pro-Russian separatists in the eastern Donbas region of the Ukraine. Despite criticism by leaders in Western countries, the U.S. recently has delayed delivery of military and technological support to Ukrainian forces seeking to contain the conflict in the east, a controversial move at the center of the 2019 partisan impeachment of President Donald Trump.

Political Legitimacy in the Middle East and Beyond

Beyond Russia and China, the notion of political legitimacy also operates in contested terrain. Rising authoritarian nationalism is evident and troubling, to say the least.

In the Middle East, since the collapse of the Ottoman Empire in 1920, an ongoing struggle has been taking place to determine whether a religious state or a secular one would be politically legitimate. In both cases, authoritarian governments have dominated more often than decentralized ones. Newly emerging nation-states whose borders reflected the imprint of Western power economic interests in the Middle East comprised the new regional geo-political map. While some such as Egypt have a storied past, elsewhere, newly formed nation-states such as Iraq and Kuwait were as often occupied by foreign regional and international powers as they stood as independent countries.

Gertrude Bell, an early 20th century English scholar on the Middle East and British civil servant, helped to craft Iraq's post-Ottoman borders, just as Lawrence of Arabia played a similar role in helping to shape the contours of Saudi Arabia.[12] A May 1916 secret agreement between British agent Mark Sykes and his French counterpart Georges Picot marked off spheres of influence of the two leading European powers in the region, well before the collapse of the Ottoman empire in 1922.[13] The Sykes-Picot Agreement has marked competing regional power struggles ever since.

Following the withdrawal of British forces from the World War I Palestine mandate in 1947, war broke out with the declaration of the State of Israel in the following year. Led by Zionists seeking to establish a homeland for Jews, many of whom had escaped the Nazi German holocaust, the country quickly became embroiled in war with Egypt, Syria, Jordan, and Iraq, each determined to prevent an independent State of Israel from survival in their midst. It did not work, and with renewed wars in 1956, 1967, and 1973, it became clear that Israel was able to defend its borders as well as its commitment to a Jewish homeland.

As with several neighboring states in the Middle East, Israel faces a contradiction as to what constitute its borders. Established as a Jewish homeland in 1948, it has guaranteed a right to return to Jews living elsewhere. At the same time, since the 1967 war, Israel has held territory that was formerly under different rule: the Golan Heights in Syria, the Gaza Strip under periodic Egyptian rule, and the West Bank under Jordanian rule. While Israel has removed its settlements in the once occupied Gaza

Strip, it has declared the Golan Heights as part of Israel, and has fostered Israeli settlements in the West Bank. Were Israel to fully annex the West Bank, it would soon find a Palestinian majority, thus changing the reality of Israeli as a Jewish State. As elsewhere, defining borders along religious lines is part of the larger question of political legitimacy for which religious affiliation as a criterion for citizenship is problematic.

What kind of state in the Middle East meets a test of legitimacy? Egypt has largely followed a secular tradition, but often with authoritarian rule. In Saudi Arabia, the Saudi monarchy has asserted its political legitimacy as guarantor of the integrity of Moslem holy sites in Mecca, Medina, while granting exclusive religious authority to Wahabi clerics who have pursued a conservative interpretation of the Koran. In contrast, following an early effort to achieve a secular democracy, Iran witnessed a CIA sponsored overthrow of the regime of Mohammed Mossadegh in 1953 and the installation of Shah Reza Pahlavi as ruler of the country. As elsewhere, many Iranians viewed this as politically illegitimate, and a conservative opposition, initially in exile, began to work to overthrow the regime, succeeding when the Shah became ill and left the country.

When the Shah fled in 1978, Ayatollah Ruhollah Khomeini led a conservative revolution in which an Islamic Republic under the control of Shi'a religious leaders would lead the country in a new direction. Some have seen the idea of an Islamic Republic as contradictory, and contrary to political legitimacy, but this has not prevented the government from continuing to assert its authoritarian rule, including the sponsoring of military conflicts in Lebanon, Iraq, Syria, and Saudi Arabia as part of an historic division between Shi'a and Sunni communities.

Israel, and its expansion of settlements in the West Bank, are seen from Tehran as politically illegitimate, and the potential for conflict remains substantial. Taken together, states in the Middle East are torn between nominally democratic states with largely authoritarian regimes and fundamentalist states that view democratic institutions as a Western imposition. Given the prevalence of religiously defined states and authoritarian ones, the potential for ongoing conflict puts the region at greater risk than elsewhere.

Challenges to Political Legitimacy are Widespread

The fissure of nation-states is not limited to the EU or the Middle East. China has undertaken a process of laying claim to outlying areas near the mainland. Taiwan, once under Japanese control, has a long history of independence, and for decades was home to Chinese nationalists who opposed Mao Tse Tung's regime in Beijing. Today, Chinese authorities consider Taiwan as part of China, just as they have asserted control over former colonial outposts in Hong Kong and Macao.[14] As they have done so, they also have looked to impose control over minorities in their midst, notably the Falun Gong spiritual movement,[15] the people of Tibet,[16] and more recently, the Uighur Moslem minority.[17]

In Myanmar, the government under Aung San Suu Kyi has persecuted the Moslem Rohingya minority, with many fleeing to refugee camps in Bangladesh. Charges of anti-Moslem abuse and genocide have been rising.[18] In India, Hindu Prime Minister Narendra Modi, of the nationalist Bharatiya Janata Party, recently has removed citizenship protection for Moslems in the country, in an echo of the partition of British India in 1947 when India was separated from Pakistan and then East Pakistan, now Bangladesh.[19]

The list of nationalist movements and the treatment of minorities could go on. Despite repression, many of these countries benefitted from globalization, drawing significant foreign investment and expanded international trade from which per capita incomes grew considerably.[20] Now they face potential isolation as nationalist populism tears away at the fabric of international cooperation which has been the norm since the Second World War.

Divergence of Inequality and Prosperity Undermines the Social Contract

A second factor that has shaped political legitimacy is changes in income and wealth inequality. Following the end of the Second World War, per capita incomes around the world have raised living standards for millions of people and reducing world poverty levels. At the same time, the distribution of income has been highly uneven.[21]

While global income inequality has declined, within-country inequality has increased in many countries, as can be seen in Figure 1.1. As this inequality has increased, political alienation by large sections of some countries has grown, thus undermining political legitimacy.

Figure 1.1 Rising International Income Inequality.

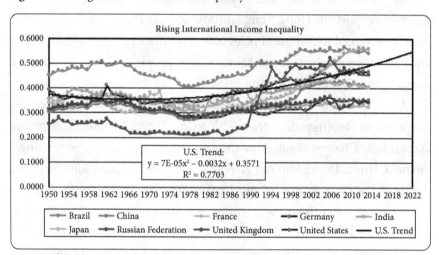

Source: https://wid.world/data/#countrytimeseries/sptinc_p90p100_z;sptinc_p0p50_z/GB/1980/2016/eu/k/p/yearly/s

Tracking inequality of income and wealth has been undertaken by a number of institutions, one of which we note here is the World Inequality Lab based at the Paris School of Economics. Pretax data, shown here, demonstrate the increase in income inequality for a sample of countries over the past seventy years.

While post-tax income that takes transfers into consideration indicates a lower degree of inequality, an upward trend still exists. As it does, unless real per capita income is rising at a significant rate, social unrest often increases, placing pressure on governments to enact economic reforms. More democratic governments responds through both legislative initiatives as well as by elections, while more authoritarian regimes can often defer or ignore rising levels of inequality where they appear.

Figure 1.2 Wealth Inequality Levels Not Seen in a Century

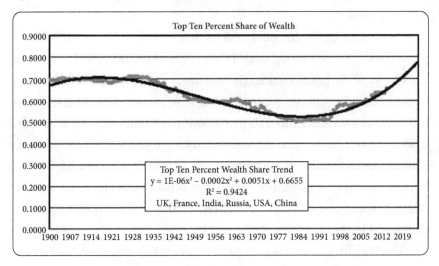

Source: https://wid.world/data/countrytimeseries/sptinc_p90p100_z;sptinc_p0p50_z/ GB/1980/2016/eu/k/p/yearly/s

Whether measured at the ten percent or one percent share, income inequality since reaching a low point in the mid-1970s.[22] Wealth inequality has also tended in the same pattern, increasing by up to 25 percent between 1980 and 2015. The point here is that rising inequality in the face of economic prosperity contributes to social alienation, and thus the rise of either far Right or far Left political movements.

Political Legitimacy Depends on the Level and Distribution of Information

A third factor that affects political legitimacy is how individuals respond to information. Information is an asset. Governments and individuals often have limited information on which to make decisions. This is why we see calls for greater transparency in both the public and private sector. But information is not costless. Who should bear the costs of greater transparency carries important implications for what kind of government may be acceptable to a population over time? Governments may bear the expense of acquiring greater information but not necessarily greater transparency, in which case, the prospect for totalitarian rule becomes greater.

Secrecy, the concealment of information from broader scrutiny, may be an essential tool for making decisions, even in ostensibly democratic societies. In wartime, governments rely on secrecy to conduct military strategy. In private markets, firms contemplating new innovations often seek protection of information through patent and copyright laws. What remains is an open question—how can one pursue a greater level of transparency without compromising the likelihood of success. It is a conundrum that leads many critics of government to accuse officials of lying on any number of matters, and not without foundation, as to why some secretly pursued choice was in the best interest of society.

The War in Vietnam serves to illustrate the question of information transparency, secrecy, and political legitimacy. From 1954 to 1975, the U.S. suffered 58,220 military casualties in the War in Vietnam. U.S. involvement, a product of the Cold War, seemed over time less and less relevant to vital U.S. interests, even as Presidents Kennedy, Johnson and Nixon pursued an elusive military victory. Daniel Ellsberg, a U.S. military analyst working for the RAND Corporation, released a secret Pentagon study on U.S. involvement in the war, and when published in the *New York Times* in 1971s, came to be known as *The Pentagon Papers.*

The *Pentagon Papers* revealed how various U.S. government officials had misled the U.S. public regarding involvement in the war. The decision to go to war was not based on clearly known facts, and once engaged, the study showed that the war was not winnable on conventional terms. Once published, public opposition expanded rapidly, leading to a decision by President Gerald Ford to terminate U.S military involvement in Vietnam in April 1975. The Vietnam War left a bitter legacy of mistrust of U.S. military engagement in overseas conflicts, even though it has not stopped subsequent involvement in two wars in the Middle East and ongoing military engagements in Afghanistan and Iraq. When an overseas military mission is not seen as vital to U.S. national security, ongoing commitments undermine political legitimacy at home.

In contrast, during the Second World War, the U.S. developed the first operational nuclear weapon, and then used it in the bombing of Hiroshima and Nagasaki, Japan in August, 1945. This controversial program decision is thought by many to have foreshortened the war while opening the door to the spread of nuclear weapons. During the war, other countries, notably Nazi Germany, had made some progress in developing a nuclear weapon, only to be thwarted by subversive destruction of the heavy water reactor technology then being pursued.

After World War II, during the early days of the Cold War, Russian agents were able to acquire knowledge of the U.S. hydrogen bomb research program, even though the Russians never used nuclear weapons in any theater of conflict. Despite nuclear disarmament treaties, the spread of nuclear weapons technology has increased global insecurity. This is why so many decisions today have revolved around efforts to contain their spread, most notably, in North Korea (which has operational nuclear weapons), and Iran, which has been on the threshold of acquiring nuclear weapons capacity. It also is why political legitimacy is being questioned in terms of what countries possess nuclear technology and which do not, along with the extent to which a regime is based on transparency and accountability for nuclear decisions.

Central to this question is not just the cost of generating information but also how political legitimacy is affected by the degree of transparency a government provides. Critics who accuse governments of lying often base their case not just on the behavior of a single individual but on the broader question of why important policy decisions are not exposed to greater public scrutiny. Conservatives are divided as to how much should conceal from the public, but often support measures to reduce the size of government as a solution to mistakes from secret decisions rather than on insisting on greater transparency in decision-making.

On the Left, critics of government declare that government could and should engage in greater supervision and oversight of the economy but also in providing greater transparency and exposure of government secrets. Julius and Ethel Rosenberg were executed in 1953 for having revealed knowledge of U.S. nuclear technology to Stalin's Russian Communist government. This took place during the heyday of the Cold War, and when Wisconsin Senator Joseph McCarthy pursued a witch hunt against suspected Communists and fellow travelers in public and private life.

In the 1980's, Oliver North, a U.S. Marine Corps Lieutenant Colonel, was enmeshed in a secret arms deal to sell weapons to Iran in hopes of a release of U.S. hostages taken in 1979, and to take the revenue from arms sales to support contra rebels fighting against the Leftist Sandanista regime in Nicaragua. It was later exposed. President Ronald Reagan then was forced to curtail the scheme. Secrecy in the conduct of government decisions feeds suspicion of government officials, and thus calls into question the legitimacy of a given government.

Perceptions of Risk Shape the Political Legitimacy of Governments

A fourth basis of political legitimacy derives from changing perceptions of risk. In any market, prices may not fully embody all relevant information. Imperfect information translates into risk, which in turn, raises the question of who should bear risk. Private markets often can insure against risks through collateral or other risk-sharing arrangements. Option contracts enable one to hedge against any number and types of risk. But even when the level and distribution of information is symmetric, insurance markets can fail when perceptions of risk diverge. Here we have another example of how markets can fail to price resources in an efficient manner, namely, in the presence of moral hazard, which we will take up later in greater detail.

As an example, when banks are required to join an insurance pool to cover losses, as in the case of Federal Deposit Insurance Corporation standards, individual banks may choose to undertake higher risk lending than they would in the absence of such mandatory insurance levels. The FDIC, along with the Federal Savings and Loan Association Insurance Corporation, or FSLIC, were created in the depths of the Great Depression of the 1930s to reassure depositors, and thus to promote financial intermediation in response to panic withdrawals that had been taking place and causing many banks to fail. FDIC was established by the Banking Act of 1933, while the FSLIC was established by the National Housing Act of 1934. The FDIC would cover commercial banking, which by the Glass-Steagall Act of 1933, separated commercial from investment banking, while the FSLIC covered insurance for the housing market, leaving unsecured risk to purely investment banks.

These insurance programs, backed and administered by the U.S. government, worked reasonably well for decades, but through a series of deregulatory moves in the 1980's, led many financial institutions to take on risks that would eventually lead to financial failure. The 2007–2009 financial crisis was marked by a financial and housing bubble in which prices did not correspond to the underlying capacity of firms to sustain sufficient growth to amortize the underlying levels of debt that were being created.

Among the responses to the crisis of 2007–2009 was an increase in the level of insurance coverage mandated by the U.S. government, which in the case of FDIC insurance, meant that henceforth deposits would be insured up to $250,000 in deposits in comparison to the old standard of $100,000. This expanded coverage helped to stem what could have been a new panic in which massive withdrawals could have forced banks to close. But what it also did was to encourage banks to take on additional lending risks, given the higher level of coverage that the new coverage levels afforded. This example illustrates another way that markets can fail, and which is known as moral hazard. An economic agent takes on additional risks that would not otherwise be assumed, given that a third party has given either implicit or explicit coverage for losses.

Perceptions of risk vary with time. At the time of the 2007–2009 financial crisis in the U.S. Ben Bernanke served as head of the Federal Reserve Bank.

Having studied the Great Depression, he drew the lesson that when the stock market crashed in 1929, the solution was not to tighten credit but to do just the opposite. Not all institutions have been guided by such longer-term perspectives. Many still operate with much shorter time horizons. Moreover, governments may frame decisions that are relevant only through the next election rather than consider the longer-term consequences.

Today, in the U.S., both GOP and Democratic politicians propose, respectively, massive tax cuts and greatly expanded government expenditures. The result is the ballooning of ever large budget deficits and a rise in the overall level of federal debt relative to the Gross Domestic Product. This behavior will continue as long as politicians do not perceive, or experience, default in federal debt service. Yet, at the state level, and abroad, unsustainable debt is a major reason why many governments have failed to continue, replaced in many cases by different regimes that either renegotiate debt obligations or seek debt repudiation.

The collapse of the Weimar Republic regime in post-World War I Germany was due to unsustainable debt service levels imposed by the Treaty of Versailles, and when the Great Depression expanded into Europe, it gave rise to Adolf Hitler's Nazi totalitarian regime. A similar experience took place in Russia, when crushing debt created by the First World War led to the collapse of the Romanov regime and the replacement by Vladimir Lenin's Communist revolution of 1917. It was not just the rise of these authoritarian regimes that should be of concern. It is that the rest of the world can be embroiled in adopting a response, be that World War II, or the Cold War, and for which the economic costs can be considerable.

Few today think the U.S. is in a similar position in terms of deficits and debt. However, the ability to sustain rising government debt levels in the U.S. depend ultimately on the confidence of domestic and foreign buyers of U.S. treasury securities. Incoherent and inconsistent U.S. government leadership can lead to a decline in confidence in U.S. economic policies well before an actual default were to take place. If there is a reason why the political legitimacy of the U.S. government is at risk today is that few, if any, voices are to be heard regarding fiscal policy management, with opposing parties choosing instead on other issues that detract from what could undermine the ability of the U.S. to continue to borrow in financial markets.

Incomplete markets, and how perceptions of risk can lead to a mis-specification of policy choices can result in market prices failing to allocate efficiently an economy's scarce resources. The political rhetoric we see today is tending toward ever more divergent positions regarding how much government should intervene in the economy, and equally important, how much it should intervene over a sustainable time path. While how well an economy performs is linked to how public policy choices are made, political legitimacy also extends to our attitudes toward risk.

Where does this leave us? We thus have political legitimacy under trial from questions of borders and national identity, from rising economic inequality, from the way in which information is gathered, managed, and disseminated, and from varying perceptions of risk. All of these factors shape the nature of political legitimacy by which societies may either choose or accept to be governed.

CHAPTER TWO

STATE FORMATION
IN SPACE AND TIME

A Brief Geography of States Over Time

Let us first take a quick look at the geography of states in an historical context. At the end of the Second World War, empires fashioned in the previous century, already frayed by the First World War and the Great Depression of the 1930's, slowly began to fade as a model of governance. As empires receded, nation-states took their place, playing various roles in coalitions that emerged and receded during the Cold War from 1945 to 1991. As long as the Cold War prevailed, geographic boundaries, often fashioned either after World War I or after decolonization after World War II, tended to remain largely unchanged.

With the collapse of the Soviet Union in 1991, new states were formed around a much smaller Federation. Since then, we see Russian efforts now directed at redrawing national boundaries in an effort to reconstruct a Soviet empire. The fighting taking place between Russian separatists and an independent government in Kiev is part of a larger process of political devolution and reconstruction.

Ending the conflict depends on a political agreement, namely, crafting an arrangement that achieves a measure of stability, with some degree of acceptance of the goal of economic growth. Whether Vladimir Putin succeeds in his effort to rebuild a Russian empire somewhat in this image depends in part on the response of Russian citizens as well as populations in former satellite countries, in addition to the response of the West, notably EU member countries.

The current conflict in the Ukraine should be seen against the larger backdrop of efforts elsewhere to redraw political boundaries. In the Middle East, ever since the collapse of the Ottoman Empire at the end of World War I, nation-states emerged in various forms as a model of governance. Some such as the rulers of Saudi Arabia adopted monarchy with an over-arching goal of preserving and expanding Sunni Islam throughout the world. Elsewhere, more secular nation-states emerged, though paying varying degrees of homage to religious customs within their domain. Egypt, Syria, and Iraq evolved along the lines of secular nation-states, as rulers put into place some degree of electoral mechanisms found outside the Middle East.

Some found these regimes to be politically illegitimate, as they were not founded on strict religious principles. It was out of this the Muslim Brotherhood emerged in Egypt, first in opposition to Gamal Abdel Nasser's regime, continuing through Anwar el Sadat, and then Hosni Mubarak until he was forced to step down in 2012.

Although Mohammed Morsi's Muslim Brotherhood then was elected to government, within a year, the Brotherhood were ousted by a military coup with a restoration of a secular regime under General Abdel Fattah el-Sisi. Thus, Egypt, like other states in the region, faces a challenge of whether religion should constitute the basis of political legitimacy or whether monarchy, military dictatorship, or some form of secular electoral democracy should serve.

Similar divisions can be found elsewhere, as in Iran. After the collapse of the secular monarchy of Reza Pahlavi in 1979, Ayatollah Khomeini proceeded to adopt a theocratic republican model of government in Iran, whose ultimate decisions would be supervised by Shi'a clerics who were the driving force against the secularism of the Shah.

Out of the Iranian revolution came a renewed Islamic conflict between Shi'a and Sunni groups in the Middle East, starting with the Iraq-Iran war in the 1980s. Two Gulf wars led to the downfall of Saddam Hussein's government in 2003, from which a Shi'a dominated Iraqi government emerged. Since Shi'a account for the vast majority of Iraqis, the new regime had the nominal appearance of a more representative government, and thus political legitimacy. Yet, as more recent events have shown, a more representative government does not guarantee an inclusive one, and this is where the question of national boundaries began to fray.

When Nouri Al Maliki assumed the leadership in Iraq, he adopted a policy of excluding minority population factions from government. This exclusion stoked traditional separatist sentiment among the Kurdish minority, itself a victim of genocidal action under the previous regime of Saddam Hussein.

The overthrow of Saddam Hussein's government also spawned the emerge of IS, the Islamic State, a Sunni group that began fighting against the regime of Bashir al Assad in Syria and then the Shi'a dominated government in Baghdad. The Islamic State aims for no less than the overthrow of regional nation-states of Syria and Iraq in a declared effort to construct a Sunni dominated Islamic Caliphate, much in the model of the older Ottoman Empire. As such, they would overturn colonial era boundaries dating back to the Sykes-Picot Agreement of 1916 that formed the boundaries of Iraq and Syria.[23]

In all of these examples, whether it is a regime under attack or an attacking group of forces, the goal is to secure power and stability over resources in a region. But not everywhere do we see examples of political boundaries being redrawn through military conflict. In 1993, a referendum in Czechoslovakia led to a peaceful separation of what became the Czech and Slovak Republics. And in 2014, Scots go to the polls to decide whether to remain in Great Britain or go their separate ways for the first time since the creation of the Union of 1707. Elsewhere, efforts to draw political boundaries have been shaped by a mix of military and political choices.

Within Europe, Basque separatists fought for decades a guerilla war against the government of Madrid, Spain. Within Spain, Catalonians are now contemplating a redrawing of borders as a separate entity. Farther north, ever since the 1916 Easter Uprising in Ireland, the borders of Ireland and Northern Ireland have been subject to dispute, yet now have moved to a more political phase of governance. Outside of Europe and the Middle East, India and Pakistan agreed to a partition in 1947, only to be followed by the separation of Bangladesh from Pakistan in 1971.

Within Africa, national borders that emerged from colonial boundaries in the late 1950's became subject to ongoing conflicts over resources. Whether the efforts of Katanga to secede from the Congo in the 1970s, the Biafran separatist war in Nigeria from 1967 to 1970, the Ethiopian-Eritrean war from 1962 to 1991, the breakup of Sudan in the 1990s, or the recent efforts to constitute an Islamic state in Mali and now by the Islamist group Boku Haram in Northern Nigeria, the pattern has a discomforting similarity.

Elsewhere we see a similar pattern. Political boundaries are subject to redrawing either through democratic procedures or through the use of military force. Whether nation-states with nominal or substantive adherence to democratic procedures, or budding empires, the problem with most modes of governance is an exclusionary model of power, a point we will take up further at a later point. For now, where Islamic fundamentalist conflicts unfold, it often results in the subjugation and persecution of religious minorities, though nothing requires that this be so.

Religion alone is not the driver of all state and non-state conflicts. Nationalism also is a powerful driver. The ethnic cleansing that unfolded during the Serbian-Bosnian conflict in the 1990s is one example. More recently, Vladimir Putin's efforts to gather those populations that qualify as ethnic Russians within one political state is not unlike Hitler's claims in Czechoslovakia and Austria in the years prior to World War II. This does not equate Putin with Hitler. It simply draws a parallel in which ethnic nationalism is used to define what constitutes the politically legitimate boundaries of a state.

Quantitative Measures of States

What size and role should governments play in economic and social affairs? This perennial question has not only produced revolutions and civil wars. It also is pursued even within the norms of a democratic society. To invert the 19th century Prussian military strategist Von Clausewitz, politics is the continuation of war by other means. Of course, that notion assumes an antagonistic relationship between government and the population, which is not necessarily true in all cases. As we have already noted, much of this relationship depends on how individuals perceive risk and what in turn they expect government to do in response.

Is there an optimal size of government? The question is best posed in terms of the size of government relative to the economy that is its foundation. But that also begs the question of whether government is too large or too small, and in terms of the level of centralization. In the context of our discussion of globalization and authoritarian nationalism, one underlying issue is whether sovereignty resides exclusively at the local, or even national, level, and to the exclusion or inclusion of international governance.

Under globalization, some degree of delegation of national sovereignty operates at an international level to coordinate the expansion of international trade, investment, and cooperation. Few have argued that globalization means the abdication of national sovereignty, but rather the extent to which international agreements should be binding on otherwise sovereign national governments.

Given that governments vary significantly in both economic and political size, some degree of cooperation is essential if individual states are to survive. When faced with the question of international economic and political agreements, authoritarian nationalists would argue that they impinge on national sovereignty and should thus be repudiated wherever possible, if not minimized to a great extent. When withdrawals from international agreements take place, global governance falls back to individual nation-states, or in some instances, a reversion to empire, as a means of decisions on the flow of trade and investment, and international cooperation on matters ranging from international security to global climate change.

On the Scale and Size of Government

Before we can address the question of the optimal size of government, we need first to look at the range of institutions. Putting aside the degree of decentralization within a given nation-state, consider, for example, the number of sovereign states. At its founding in 1945, the United Nations comprised 51 countries, around which a permanent Security Council of five members could exercise veto power over any resolution. The five states are: China, France, the Russian Federation (then the Soviet Union), the United Kingdom, and the United States. And, until 1972, the seat held by China was by the nationalist government in Taiwan, following the civil war in that country and the victory of the Communists under Mao Tse Tung in 1949.

Given the changes in Russia and China, if we look at population, the cumulative permanent members represent a declining share of global population while at the same time, accounting for just under half of global Gross Domestic Product. In effect, while UN overall membership has accounted for a growing share of global population, the declining share of the permanent Security Council member countries makes the institution less democratic. Although the UN Security Council structure has become less representative over time, this is not to state that its functions are unimportant. Few would question its role in global peacekeeping, health, refugees, climate, and related issues.

For this purpose we can look at the growth of membership in the UN in the period since 1945. Fifty-one countries formed the original core of the UN membership at its founding, increasing gradually to 193 today.

If we look at these data in terms of the population per country, the average was 44 million in 1945, falling to a low of 27.9 in 1966 as the number

Figure 2.1 Relative Size of UN Security Council Permanent Member States.

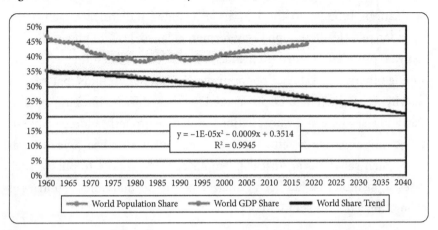

Source: World Indicators, the World Bank. https://databank.worldbank.org/reports.aspx?source=world-development-indicators#

of post-colonial states expanded, and then slowing in more recent years to a ratio of 36.7 million today as population growth has increased. Of course these numbers do not reflect some of the enormous differences in states.

China's 1.3 billion population readily overwhelms Malta's 420,000 population, for example. Counting the number of nation-states does not take into consideration the number of sub-national governmental units, which in the aggregate may far exceed the number of national units. So we need to look beyond a simple tabulation of governmental units to how they fit in economic space.

Although the United Nations has become an enduring international institution, member countries participate on the principle of retaining national sovereignty save for the collapse of political order. Yet even when political collapse is not at issue, countries may choose to collaborate in a time of crisis, while at the same time, resisting even symbolic reductions in national sovereignty.

A case in point is the role of the UN International Criminal Court, an institution established in 2002 to consider cases of individuals charged with violations ranging from theft to homicide and forcible transfers of populations brought to the ICC have included indictments against the Ugandan rebel leader Joseph Kony, former Sudanese leader Omar al-Bashir, Kenyan president Uhuru Kenyatta, Libyan leader Muammar Gaddafi, among others. The U.S. has opposed the ICC on the grounds that Americans living abroad could be prosecuted for alleged war crimes in Afghanistan and elsewhere and whose actions should be properly addressed by the U.S. criminal justice system. The Trump administration has gone so far as to threaten sanctions against ICC employees who choose to pursue such cases, a position that has been criticized by the EU and other countries as promoting a double standard of justice.[24]

States as Expressions of Economic Size

As we have noted, with the increase in the number of sovereign states, the average size of countries is declining. What, then, about the size of government? One way to answer this question is in terms of the fiscal weight of sovereign states. The simplest way to do this is in terms of the ratio of tax revenues to a country's GDP, or in terms of the ratio of government expenditures to the GDP. The size of government relative to its GDP at any one time reflects in large part the role of fiscal policy in pursuit of a policy of full employment stabilization and growth.

During the 1980s, which represented the twilight of the Cold War, most OECD countries saw a decline in the weight of government expenditures, only to rise again in response to the Great Recession that began in 2007. But it also reflects the extent to which states are charged with functions that transcend the primary function of stability we have evoked at the outset. As to the United States, it stands on the lower end of the scale, reflecting the institutional heritage of viewing economic functions of the public sector as more limited in scope than many of the countries with which it maintains economic and diplomatic ties. Responses to the current coronavirus pandemic point again to an upward trend.

Figure 2.2 Central Government Expenditures as a Percentage of GDF.

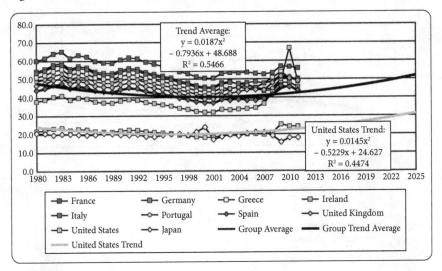

Source: The World Bank, *World Development Indicators.*

Against the backdrop of stabilization, most countries in our sample also underwent a lowering of tax revenues relative to GDP such that public debt as a percentage of GDP expanded. This is the context in which today's discussion of how to create sustainable growth has emerged, namely, how to keep debt management at some sustainable level, a topic we also will take up in due course. In this sense, the weight of governments expands or contracts in part through economic cycles over which government policies are supposedly designed to stabilize.[25]

But even considering the weight of government expenditures and taxation does not capture the overall weight of government in the economy. What is missing is the impact of regulation. Here there are additional expenses borne by producers and consumers that may add as much to the size of government as either tax revenues or government expenditures. Some have estimated that Federal regulations alone have reduced current U.S. GDP by as much as $39 trillion dollars per year at current levels of GDP,[26] and if accurate, a figure that dwarfs current GDP in 2011 of $15.1 trillion dollars. Whether any or all of this could be justified in

Figure 2.3 Ratio of Central Government Tax Revenues to GDP.

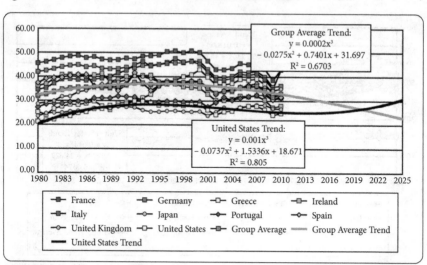

Source: The World Bank, *World Development Indicators.*

economic terms depends on what benefits have been derived in terms of environmental quality, the mix of goods and services, as well as in the distribution of income affected by such regulation.

Lastly, one can look at the size of states in terms of military or economic power. While military expenditures are subsumed under overall government expenditures, some choose to measure military power in terms of weapons and equipment, or the number of personnel in armed services units. If you look at states in terms of the number of people serving in the active military, China is first, with 2.285 million, followed by the United States with 1.369 million, India with 1.325 million, and North Korea with 1.19 million.[27]

These figures are less meaningful unless taken in comparison to what percentage of the population is serving in the armed forces, and in terms of the lethality of weaponry, as well as in terms of what percentage of a country's GDP is devoted to military expenditures. The United States does not spend as large a percentage of its GDP on the military as Saudi Arabia (9.3), Russia (4.1), or the United Arab Emirates (4.7), but in absolute terms, its annual military expenditures of $640 billion is larger than the total expenditures for the next nine largest military budgets in the world. And while the Russian Federation has more nuclear missiles in its stockpiles than the U.S. (8,500 vs. 7,700), overall military strength in the U.S. still places it above any other country.[28]

Regardless of the combination of government spending, taxation, and regulation, the larger is the size of government, the lower is likely to be its level of economic freedom, and which to some extent may parallel its political freedom as measured by the level of political and civil rights.

Political conservatives view the costs of regulation as outweighing benefits in general. They often cite the insurance mandate of the 2009 Affordable Care Act adopted during the first term of the Obama administration as a further reduction in individual economic rights even as coverage is extended to a larger percentage than before. Those on the Left view the Act as promoting distributive justice through greater access to health care insurance.

How can we compare the economy and the size of government? We already have cited some common measures above. But in addition, some address this question in terms of the level of economic and political freedom.

The U.S. Heritage Foundation, a politically conservative think tank in Washington, D.C., for years has tracked an index of economic freedom.[29] The index is based on weighted scores for property rights, and indices for economic freedom as measured though: the degree of corruption, the level of government spending, business freedom from regulation, labor freedom, monetary freedom (the independence of a central banking authority), trade freedom, investment freedom, and financial freedom. While one can argue about weights given to these characteristics, the index provides a first-order gauge of the degree of economic freedom across a range of countries.

Though these are qualitative indicators based on a combination of survey data and professional estimates, they are designed to illustrate the burden of government in the economy and society. Using survey data and professional estimates, for the period 1995 through 2013, the trend of economic freedom in the U.S. using the Heritage Index points to a reduction in the future, much as is predicted for a sample of major industrial countries,

Figure 2.4 Composite Index of Economic Freedom, 1995–2014.

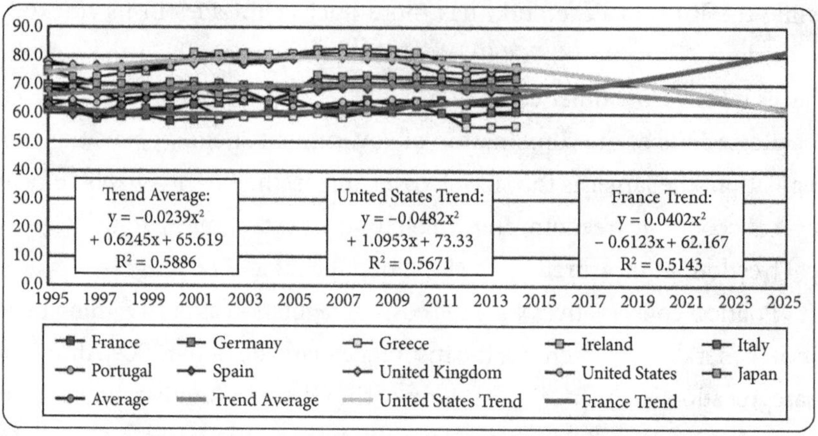
90.0
80.0
70.0
60.0
50.0
40.0
30.0
20.0
10.0
0.0
1995 1997 1999 2001 2003 2005 2007 2009 2011 2013 2015 2017 2019 2021 2023 2025
Trend Average: y = -0.0239x² + 0.6245x + 65.619 R² = 0.5886
United States Trend: y = -0.0482x² + 1.0953x + 73.33 R² = 0.5671
France Trend: y = 0.0402x² - 0.6123x + 62.167 R² = 0.5143
France
Germany
Greece
Ireland
Italy
Portugal
Spain
United Kingdom
United States
Japan
Average
Trend Average
United States Trend
France Trend

Source: The Heritage Foundation, *Economic Freedom in the World*, selected years.

with France serving perhaps as an exception, even with its current Socialist government.

One underlying question one might be asking at this point is: What is the relationship across economic freedom, per capita GDP, and the degree of public sector intervention? We will explore this theme in terms of a sample of countries to see to what extent a clear trade-off can be estimated, or whether the kind of data we have available do not lend themselves to such a ready interpretation. For now, we state simply that at some level there are such trade-offs. How to frame them as public policy choices typically falls far short because so little, if any, consideration is given to the level of risk.

As political boundaries expand and contract in a sometimes accordion-like fashion, questions of stability, sustainability, and ultimately, political legitimacy still determine the choice of regime in general and the choice of roles for states and markets in particular. Political divisions turn largely on perceptions of risk with different rates of discount as to future consequences of any action taken today.

Our emphasis here is not on any particular state-level political configuration, though we will draw on historical examples to illustrate how these choices are shaped. Instead, we are interested in exploring how markets are central to political choice and whether market structures and conduct imply a larger or smaller role for states in the overall framework of governance. In so doing, we pursue the question of what constitutes a natural political order. As we do so, we look at the relationship between government size and form, economic freedom, risk, and ultimately, political legitimacy.

Markets as Foundations of States

Markets operate as the glue for most geographic political boundary choices. Not only do trading relationships bring geographic units together. They also undergird a sense of mutual self-interest that lends itself to a choice of polity. Capitalist economies built around principles of private property and free trade have created more wealth in the world over time than any alternative system.

Given the ability of capitalist economies to generate wealth, does it follow that they do so with no adverse effects on society or the environment? It is at this level that we confront the question of whether private property rights and individual liberty produce outcomes that are sustainable, efficient,

Figure 2.5 Country Shares of Global GDP in $2005 Constant Prices, 1960–2013.

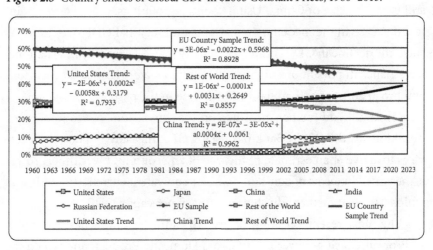

Source: The World Bank, *World Development Indicators.*

risk minimal to some desired and acceptable degree, and ultimately fair. To the extent that they do, they affirm a particular political order in which the functions of the state are minimal. If not, then distortions in market processes generate outcomes that lead to pressures for government intervention, even at the risk of loss of some measure of individual freedom.

At the simplest level, the size of government logically would be driven by the extent of economic integration. Economic integration can be measured in terms of overall Gross Domestic Product as well as through trade. As such, it can serve as a key factor in political governance even though a broader array of singular characteristics would create a more sustainable foundation as well.

One way of looking at this question is in terms of country and country-grouping shares of global GDP. Using World Bank data, we find that a sample of current European Union member states has the largest share of global GDP, though it is on relative decline. Behind the EU is the Rest of the World outside of the U.S., China, Japan, Russia, and India, and its share is slowly rising, as is the share of China in Global GDP. Finally, the U.S. comes in as the still single largest national country economy, though its share also is on the decline.

As to the U.S., its share of global GDP is on the decline, though it is still twice the size of China. Using country-groupings, these figures point to a decrease in the inequality of national and regional GDP over time. As such, the decline in GDP country inequality may explain why international governance in pursuit of stability will require greater reliance on coalitions and broad consensus than has been the case in the past.

We could add further measures on the dimensions of economic size. Traditionally, the World Bank has used a GDP measure of goods and services to arrive at an estimate of the size of an economy. Over time, growth is measured in terms of constant dollar or equivalent currency growth, and which has been further adjusted in terms of per capita GDP.

The most recent variation of growth estimates and economic size is PPP, or purchasing power parity Gross Domestic Product, and which the

Figure 2.6 Global Country-Region GDP Inequality 1960–2012.

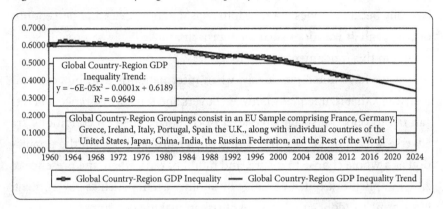

Source: The World Bank, *World Development Indicators.*

World Bank also tracks. A PPP GDP measure is designed to filter out distortions created by exchange rates and pricing policies to give a more representative picture of an economy. Now all of this said, this still leaves us with the question we raised at the outset, namely, how can one arrive at some estimate of the size of government, and in so doing, provide a framework that satisfies the criterion of political legitimacy.

Beyond a PPP GDP measure, whether in the aggregate or on a per capita level, economists have spent some time wrestling with how much of a country's well-being can be captured in a measure of economic output. Many economic activities do not enter into the calculus of the GDP, and not all of the consequences of a country's GDP will be reflected in official statistics. Moreover, a GDP measure does not take into consideration other metrics such as life expectancy, or the in-country distribution of income and wealth.

Some have suggested that we use a social-welfare index that incorporates other factors alongside a GDP measure. The UNDP's Human Development Index provides one such measure. For any level of development, the degree of access to potable water, participation rates of women in the economy, and life expectancy serve as complements to per capita GDP to provide a broader basis of the quality of life. But even here, an indicator such as the Human Development Index still falls short of enabling us to answer the question of the optimal mix of states and markets. It falls short basically because it does not take into consideration levels and perceptions of risk. Only if we adopt such an approach are we likely to provide some insight in this fundamental question.

As we have noted previously, when information is distributed asymmetrically, that is, unequally between buyers and sellers, insurance markets can fail to obtain a sustainable level of coverage. The two conditions are adverse selection, when those with a higher probability than the population as a whole choose to insure, and moral hazard, where the presence of either implicit or explicit coverage by another agency such as government, leads firms to adopt a higher level of risk in making decisions.

All economic activity unfolds in the presence of some degree of risk. We do not know what the future will hold down to some engineering level of precision, but we know that it will most certainly affect our prospects for the future. When perceptions of risk increase, this typically results in increased pressure on government to provide a measure to reduce the level to some acceptable level, even though this may not be the most efficient or equitable choice to adopt. The problem is that we often do not have a clear notion of what is acceptable risk. As a result, government policy often is framed with a momentary benchmark of acceptable risk that in turn, rises and falls with economic and political events.

Economists define beta risk as asset-specific whereas alpha risk applies to systemic risk that affects the overall behavior of individual assets. While we have become quite adept at generating beta risk measures, our understanding of alpha risk is more challenging, and it is at this level that we often find calls for greater government intervention to bring this kind of risk to some underlying level of acceptability.

Risk is factored into market indices such as bond ratings or aggregate country risk, where various types of risk are subsumed at a country level. Bond ratings often change in response to events rather than in anticipation of them, and for which agencies often have been criticized for failing to anticipate some underlying probability of default. This has been true at various points in history for sovereign government bonds, the greatest form of bond holdings. And, as is so often the case, as with reactions in the stock markets, one may downgrade bond ratings beyond what a more fully informed set of information would lead one to adopt, in which case, adjustments in bond prices and interest rates fluctuate in a never-ending effort to reach an efficient pricing level.

One increasingly cited index of risk is the Chicago Board of Trade's Volatility Index of Assets, and which is known as VIX. Launched in 2003, VIX provides a market-price driven proxy of aggregate risk not just in financial commodity markets but also the larger set of political events that can add or subtract from the level of volatility. As one example, the CBOE provides daily data on the S&P 100 pricing in terms of the underlying degree of volatility on this sample of equity firms, a project that has been back-dated as far as 1986 and now up to today.

The VIX displayed extraordinarily high levels of risk when the New York Stock Exchange took an unexpected drop of 22 percent on October 19, 1987. The stock market quickly rebounded, and volatility moved closer

Figure 2.7 CBOE S&P Vix Index 1986–2014.

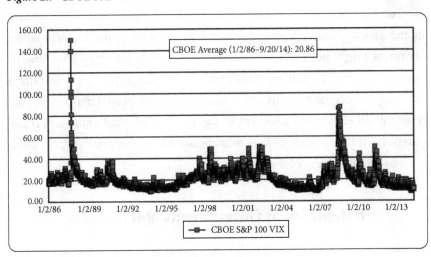

Source: http://www.cboe.com/micro/vix/historical.aspx

to its long-term average of 20. Investigations into why this took place soon placed blame on program trading in which large blocks of stock were either bought or sold if some unanticipated trigger price threshold was reached. This brought rules that allowed exchanges to temporarily shut down if extreme events were to unfold. Yet when the Great Recession of 2008 began to unfold, financial markets did not close even as volatility increased. Volatility rose in November 20, 2008, reaching a high of 87.24, and then falling quickly back to a more normal level.

Sovereign bond ratings represent a similar effort to factor in the various types of risk. By raising or lowering ratings, these financial agencies can affect the ability of government to issue new debt and pay off obligations in a timely fashion. Standard and Poor's, Fitch, and Moody's are the primary sovereign debt ratings agencies in the U.S., but which issue bond ratings for sovereign debt over a broad range of countries.

In an attempt to capture some of the broader underlying dimensions of risk, some ratings firms generate estimates of aggregate country risk assessments that overlap with sovereign debt ratings. The Economist Intelligence Unit is one such organization, but there are many others. One of them is the PRS index of aggregate country risk.

For a while, the PRS Index of Aggregate Country Risk was included in the World Bank's World Development Indicators, particularly where countries might not have full sovereign debt issue capacity. As domestic financial intermediation expands across countries, sovereign debt ratings are likely to become more frequent and transparent, even if national economies still differ as to their respective standards of accountability and transparency. And agencies are likely to issue complementary risk indicators for various sectors of any economy.

Rationality in Governments and Markets

Economists like to affirm rationality in human behavior. They do so because in the end, rationality makes for a much more compelling narrative than the alternatives. Rationality also fits well with the empirical models that are used to examine various events. Yet what even economists now acknowledge is that rationality depends on the level of information. And so in a world of imperfect and often asymmetric information, markets can work inefficiently to achieve what in the end citizens expect from them.

If markets can generate efficient levels of information for rationality to prevail, then governments would have a smaller role to play than is so often the case. It is under what conditions when it fails to do so that rational decisions may not result, with efficiency being the casualty. What this suggests is that we consider the role of governments in our examination of risk. In so doing, we need to ask whether governments exist essentially for reasons tied to risk and economic behavior, or primarily for other reasons.

From the time of Plato and Aristotle, we have a rich body of thought on the rationale for government. One need only think of Plato, Aristotle, Machiavelli, Hobbes, Locke, and Kant, among others to appreciate just how this literature informs out current attitudes toward the state.[30]

Many of the arguments put forth concentrate on the extent to which a greater or smaller role of government expands the potential for human freedom and the capacity for ethically constructive behavior. Yet while these debates contribute much to our perceptions of the political legitimacy of states, they often have little to say about the costs and economic benefits of government, let alone perceptions of various levels of risk.

Although one can find economic content in some of the classics in political thought, it is largely during the 18th century that distinctive economic contributions to our understanding of government emerge. What economists bring to the table is an explicit consideration of the incentives that various types of government decisions produce on economic behavior. Beginning with the classical economic writings of Adam Smith (1723–1790), David Ricardo (1772–1823), and John Stuart Mill (1806–1873), we find a conceptual framework for understanding the economy as well as the impact of government intervention.[31] It is here that we begin to find insights as to whether government should be engaged in managing risk.

What distinguishes these writings from political thought is an explicit consideration of the impact of government incentives on human behavior. At the same time, because more recent economic theorists have concentrated on incentives, they often have gone to some length to distinguish the normative judgments that accompany an analysis of incentives from the objective impact that incentives can produce. At times, this has left a body of work in which the normative political economy pre-occupations of earlier writers have been largely set aside. In an atmosphere of pure economic theory, the relationship between economics and politics has often been obscure.

When economic crises prevail, it is then that economists return to political economy. At such points, we get a renewed perspective on the state in which greater or lesser intervention can be viewed more clearly as expanding or reducing some measure of social welfare. When such events as the Great Depression of the 1930's strike, political economy takes on another life as the debate on the economic role of the state is once again joined. It is also under such circumstances that the role of risk in economic decisions becomes clearer.

While many economists have written on the Great Depression, two of them illustrate the role of risk and political economy, namely, John Maynard Keynes (1883–1946) and Milton Friedman (1912–2006). Consider, for example, Keynes' most famous book, his 1936 publication of the *General Theory of Employment Interest and Money*. At that time, the global economy was in the depth of the Great Depression. Few saw how markets could bring about world economic recovery. Yet this was precisely the prescription of most economists at the time, and against which Keynes set about to change. The question is whether markets were sufficiently rational to achieve fully employment automatically or whether government intervention would be necessary. The answer, as it turns out once again, depends on perceptions of risk.

Keynes took exception to the classical view of economics. To do so, he put forth a theory of expectations regarding how consumers and investors behave in the face of perceived risk. In Keynes' view, extreme risk aversion set in once the stock market crash of 1929 took place. In his view, market institutions were incapable of generating a recovery, so strong was the level of risk aversion at the time.

For Keynes, the solution lay in discretionary and, where needed, deficit government spending to stimulate aggregate demand. He argued that such intervention was essential to restore consumer and investor confidence. Indeed, Keynes concluded his treatise with the pithy phrase, "In the long run, we are all dead" to underline his emphasis that self-correcting market mechanisms would work slowly at best, and that government intervention was the answer. In all of this, Keynes argued that monetary policy was essentially useless.

Keynes' views were first greeted with skepticism. Not since the time of Malthus had economists looked favorably on government intervention.[32] At the same time, during the Great Depression, there was widespread belief that market capitalism was failing, and that something drastic needed to be done. For some, the answer was socialism. For others it was fascism. In between were those still in favor of limited government, but whose voices were crowded increasingly by the intensity of pressure for government to do something.

If there was an American Keynes, it was Franklin Delano Roosevelt, and the New Deal legislation of the 1930's. Roosevelt argued for government intervention to "save capitalism" from itself. Following the defeat of Herbert Hoover in the election of 1932, FDR's New Deal programs enshrined public works as a tool to bring about economic recovery. Similar programs were adopted in England and France, while more totalitarian models were adopted in Nazi Germany and in Soviet Russia. At the time, few saw any contradiction between the expanding role of government and the limiting consequences on individual freedom.

For those skeptical of government intervention based on Keynes theory of expectations, the idea that government should play a smaller role first got at best a small hearing. Among critics of big government at the time were such writers as Ludwig Von Mises (1881–1973) and Friedrich Hayek (1899–1992), both émigrés from Europe who had seen government intervention as diminishing individual freedom. Hayek's 1944 treatise, *The Road to Serfdom*, looked at rising government intervention as not just inefficient, but also leading to a reduction in individual freedom. In Hayek's view, such intervention was politically immoral.[33]

Hayek's writings also focused on the role of information in economic decisions, and this was more critical to our notion of a stochastic economy. In his view, governments rarely had as much useful information as markets in making economic decisions, regardless of the underlying political values on which such claims were being made. In this context, he joined in an ongoing debate as to whether a collectivist economic order could arrive at a more efficient allocation of resources than a market system could. In Hayek's view, government transactions costs to obtain enough information to efficiently manage risk by definition would work far less well than market-driven mechanisms. Yet, as important as Hayek's insights were to the field of risk, they were largely ignored in the larger debate over government's impact on economic and political freedom.

Though inspired by Von Mises and Hayek's notion of freedom, Milton Friedman focused first on the larger economic debate over government intervention posed by Keynes' theory of expectations. Friedman concentrated on the role of monetary versus fiscal policy, and how in his view, monetary policy carries more profound effects than fiscal policy alone. Although Friedman made a case for limited government in his 1962 book, *Capitalism and Freedom*, it was in the field of monetary policy that he offered a more engaging critique of Keynesian economics.[34]

To do so, Friedman first concentrated on the role of money in explaining the Great Depression of the 1930's. Toward that end, with Anna Jacobson Schwartz, Friedman argued in *A Monetary History of the United States, 1857–1960* that the Great Depression of the 1930's was in the first and last instance caused by a contractionary monetary policy pursued by the Federal Reserve.[35]

At the time when Friedman's book was published, the prevailing view was primarily that the Great Depression was caused largely by the excesses of stock market speculation, epitomized in such works as John Kenneth Galbraith's 1954 best seller, *The Great Crash*.[36] With Friedman's measures of money stock, it soon became possible to test the effects of the Great Depression in terms of monetary policy. What came of this work is that money does matter in affecting the level of economic activity, even if the role of risk is not explicitly identified.

Today, few would argue that monetary policy is central to economic activity. While fiscal policy carries important consequences on the supply of money, on the distribution of income, and on the composition of goods and service, in the end, it is monetary policy that is the major determinant of the overall level of economic activity.

When investors and consumers can form rational expectations based on past activity, the level of risk in the economy is reduced. In this sense, the stochastic economy operates with some unanticipated events, but if they are sufficiently small in scale, they individuals will tend to behave not just in boundedly rational fashion, but also in socially rational ways. The question is: What shapes the contours of this stochastic political economy, especially in the world of globalization in which we now are living? The answer lies in part on how individuals respond to risk, as the following illustration will serve.

Stochastic Political Economy

In a globalizing economic environment, as long as growth proceeds without major episodes of risk, few seem to pay attention to the classic concerns of political economy. Yet even here we have periodic reminders that risk matters. A good example is the 1997 East Asia financial crisis and the fallout that it produced.[37] The reason why we take up stochastic political economy with this example is that it reminds us that no expectations are perfect, even if they have the endorsement of major financial and policy institutions.

East Asia presents a success story for economics. Beginning first with postwar Japan, South Korea, Hong Kong, Singapore, Thailand, Malaysia, and now China all have adopted policies to increase per capita incomes through export-led growth. While export-led growth is tied to some extent to a version of mercantilist doctrines of the eighteenth century, the successes of export growth seemed to offer the key to global prosperity.

During the 1990's the external indicators of most of these economies looked good. In fact, reports by the World Bank and the IMF all pointed to continuing success. However, in July 1997, Thailand devalued its currency, the baht. What provoked this action was that investment in the economy had been leveraged by rising stock and property values, something also that had propelled Japanese economic growth in the 1960s and 1970s. However, as Japan experienced in the early 1980's, when stock and property values went through a price correction, the flow of loans dropped sharply. As this happened, credit stalled and exports slowed, thereby causing a severe recession.

In the months following the Thai baht devaluation, contagion overcame the Korean, Hong Kong, Philippine, Singapore, and Malaysia economies. In each of these cases, the standard recipe was for greater transparency in asset valuations, stimulated in part by greater access of foreign direct investment under globally accepted accounting standards. In the short run, no such moves took place. In fact, Malaysia's then Prime Minister Mohammed Mahathir imposed capital controls that limited outflows of investment, and suggested that a sinister plot masterminded by western financial interests was the reason for the financial crisis.[38]

In the events that followed, a number of highly leveraged firms faced bankruptcy. One of them was LTCM, Long Term Capital Management, based in Greenwich, Connecticut. Under the direction of former Salomon Brothers partner John Meriwether, its board included economics Nobel Prize laureates Robert Merton and Myron Scholes, along with other distinguished figures from Wall Street and the U.S. Treasury.

Although LTCM was based on the idea of managing financial risk by dynamically hedging geographically diverse assets so that risk could be effectively eliminated. In an engaging account, Wall Street writer Roger Lowenstein describes how LTCM 's initial capitalization of U.S. $6 billion dollars produced exceptional returns, but then began to decline.[39] The reasons for its decline were threefold.

First, LTCM returned half of its initial capital after three years, leaving it more vulnerable to shocks. Second, once Wall Street firms learned of LTCM's hedging strategy, imitators emerged to make the market more competitive. And third, LTCM was not a perfect hedging instrument. It was not perfect in that the bets placed in various markets were based on historical patterns in different markets across different assets. If future events did not correspond to past behavior, the bets would turn up wrong, and they did.

What drove LTCM down was first the East Asian Financial crisis of 1997. As long as LTCM could hedge its bets elsewhere, however, there was a chance that it could weather the storm. However, in August 1998, Russia suddenly stopped payments on its external debt, an event last seen only in the dying days of Czarist Russia. With such turmoil unfolding, creditors began lining up to withdraw their money, but LTCM was already leveraged for some $U.S. 1.25 trillion dollars. Faced with bankruptcy, New York Federal Reserve's Roger Fisher headed a team that organized a bailout of LTCM, and proceeded to place it in receivership. In the process, some investors lost millions, especially once LTCM was quietly closed down in 1999.

The LTCM experience affords yet another example of how the stochastic economy plays out. In this case, the use of dynamic hedging in financial portfolios shows that no quantitative model, however sophisticated in its construction, can eliminate risk. There always will be room for human judgment that quantitative models are unlikely to capture. In this instance, shifting investor sentiment reflected changing perceptions of risk, and the result was socialization of risk through a quasi-government institution, namely, the U.S. Federal Reserve. Since John Meriwether and others in the field declared that they would resume hedge fund management after LTCM, the real question is whether a Federal Reserve bailout simply created market failure through moral hazard. Time and again, we will have ample opportunity to see if government as a bailout institution proves this true or not.

As a more recent example, consider how states and markets responded to the Great Recession of 2008–2012. With excessive valuations in both the housing and stock market in the U.S., a sell-off began in late 2007 and accelerated throughout 2008. This event precipitated a series of crisis responses, beginning with the TARP, or Troubled Asset Relief Program while then President George W. Bush was still in office. TARP authorized government agencies, notably the Federal Reserve Bank to purchase assets in banks and in Fannie Mae and Freddie Mac, the two principal agencies that helped fund housing purchases, to restore confidence. It was a tepid response that seemed to offer little change in the downturn.

Signs of a weak recovery induced the newly elected Obama administration to push Congress to pass the American Recovery and Reinvestment Act in 2009. ARRA used substantial increases in deficit spending on road and other infrastructure construction, while the Federal Reserve then adopted a program of Quantitative Easing to further stimulate the economy. Unlike previous uses of open market purchases of Treasury securities to provide economic stimulus, Quantitative Easing involved government purchases of financial assets from banks and other financial institutions in an effort to increase liquidity and stimulate renewed lending by banks.[40]

In the process, the U.S. Treasury also took an ownership position in General Motors and Chrysler, while letting investment bank Lehman Brothers fold as a signal that the U.S. was not prepared to bail out every institution because it had become "too big to fail". As all of this unfolded, hitherto unregulated investment banks scrambled to recapitalize themselves with commercial bank operations so that they could qualify for Federal Deposit insurance and access to the Federal Reserves' Discount window facilities.

Public response to the Great Recession was driven in part by the magnitude of Federal government budget deficits, which some saw as getting beyond control. To facilitate a more orderly return of the economy, Congress adopted the Dodd-Frank legislation in 2010 that provided for orderly liquidation of failing firms, regulation of hedge fund advisors, a transfer of powers to the Comptroller of the Currency, the FDIC, and the Federal Reserve, along with creation of a Bureau of Consumer Financial Protection. It was as controversial as the ARRA legislation of 2009, and along with the passage of the Affordable Care Act of 2010, represented an increase in government oversight in the management of risk in the economy. As the U.S. economy has gained renewed strength, traditional arguments of whether government is intervening too much at the expense of individual liberty or whether it is assuming risks that markets seem unable to bear have once again shaped public discourse.

Currently, the U.S. faces yet another crisis that threatens to unhinge markets to a level not seen since the Second World War, namely, the coronavirus pandemic now sweeping the world. Originating first in Wuhan province in China, it soon began to spread to other regions of the world, causing havoc in countries least prepared for such an outbreak. Because symptoms of the coronavirus are not first evident in someone who has become infected, testing is essential, followed by the development of an effective vaccine.

In the U.S., as elsewhere, testing has been taking place at a relative slow rate with the result that infection rates have begun to spike. Panic among citizens has led to hoarding of household items, with supermarkets often emptied of stocks as fear drives consumer purchases.

Emergency measures of social distancing and attention to hygiene are the most effective responses thus far, but for which production and employment are taking a toll. The Dow Jones industrial average has lost 30 percent of its value from early March to the end of the month, and calls for emergency government intervention have led Congress to enact extraordinary spending measures to contain the economic impact of the outbreak. Limited and often distorted information have only made matters worse. What the coronavirus illustrates is the impact of a sudden shift in perceptions of risk and what citizens expect government to do in the face of a sudden economic downturn.

CHAPTER THREE

HOW NEUROSCIENCE INFORMS POLITICAL LEGITIMACY

Neuroscience and Human Behavior

Most social science is built on the notion of rationality in decision-making. In recent years, much of this has been contradicted by observation and experimentation. From this, neuroscience has emerged to provide insights that link how we perceive information and then choose to act. What social science has tried to retain is a normative framework from which in the presence of perfect information, our perceptions can lead us to make rational and positive decisions. We are far from that reality. Political legitimacy is as handicapped as other areas in its ability to provide us with a normative approach to decision-making. So let us consider what neuroscience and its antecedents has to say about human behavior, how it affects our notions of political legitimacy, and whether there are useful normative insights to be drawn.

As far back as the eighteenth century, Swiss mathematician Daniel Bernoulli (1700–1782) and Scottish economist Adam Smith (1732–1790), it is clear that emotions drive many decisions. When in 1738 Bernoulli observed the gambling behavior of individuals at the St. Petersburg, Russia, casinos, he noted a distinction between the notion of maximization of wealth and maximization of utility.[41] In a game in which successive plays could lead to an infinite payoff, he noted that many would stop at different points in the game. His conclusion is that gambling was a process of deriving satisfaction from the game but that different individuals had differing attitudes as to how much they were prepared to gamble. From this, we have his noting of risk averse, risk neutral, and risk lover decision makers. Bernoulli's insights have shaped modern game theory in Economics, leaving open how and why risk preferences change with circumstances and time.

Years before he wrote the *Wealth of Nations*, Smith had written an essay in 1759, *The Theory of Moral Sentiments*. Drawing on Enlightenment thinkers of the 18th century, Smith wrote on the complexity of human inter-actions that was latter distilled into the notion of the social benefit of the individual pursuit of self-interest as beneficial to society.

In his 1759 essay, Smith noted that acts of compassion for others could derive from one's sense of belonging to a larger social order, and that belonging, and being accepted, had much to do with the morality of one's individual conduct. As such, Smith was evoking notions of social psychol-ogy as a more insightful guide to moral action rather than pure reason alone. While Bernoulli's evocation of types of individual personalities has been information, when blended with Smith's notion of moral conduct, we have a more complex portrait of human interaction than a simple self-sat-isfying maximizing individual might explain, as is often portrayed in many texts in Economics.

Today, insights from historical observation have been grounded more recently into findings from neuroscience. Neuroscience helps to explain many anomalies that are otherwise puzzling. A joke in Economics helps make the point. Two men walking down the street come across a $20 bill on the sidewalk. One says to the other, "Look, there's a $20 bill on the side-walk. Let's pick it up." The other replies, "No, it cannot be a $20 bill because if it were, someone would have taken it already." In another vein, how is that individuals who observe declining values in a portfolio stock refuse to cut losses and rebalance. The answer, as many behavioral economists have noted, is that people may value losses greater than they value gains.

Instead of a calculus based on maximizing expected value, individuals are making choices in which they attach different weights to gains and losses. As Daniel Kahneman and Amos Tversky wrote years ago, individuals make choices on the basis of prospects, which allow for differing weights.[42]

Kahneman's work has pointed out how in a less than perfect information universe, we make choices on the basis of proxies. These proxies are built around heuristics, that is simplified ways that we perceive information, but which are subject to cognitive bias.

There are three types of cognitive bias present when we use heuristics to make decisions, namely, representativeness, availability, and anchoring. Faced with limited information from which to make a decision, the representatives bias leads us to ignore prior probabilities of an event, to ignore the sample size from which a probability is assigned, a misconception of chance and predictability, and thus the illusion of validity.[43]

Behavioral economics, and behavioral finance, now provide greater insights into human decisions than earlier notions of decisions made under conditions of risk. What neuroscience has done is to build on psychological insights through direct observation of chemical signals emanating from the brain. Scans of individual responses to various stimuli reveal that of the various parts of the brain, some rely on one part of the brain more than the other.[44]

The oldest part of the brain is the stem, which contains the medulla, oblongata, the midbrain, and pons. These organs control primal functions of breathing, heart rate, and blood pressure. The brain stem determines primal survival responses unrelated to reason. In contrast, the cerebral cortex, and basal ganglia make up the forepart of the brain. The cerebral cortex provides a control mechanism that responds to new information before adopting a response. The forebrain generally works more slowly than the amygdala, and it enables one to modify behavior through reasoning in response with new information.

Individuals vary according to whether they rely more intensely on the stem, the midbrain, or the frontal cortex in making decisions. This adds a more complex dimension to Bernoulli's notion of individuals who may be risk averse, risk neutral, or risk loving when faced with gambling prospects.

Politics, and attitudes on politics, are profoundly shaped by whether individuals are more responsive to the more emotional amygdala or the more rational frontal cortex in making decisions. The conduct of politicians often is grounded in emotional manipulation, and thus prone to more strictly emotional decisions than when driven by the frontal cortex. We may observe a politician who is adept at manipulating emotions to garner and retain power, even if the emotions may not be the best guide for making decisions.

In his 1933 inaugural address, President Franklin D. Roosevelt noted that the only thing we have to fear is fear itself. In contrast, when Niccolò Machiavelli issued his essay, *The Prince*, in 1532, he was pointing to the value of using intimidation by a ruler, to marshal support and retain power. The juxtaposition of these two views illustrates the complex nature of political decision-makers and the political order in which they operate.

As we have posited here, political legitimacy remains a conundrum. When an economy is faltering, political leaders often offer up strong positions in response. They may or may not be authoritarian ones, depending on the state of mind of citizens. If the public holds expectations that transparency and knowledge should prevail, they are making a front cortex argument as to how decisions should be made in the face of an economic crisis.

When an economy is enjoying buoyant results, the need for fundamental change should be less compelling as long as individuals are relying on frontal cortex decision-making. That is what we would expect in the polity. Yet we see that even in improving times, political discourse can turn inward, even vindictive, as though matters are far worse than they seem. It is a phenomenon most found in far-Right and far-Left ideologies, and problematic for democratic institutions, to say the least.

The fields of behavioral economics and behavioral finance provide a more complex framework through which decisions are made. Instead of the perfectly rational individual who seeks to maximize his or her own satisfaction or income, choices depend on how we perceive information and around which we display various types of cognitive bias that are linked to how our brains are wired.

One way around a fully informed logical decision framework is through local order rationality. Under such conditions, people may make decisions that are boundedly rational, that is, rational within the local confines of knowledge that an individual perceives. Where bounded rationality diverges from globally informed rationality, markets can fail to achieve a socially desired outcome, from which calls for government intervention can often arise.

Daniel Kahneman (1934–) and the late Amos Tversky (1937–1996) undertook pioneering work in the field of behavioral psychology. Linking cognitive psychology to economics, they reformulated a standard paradigm in economics, namely, that individuals maximize utility or income but in which other factors determine a decision. They summarized this new perspective in a 1979 article entitled "Prospect Theory", to account for observed anomalies in the standard theory of human behavior.[45]

They came up with three types of bias that influence how decisions are made: representativeness, availability, and anchoring. We are prone to make judgments about a decision based on anecdote and hearsay more often than on scientific sampling. We thus formulate a relationship that may be counterfactual to scientific evidence. Such thinking can lead to herd behavior in which we make decisions because we think others are doing so. One result of this is speculative asset bubbles, which we will take up later in greater detail.

A second bias in decision-making is the availability heuristic. We often are more heavily influenced by something that just happened rather than by an event some time ago or one possibly in the future. When the dot.com boom took place and when the Great Recession of 2008 unfolded, most looked only at the current behavior of the stock and housing markets. Few considered whether the stock market crash of 1929 had any relevance to mistakes that might be repeating themselves in a recent event. Judgments thus can be heavily influenced by the most recent headlines rather than by a longer-term perspective where the consequences were more evident. And much of this bias derives from our ability to recall the larger range of experience that might more usefully inform our decisions.

The third source of bias derives from the anchoring effect. We tend to make decisions on the basis of the first piece of information received. Factors that drive the anchoring effect are mood, experience, personality, and cognitive ability. One corollary dimension of the anchoring effect is the endowment effect. We weigh decisions more strongly for items that we own rather than when we do not. This explains, for example, why individuals who own a share of stock that is losing value to avoid selling it at some point to cut losses. This implies that loss aversion is valued more than a gain.

In the words of Daniel Kahneman, we make decisions at two possible levels: System 1, which is fast, instinctive and emotional; and System 2, which is slower, more logical, and deliberative. System 1 behavior is easier to follow, but prone to the kinds of bias in decision-making we already have noted. System 2 takes longer but can reduce the level of bias in our decision-making. The question is whether we simply are too lazy and habit-driven to tackle the harder task of System 2 thinking, in which case we may wind up with decisions we may later come to regret once more information has become available.

Taken together, we find that because making rational decisions is complex, we rely on heuristics and heuristics can be misleading. Any number of studies have illustrated how bias influences our decisions. When we make biased decisions in economics or politics, we may wind up undermining foundational notions of political legitimacy, namely, that government actions can guide the allocation of resources to best satisfy societal wants. And that leads us directly to neuroscience, how the brain processes information, and thus to what extent does our behavior translate into a legitimate form of governance.

Biology and Human Nature

Biology is a foundational discipline for neuroscience. Research has come a long way since the work of nineteenth century British naturalist, Charles Darwin. Looking back, in his 1859 book, *Origin of the Species*, Darwin spelled out a framework of human evolution, a radical notion at the time and at odds with prevailing theological teachings. For humans, our ancestors descended from primates that include apes and monkeys. This shocked many at the time, for whom biblical teachings state the origins of humans within the creation of the earth in six days. Believers in a literal interpretation of the Bible then undertook a concerted campaign to discredit Darwin's teachings, and whose legacy is still with us today.

In the U.S., the evolution of species was the focus of the famous Scopes Trial of 1925. John Scopes, a Dayton, Tennessee, schoolteacher, was charged with violating the Butler Act, which then strictly forbade the teaching of human evolution in any state-funded school.[46] Scopes was found guilty and given a fine of $100, which was later overturned. Yet it set the stage for generations of conflict between religious groups and the scientific community, one of whose consequences has been the rise of private religious schools instead of state-funded public education.

The science of evolution has been validated through observation of how species have adapted over time to changing environments.[47] In 1974, paleoanthropologist Donald Johansen's discovery of a 3.2 million-year-old female hominin australopithecine, to whom he and his co-discoverers Yves Coppens and Maurice Taleb, gave the name of "Lucy".[48] Continuing research has revealed other fossils that provide a more complete table of human evolution.[49]

Evolution stands in contrast to Creationism, which attributes all varieties of species as a reflection of divine will. For Christian creationists, it draws its narrative from the Book of Genesis, that the world was created in a very short span of time, six days in the extreme, and something on the order of 10,000 years at the other end. This stands in contradiction

Figure 3.1 Display at the Creation Museum, Petersburg, Kentucky, 2020.

Source: https://creationmuseum.org/?gclid=EAIaIQobChMIncvultCJ6gIVDI_
ICh3KoQlCEAAYASAAEgKaWvD_BwE

to archaeological discoveries of fossils that date back to millions of years, well before humans were living in bands of small communities as hunter gatherers.

Despite accumulating scientific evidence, evolution is still viewed with suspicion by those who see it as contradicting a literal interpretation of biblical teachings. To re-affirm a literal interpretation, some have gone so far as to construct a Creation museum in Petersburg, Kentucky, in addition to finding various public images of an anti-evolutionist view of the world. Founded in 2007 by Ken Ham, an Australian born Christian fundamentalist, whose exhibits portray the earth as not older than 6,000 years.[50] This differs from the scientific consensus that the early is approximately 4.5 billion years old, and the universe dates to 13.8 billion years.

Opposition to evolution continues for those who view society as threatened by scientific inquiry. This opposition has propelled not just an aversion to public school education. It also has fueled a conservative view of government, as subversive, amoral, and inimical to human liberty.

This aversion translates into opposition to a separation of church and state, out of which is a range of issues that continue to animate conservative political discourse, ranging from school prayer, second amendment gun rights, to abortion rights. And, needless to say, political rivalries often are driven by efforts to appeal to sentiments regarding these issues.

Political considerations aside, how can religious beliefs be reconciled with the weight of science and constitutional principles? How can one preserve the right to practice religion while at the same time defining a constitution that stipulates a separation of Church and State? The late paleontologist Stephen Jay Gould offered a more nuanced theory that could provide a bridge to an answer. He argued that random events can affect the evolution of species, and which is known as contingent evolution.[51] Contingent evolution helps to explain the absence of a literal line of progression, leaving open the question of religious beliefs. But this is far from complete.

Creationism has drawn broad criticism from the scientific community. Some, such as Richard Dawkins, have argued that in his 2006 book, *The God Delusion*, that God does not exist and that the state of the world is purely a result of evolutionary forces.[52] Others have taken a less critical stance, notably Stephen Jay Gould and Frances Collins, in which belief in a supreme being can stand alongside the weight of scientific inquiry.[53] Collins was appointed Director of the National Institutes of Health during the Obama administration, and was instrumental in the discovery of genes associated with several diseases. He has affirmed that religious belief can co-exist with scientific inquiry. Gould has argued that science and religion constitute two separate domains of understanding: science defines the natural world, and religion the moral one. As they are separate domains, there is no conflict, and which he characterizes as non-overlapping *magisteria*.

For many, religion is the only guide to a moral and just society, and thus a politically legitimate state. This belief has led to the organization of Evangelical Christian groups that openly advocate politically for greater expression of religion—in schools, on public spaces, and in terms of how political candidates meet tests of authenticity. It infuses a fractious debate

Figure 3.2 Rejection of Evolution.

Source: Billboard on Route 13 north just south of Seaford, Delaware, June 2020.

over rights to an abortion and to the treatment of non-heterosexual individuals and household units.

The 1973 Supreme Court decision in *Roe v. Wade*, which declared that the right to an abortion is guaranteed by the Constitution, has been a flashpoint of contention every time someone is nominated to the Supreme Court. While not all opponents of abortion are Evangelicals, the drive to overturn *Roe v. Wade* has been driven largely by religious conservatives. Political observers call abortion a wedge issue that can spur voters to support or oppose a particular candidate on that question alone. It has been used by Conservatives and Liberals alike as an organizing tool to increase voter turnout, even if recent decisions by the Court have affirmed *Roe v. Wade* as a settled precedent. Whether that will be the case in the future depends critically on the composition of justices on the Supreme Court, and which becomes a battleground every time a vacancy on the court opens up.

Individual and Collective Identity

The evolution-creationism debate illustrates something about the human brain and our ability to reconcile factual evidence with instinctive behavior. Advances in neuroscience have enabled us to acquire a more complex understanding of human behavior. In the process, it can help us to arrive at a more satisfactory definition of political legitimacy.

Neuroscience draws on physical chemistry and experimental psychology to examine interactions of the nervous system and the brain. Brain scans and other techniques enable scientists to examine how various stimuli affect the nervous system as well as brain functions. As such, it has spawned several parallel scientific disciplines that include behavioral economics, behavioral finance, and behavioral political science. In the process, it has broadened standard notions of rational choice in the social sciences to provide a more complete account of human behavior.[54] Research in this area is foundational to an inclusive framing of political legitimacy.

From evolutionary biology, we now know that human motor skills and brain functions have become more complex over time. What neuroscience brings to this perspective is how the brain has evolved in terms of processing information and emotional responses.

Evolution of the human brain has evolved in three stages. The first and oldest is the reptilian, or survival brain, found at the stem atop the spinal cord. The survival brain operates at an unconscious level, managing heart, breathing, eating, and other basic functions. It also senses risk and leads to unreflective action, whether aggressive impulsive conduct or flight. It reflects no thinking about the future and is predicated simply on an immediate drive to survive.

New Yorker Magazine writer Malcolm Gladwell has written about impulsive behavior in such books as *Blink*, and *The Tipping Point*, while Princeton Psychologist Daniel Kahneman won a Nobel Prize in Economics for his research summarized in the best-selling book, *Thinking Fast and Slow*.[55] Sometimes, instincts can work well for survival, while in other circumstances it can lead to disaster. Whether one or the other depends on how much information is available at a given decision moment and how much of it an individual has understood when received.

Beyond the reptilian brain, we find the limbic system. It governs the emotional brain via the auditory, visual, and memory functions. The limbic

Figure 3.3 Tripartite Division of the Brain.

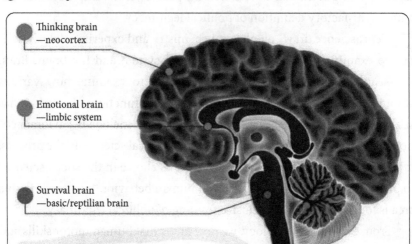

Source: Vanessa Elliott and Ken Horrigan, "Neuroscience: The Brains behind Behaviour Based Safety", Proceedings 19th Triennial Congress of the IEA, Melbourne, 9–14, August 2015, p. 3.

system incorporates language comprehension and provides a basis for decision-making based on habit and experience. The limbic system comprises the amygdala, the hippocampus, the thalamus, the hypothalamus, the basal ganglia, and the cingulate gyrus.

The amygdala shapes perception of emotions such as anger, fear, and sadness, and serves as a regulator in controlling aggression. It helps store memories of emotions and events, thus enabling decisions to be made based on familiar experiences. The hippocampus consolidates information from short-term memory to long-term memory to provide spatial memory that enables navigation in decisions.

The hypothalamus regulates metabolic processes that affect temperature, blood pressure, hunger, thirst, and sleep. The hypothalamus transmits metabolic information to the thalamus. The thalamus consists of two lobes, one in each hemisphere of the brain, and sends signals to the cerebral cortex, the outer layer of the brain where higher reasoning functions take place.

Although the cerebral cortex is physically the largest component of the brain, it operates more slowly than the limbic system, and which in turn even more slowly than the reptilian section of the brain. The cerebral cortex guides rational decisions based on available information. It has shaped much of how we view scientific research and discovery. Moreover, the rationality dimension of the cerebral cortex has driven not just physical science but also the social sciences, where observation and testing lead to informed conclusions about human behavior.

Given the differential operational speeds of different parts of the brain, because the cerebral cortex operates more slowly than the limbic or primal parts, our ability to make rational decisions is often subject to the distorting effects of habit and basic instincts. This confounds our perspective regarding how science can inform our decision-making. When confronted with novel or counter-intuitive informative that is based on scientific observation, our

Figure 3.4 Functions of the Brain.

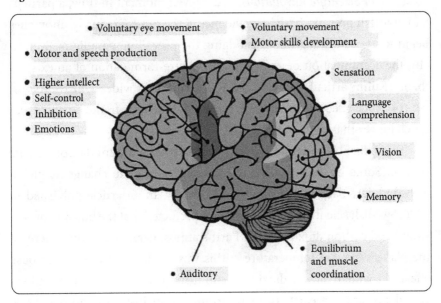

reactions may not respond in a rational fashion. We may respond with dis-belief and skepticism, even if the evidence we note is contrary to our tra-ditional perspective. For this reason, when it comes to allocating scarce resources, or adopting a collective decision through government, we may not display the necessary rational basis on which such decisions are made.

Climate Change and Neuroscience

Perhaps nothing illustrates the rational vs. emotional mental processes bet-ter than the question of climate change. In a debate similar to the helio-centric theories that Galileo and Kepler put forth centuries ago against the traditional geocentric formulation, climate change today is viewed by some as nothing more than as part of a cyclical pattern that will revert to some norm that we have been accustomed to observing. What remains is whether scientific investigations validate cyclical patterns or something that is bringing about a more fundamental structural change.

Years ago, Thomas Kuhn noted this phenomenon in his book, *The Structure of Scientific Revolutions*.[56] At a given moment in time, a particu-lar paradigm prevails, based on evidence at the time. Gradually, anomalies begin to appear, though not dislodging the prevailing paradigm. Eventu-ally, the accumulation of anomalies forces a re-formulation of an existing theory. Kuhn's articulation of how science evolves provides a mirror to how neuroscience affects our thinking, except that the time frame he noted was much longer than so many decisions we face today.

The farther back in time one goes, the less reliable are any data on climate change. Some of the first characterizations of climate change as global warming date back to the nineteenth century. In an article published in 1896, Swedish scientist Svante Arrhenius predicted that the burning of coal would add carbon dioxide to the Earth's atmosphere, and in turn increase the planet's average temperature.[57] This was the basis of the "greenhouse effect" in which carbon dioxide accumulating in the upper atmosphere would prevent the earth from returning to an historical normal level.

However, data collection to validate Arrhenius' conjecture was limited at the time. As a coal-based industrial revolution was creating unprecedented levels of income and wealth, many at the time chose to ignore the environmental impact that such growth was producing.

Beginning in the 1960's, research findings on climate change began to accumulate, precipitating a shift in perspective in the public policy arena. By 1970, public opinion had changed to the point of celebrating "Earth Day", and the creation of public agencies dedicated to tracking and advising on environmental quality. As a result, efforts were undertaken to mitigate global warming by 2 degrees Celsius by the year 2050, a goal enshrined in the Paris Climate Agreement of 2016 and to which 195 countries, including the U.S. at the time, signed.[58] As of 2019, the increase in global temperatures has risen by 1.2 degrees Celsius. At current rates, global temperatures could rise as much as 4 degrees Celsius by 2050, under which millions of the earth's populations could no longer survive.

Research on climate change has documented evidence of rising global temperatures associated with carbon dioxide emissions into the atmosphere. It also has documented that the polar ice caps are melting at unprecedented rates. Since 1950, sea levels have risen by 16.2 centimeters.[59] Were all of the polar ice to melt into the oceans, sea levels are projected to rise by between 65.4 and 70 meters (216 to 230 feet), putting millions of people at risk, along with the risk of extinction of many wildlife species.[60] As ice serves as a sink to sequester carbon, the melting of polar ice and the associated rise in sea levels would accelerate global climate change in ways that would challenge the ability to contain and reverse this trend.

The election of Donald Trump in 2016 resulted in a United States withdrawal from the Paris Agreement on the grounds that other countries are not in compliance and that it is harming U.S. economic growth. The Trump administration has adopted policies to promote coal production in an effort to create jobs in areas where unemployment rates were increasing as the economy moved to adopt lower carbon emissions technologies. While the economic intent has been clear, it also has buttressed groups of climate deniers who reject the science of climate change. Climate deniers reject both the science and efforts to create a more "green economy" based on more environmentally sustainable technologies.

The Trump administration has gone so far as to prohibit the release of new findings that are consistent with climate change, and to forbid the use of "global warming" in official government reporting.[61] The suppression of scientific inquiry undermines a rational path to public policy, to the dismay of many who would otherwise be sympathetic to conservative efforts to reduce government intervention in the economy.

Neuroscience provides us with a way to understand arguments by climate scientists and its deniers. To the extent that fear of the possible consequences of climate change prevails, one can seek safety in denying its existence. That position is far easier to adopt than the more difficult one of weighing the evidence of climate change and figuring out a coherent rational response.

Figure 3.5 Scientific Evidence on Climate Change.

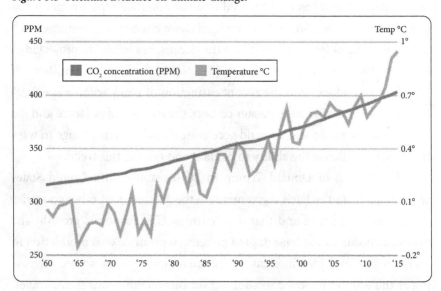

Source: https://climate.nasa.gov/vital-signs/global-temperature/

Figure 3.6 Global Sea Level Change since 1880.

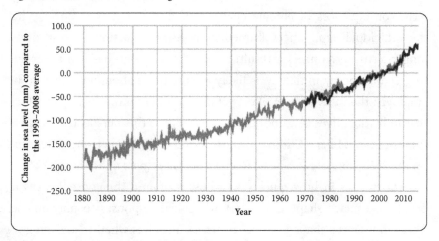

Source: https://climate.nasa.gov/vital-signs/sea-level/

We can summarize climate denial positions in terms of the following statements:[62]

1. CO_2 is not increasing
2. Even if CO_2 is increasing, it has no impact of climate
3. Even if there is global warming, it is due to natural causes
4. Even if warming is due to human action, the impact of continued greenhouse gas emissions is minor
5. Even if global warming is significant, the changes are good for us.
6. Even if climate change is not good, humans are flexible and capable of adapting when technological innovation is needed.

If one knows by experience how a physical landscape appears, and where the immediate impact of climate change seems minor, then the tendency to discount the larger long-term impact may prevail. When added to this that the immediate economic consequences of a loss in jobs due to efforts to promote a clean energy economy can be felt, then the longer-term benefits of a more sustainable economy seem less important.

An individual can be presented with compelling evidence of the long-term consequences of climate change but discount its relevance. What the individual experiences immediately displaces action to confront a longer-term horizon. As a result, the coal miner who has lost a job due to green economy initiatives is likely to care more about any effort to be employed than the broader effects of coal mining on the society in which that individual lives. And politicians who ignore this perspective do so at their peril, as Hillary Clinton acknowledged in 2017 when she stated that on the 2016 campaign trail she would put coal miners out of business.[63]

Differences in how quickly and how profound the consequences of events take place shape individual and social responses to phenomena. These differences shape political attitudes, and thus whether a given government administration is seen as legitimate.

Neuroscience provides no simple menu for political legitimacy, but it does provide insights as to how individuals respond to information. It is also important to note that these differences in responses to information do not define one political party or another, as the Great Depression of the 1930's serves to illustrate.

On Friday, October 24, 1929, the Dow Jones industrial average index fell by 12.9 percent, followed by near 13 percent drop on Monday, October 28. Yet, unlike the 22.6 percent drop on Monday, October 22, 1987, the 5 percent drop in 2000, or the 20 percent drop in 2008–2009. At the time of the October, 1929 crash, President Herbert Hoover was confronted with a mix of conflicting advice.

Some had considered the stock market to have been overvalued from the "Roaring" 1920s and that the drop would serve to purge the market of speculators and bring valuations to a more realistic level. Noted economist Joseph Schumpeter argued that to do anything would only make matters worse.[64] This stood in direct contrast to the position adopted by John Maynard Keynes in his 1936 treatise, *The General Theory of Employment, Interest and Money*, in which he advocated fiscal discretionary deficit spending to achieve full employment.[65] As he wrote as far back as 1923,

"In the Long-Run we are all dead", in response to whether government should take action in response to a crisis.[66]

In response to the downtown in the economy, the Federal Reserve bank adopted a tight money policy in hopes that it would end speculation and restore economic growth. In later years, Milton Friedman disputed this position in his 1960 book, *A Monetary History of the United States, 1867–1960.*[67] Friedman argued that the Federal Reserve bank should not have pursued a tight monetary policy in response to the Great Depression and that an easing of monetary policy could have avoided the depths of the downturn that ensued. It was a lesson that Federal Reserve Chairman Ben Bernanke would later apply in the financial crisis of 2008, and which many view as having avoided a new Great Depression.[68]

Some today have little appreciation for the policy choices made in response to the 2008 financial crisis.[69] The lack of appreciation by some can be traced to perceptions of information and how we respond. Because the economy did not go through another Great Depression, some consider that the use of quantitative easing was inappropriate not just for the increase in public debt but in the larger role of government in the economy.

In 2020, we now see a reprise of the last financial crisis of 2008, namely, the downturn in equity markets and in the economy as a coronavirus pandemic spreads from China throughout the world. As it has unfolded, limited testing capabilities have made it difficult to identify the underlying epidemiology of the disease, particularly in that an infected person may not display symptoms under several days after exposure. With millions of persons around the world now confronting the expansion of coronavirus, governments are adopting interim measures of quarantines and forced reductions in services to reduce large gatherings of populations to potential exposure.

Once again, perceptions have shaped how or whether to act. Regulations to limit public gatherings is a rational response to the perceived threat of coronavirus expansion and contamination, as are efforts to accelerate testing and developing a suitable vaccine. Yet, whether in panic selling in stock markets or in hoarding toilet paper and paper towels from store shelves, individuals are responding with fear of contamination.

Such behavior reflects signaling from the primal brain through the limbic system and displacing how our frontal cortex might lead us to behave. As with financial panics, once more information becomes available, individuals may return to a more reasoned set of responses to events, and parts of the economy's institutional structure may return to normal. Taken together, what is clear is that in the short-run, our decisions are more prone to impulsive choices driven by emotion rather than in a careful weighing of evidence from which a more accurate assessment of risk can be made, and acted upon accordingly.

If emotions can drive political decisions, and by extension, casting and shaping the framework of government intervention in an economy, where does this leave the question of political legitimacy? As noted in the outset, political legitimacy is a system by which individuals choose or accept to be governed. Those who argue in favor of greater transparency are appealing implicitly to the frontal cortex, to reason, to make political decisions. Those who favor secrecy are more likely to appeal to the amygdala in making decisions, out of which comes the notion of government by fear.

In the short-run, even those who generally are averse to government intervention, calls to do so displace longer term attitudes. When government fails to respond to the heightened magnitude of short-term events, leadership is called into question. Those who find greater government intervention over the long term are as critical as those in the short-term who would oppose such action. In a democracy, an election thus serves to either repudiate or validate a government administration, based on prevailing political sentiment. In a dictatorship or authoritarian regime, little matters up to the point where armed insurrection threatens to overturn the government.

No one should think that insights from neuroscience provide a magic key to political legitimacy. What it can do is to provide insights into attitudes and responses to a given set of events, and in turn as to how or whether a government has responded appropriately. In a normative sense, while electronic media seem to communicate more effectively the state of public sentiment, we also know that distorted perceptions can emerge, either through manipulation or through a lack of accountability for statements that influence emotional responses.

Extremist groups across the spectrum often seek to manipulate the media through emotionally charged statements that reverberate far faster than used to be the case when print media predominated. The speed with which charged statements can be sent coursing across the internet tend to bias our thinking toward the short-term, and thus to grant less weight to the burdens of reasoning through our frontal cortex rather than relying on habit and primal instincts to arrive at judgments and decisions. It is troubling for our sense of political legitimacy in that instability becomes the norm. Historically, constitutions both unwritten and written, have served to provide a framework through which governance should take place.

In the short-term, deliberative legal institutions such as the courts are burdened with reconciling momentary pressures from the longer-term need to assess and weigh evidence against established precedent. As long as short-term perspectives, driven to no small extent by the speed of technological innovation, prevail, we are likely to descend into a world in which impulse and habit dominate our choices on governance, and that does not bode well for political legitimacy over the longer term.

Neuroscience and an Economic Theory of the State

In each of the examples we have examined, we have seen how differing perceptions of risk produced various forms of government intervention. Our interest is not to argue some doctrinaire approach to political economy, but rather to show in successive chapters how these perceptions are formed, what effects they have produced, and what lessons they hold for the future of state-market relations.

For any given individual personality, we tend in the short-run to rely on impulse and habit rather than the more challenging process of complex reasoning. This is particularly true when we are confronted with scientific findings that may not be in accord with our pre-conceived notions.

It is difficult to change one's mind when confronted with counterfactual evidence. Our tendency is to dismiss findings contrary to our habitual frames of reference, particularly if they invoke sentiments of fear of the consequences. We thus find ourselves rationalizing about the significance of events, especially when the time frame is in reference to the long past or equally in the future. Unless something seems to bring immediate consequences, we are slow to change our views and take actions accordingly.

When we find that events seem more momentous than within our capacity to undertake personal action, it is then that we look to collective action, primarily government intervention, to change the likelihood of events. If, regardless of whether government intervenes in response to an event, things seems to move toward some normal state of affairs, we are less prone to demand change and to leave things as they are. This is certainly true in the case of the current coronavirus pandemic.

In light of the human health and economic impact of a virus pandemic, perceptions of what more permanent role government should play in economic affairs display an extraordinary lack of consensus. In the process, this lack of consensus bears directly on the legitimacy of government. In some cases, governments fall for failure to be seen as addressing a major crisis, while in others, governments may take on larger functions that citizens may later come to regret. To make sense of this, we now need to look at the economic functions of government in both normal and exceptional times, and whether they affirm a longer underlying social contract or whether a fundamental change is viewed as essential.

CHAPTER FOUR

AN INSTITUTIONAL FRAMEWORK
FOR STATES AND MARKETS

Government Then and Now

Governments and markets represent two alternate ways of allocating scarce resources. While markets use price discovery to match buyers and sellers, governments use regulation, spending, and taxation to achieve designated outcomes. Each responds to the presence of risk in varying ways. How those responses are made depends basically on perceptions of risk and whether markets or government provides the best way for its management. What we need to examine here is how risk is factored in market and government decisions, and how perceptions of risk shape their respective roles.

Government institutions today are engaged in a complex set of activities and goals in comparison to a century ago. If you look at government finances in the early part of the twentieth century the differences are striking.[70] First, government played a much smaller role in the economy than it has during the latter part of the twentieth century. In 1913, for example, the overall ratio of federal and state taxes to the Gross Domestic Product was just under eight percent. Moreover, the state tax ratio, which stood at 5.8 percent, was more than three times the federal rate of 1.87 percent.

Now look at where government stood as of 2004: the ratio of federal taxes to the Gross Domestic Product was 19.72 and that for the states was at 10.30, for an overall ratio of 30.1. If federal and state government ratios were at their 1913 levels, the level of tax receipts in 2004 would have been $209 billion at the federal government level and $650 billion at the state level, figures that seem almost unimaginable today when compared to the 2004 actual federal tax receipts of $2.2 trillion and state tax receipts of $1.15 trillion. The key lies in the vast expansion of responsibilities we have granted to various levels of government. In almost every case, these enlarged responsibilities have involved a shift in risk from individuals to those of society at large.

A second comparison is that the types of taxes collected in the early twentieth century differed substantially from those of today. 1913 is a useful benchmark year in that the U.S. was not yet engaged in global military responsibilities.[71] It was also when a standardized federal income tax had been adopted through passage of the sixteenth amendment to the U.S. constitution.[72] It was not until the 1930's that federal payroll withholding taxes were instituted. Without payroll taxes, it is doubtful that the New Deal programs of Franklin D. Roosevelt could have been adopted on the then modest scale that they were.[73]

A third comparison is that in 1913, almost all government functions were limited to the production of goods and service such as national defense, education, and health, activities that today would show up in estimates of national income and product accounts such as the Gross Domestic Product. In contrast, governments today account for a substantial expansion in transfer payments, that is, monetary exchanges for which at the time of the transaction, no good or service has been produced.[74] Examples include unemployment insurance, social security payments, Veterans' benefits, and temporary assistance to needy families.[75] At the federal government level, these expenditures account today for fully a third of total outlays. Again, the relevance of this distinction is the extent to which government is managing risks through transfer payments mechanisms.

How can we make sense of changes in the size of government, its composition, and the relationship of government to the market? One way to do so is to look at the economic functions of government and how these functions replace or complement functions of the market.

Economic Functions of the Public Sector

Governments perform a variety of functions. They do so with varying degrees of efficiency. Economists have spent a lot of effort to provide rational criteria for government intervention, and in the process, to devise a mechanism when government action is warranted and when it is not.[76] Each of these criteria depends ultimately on perceptions of risk and whether government intervention provides some necessary improvement over market instruments.

Governments perform five basic economic functions. They are: 1. Provide a legal and institutional framework for the efficient allocation of resources; 2. Promote Distributive Justice; 3. Promote competition in support of economic efficiency; 4. Promote stabilization and economic growth; 5. Provide for an efficient composition of goods and services. These functions expand and contract in proportion to perceptions of how markets handle the associated risks in each economic function. Let us look at each of these functions in turn and how perceptions of risk shape their roles.

Government as Arbiter of a Market-Based System

Let us consider briefly the nature of each function. The first refers to government as an umpire or referee in the marketplace. It does not imply an activist role for government, but rather one in which the setting of clearly defined rules can foster a more efficient allocation of resources.

Markets are naturally self-forming arrangements in which informal rules emerge from experience. They may later be ratified through government laws and regulations. Historically, markets operated as a function of the costs and returns over the distance involved in the exchange of goods and services. Within a given market, the spatial organization of trading reflected the importance of particular goods and services.

Legal systems evolved to enforce contracts, and to arbitrate disputes over trade and property rights. These legal systems were expected to serve some larger needs of the community such as assistance to the poor or to shape the content of what goods and services would be produced. Moreover, legal institutions were not expected to manage fluctuations in market pricing, even though ever since the Middle Ages, debates would continue over some notion of what is "fair pricing".

In the Middle Ages, St. Thomas Aquinas and other writers of his time often argued over the "just price" of a good, as well as over the role of interest, which then was viewed as usury. Although credit is not something that could not be provided at a zero cost, philosophers tended to treat it as such in the quest to achieve a form of market fairness.[77]

It would take time before the time value of money would be recognized as a legitimate basis for including interest in credit transactions. Today, religious practices often confront the role of interest with both skepticism and indeed, formal opposition in some cases. today, Islamic finance, for example, is predicated on the absence of interest. Instead of direct interest payments, ownership shares are provided as a form of collateral, and from which profits can be divided and allocated.[78] It is a way around the role of interest, and the associated risk of a given financial transaction.

The larger the geographic distance in a market the larger is likely to be the time frame of a transaction. As European countries began to emerge from the Middle Ages, the growth of far flung commerce was often a risky proposition, just as domestic markets could fluctuate in response to seasonal weather and disease. As a result, the question became one of where to find a suitable source of credit to undertake lengthy investments.

Two choices emerged. One was the rise of merchant banking, while the other was the role of central governments. In Florence, Italy, the Renaissance flourished because banking families such as the Medici provided a stream of credit to merchants trading over ever larger distances. To the north, the Fugger family of Augsburg expanded their lending power in a similar fashion and were crucial to the expansion of the Hapsburg dynasty as an agency of the Holy Roman Empire.

Banking families often faced these risks through the issuance of loans directly to borrowers in both private commerce as well as to governments. Commercial banking that we recognize today was largely nonexistent, and household savings often were in the form of accumulated physical assets on which to draw in bad times such as drought, disease, or war. Moreover, borrowers also faced direct risk in undertaking loans, with the result that credit instruments were subject to large fluctuations as economic circumstances evolved.

Two examples underscore the question of government as agent to support market institutions. Christopher Columbus (1451–1506), an Italian explorer from Genoa, came across the idea that trade with the Far East could become more profitable by finding a trade route to the far East sources of the spice trade. Marco Polo's (1254–1324) travels to China between 1271 and 1295, along with the European discovery of spice markets in such places as Damascus and Cairo, served to inspire the search for an inexpensive route to the East Indies. Having traveled aboard ships as far as the coast of present-day Ghana, Columbus noted that items found on the beaches were from some faraway place. He was convinced that there was a westward sea route to the Indies and began a search for financing an expedition.

Merchants in his native Genoa, and then in Marseille turned down his appeal for financing of such an exploratory voyage. Columbus then turned to the newly created kingdom of Spain ruled over by King Ferdinand and Queen Isabella. When he made his appeal to the king, once again he was turned down. It was only when Queen Isabella said she could persuade the King to undertake such a voyage on condition that Columbus engage in a mission to convert any person he came across to the Catholic faith. To this Columbus agreed, all the while extracting a promise that he would be the Viceroy of the as yet discovered Indies.

Figure 4.1 Christopher Columbus: Explorer, Plunderer, or a Venture Capitalist before his Time?

Source: Sebastiano Luciani del Piombo, 1519, New York Metropolitan Museum of Art.

We know the rest of the story of Columbus' several voyages to the Americas. Arriving at Salvador in October 1492, he thought he had arrived at the Indies. And while Viking explorers had landed in the New World as far back as the end of the tenth century, it was the draw of a trading empire that Spain, and almost simultaneously, Portugal, then set out to conquer.

Although Spain and Portugal agreed to separate spheres of interest in the 1494 Treaty of Tordesillas, neither kingdom became as wealthy as once thought they would. Part of this is that Spain's discovery of silver in the mines of Bolivia and Peru would lead to a vast wave of inflation from which the country seemed little able to counter at the time. In the absence of a central bank and other financial institutions, both Portugal and Spain did create imperial riches for their homeland, but it did not translate well as other countries of Europe engaged in financial innovation.

An inheritance in 1556 resulted in the acquisition of what is now the Netherlands and Belgium passing to the Spanish King Philip II (1527–1598). King Philip, who had failed to defeat the English in 1588 when they sent a naval armada to lay claim to what he viewed as his heir to the English throne, had sought to consolidate his holdings in the lowlands to prop up commercial expansion between Europe and the Americas. It was an expensive proposition. The Spanish crown underwent periodic bankruptcies, in 1557, 1560, 1569, 1575, and 1596 in the quest to build a fleet of ships and an administration to support the Atlantic trade. Against this, the Dutch in the lowlands resented the imposition of tax levies to support the crown, and declared an independent Dutch Republic in 1581.

In what would be viewed today as a guerilla war, the Dutch managed to wrest effective control of the lowlands under the banner of their Dutch Republic. By 1609, a truce was signed between Spain and the Dutch, and for which formal recognition of the Dutch Republic would be granted in the Treaty of Munster in 1648, at the end of the Thirty Years' War.

What is the significance of the Dutch Republic? The United Provinces, as the Netherlands was for a while duly constituted, had a population of barely 2 million, while continental Spain had a population of 10 million. How was it possible for the Dutch to succeed against a much larger Spain, and across the Channel, their English rivals, in creating a vast commercial trading empire?

Where the Spanish failed, and the Dutch succeeded, was in financial innovation. The Dutch pioneered in the development of limited stock companies and the world's first modern stock exchange in the early seventeenth century.[79] Begun by the Dutch East Indies company (the *Vereinigte Oostindische Compagnie*, or VOC) in 1602, and the Dutch West Indies Company (*Geoctroyeerde Westindische Compagnie*) in 1621, the Dutch were able to attract investment from all over Europe at a time when other countries relied largely on government taxation to finance state-building and commerce.

As to our example of Columbus, through the creation of joint stock trading companies and a stock exchange, the Dutch managed to build a commercial fleet of ships and an armed navy that would first take on the Spanish, and then their rivals, the English, in a series of four naval battles over the next century, and largely defeat their larger adversaries.[80] The key to their success was the limited liability stock company. By separating management from ownership liability, firms were able to take on risks that before were inconceivable without the involvement of the state. In the process, the Dutch became the wealthiest in Europe for a while, all due to their ability to attract both capital and labor to their markets.[81]

Figure 4.2 Private Stock Ownership Serves to Share Economic Risks.

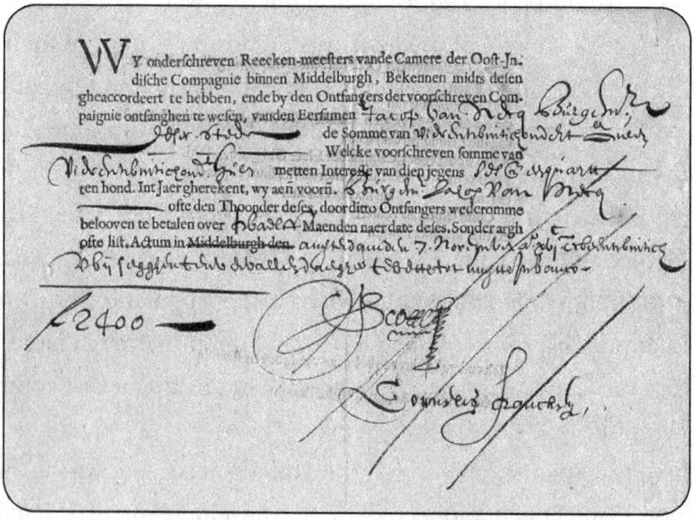

WY onderschreven Reecken-meesters vande Camere der Oost-Jndische Compagnie binnen Middelburgh, Bekennen midts desen gheaccordeert te hebben, ende by den Ontfangers der voorschreven Compaignie ontfanghen te wesen, vanden Eersamen
de Somme van
Welcke voorschreven somme van
metten Interesse van diep jegens
ten hond. Int Jaer gherekent, wy aen voorn.
ofte den Thoonder deses, door ditto Ontfangers wederomme beloove te betalen over
Maenden naer date deses. Sonder argh ofte list. Actum in ~~Middelburgh den.~~

f 2400

The above image shows a stock certificate of the VOC dated November 7, 1606, showing that the shareholder, Jan Brouwer of Amsterdam, has paid in full the last installment of 500 guilders of a share of 6,000 guilders in the capital stock of the Enkhuizen Chamber of the VOC.

Today, we recognize that both financial and productive institutions are risk-sharing agencies. They provide an alternative to dependence on government tax revenues for financing, and indeed, they often serve as a source of credit to governments themselves. Stock exchanges proliferate around the world and raise trillions of dollars in investment funds through any number of financial instruments ranging from stocks, bonds, and options. Without the initial innovations of the Dutch, it is difficult to imagine how the industrial revolution of the late eighteenth century could have evolved, let alone the extraordinary innovations of the nineteenth and twentieth centuries.

Rationality in the Presence of Asset Bubbles

Can the corporate form of business avoid all risks? The answer clearly is "no", even though they can diversify to some extent. Markets depend on a degree of transparency in conducting trade, and are not immune to fads and fashion. A classic example is the presence of stock market bubbles. In the same seventeenth century that would give rise to the creation of Dutch trading wealth, we see one of the first examples of an asset bubble, namely, the tulip bubble that unfolded between 1636 and 1637. While the Dutch already had a functioning stock exchange in Amsterdam, newly created wealth fueled a speculation in tulip bulbs that would rise spectacularly and then crash at an equally rapid rate.

At one point a single *semper augustus* bulb was trading at the equivalent of a house.[82] Then, for reasons largely unknown in changes in consumer sentiment, selling displaced buying and the price fell to nearly zero in a matter of weeks. Similar bubbles would occur in other times and places, notably the Mississippi bubble of 1720, the South Sea Bubble of the same year, the Japanese real estate bubble of the 1970s, the U.S. dot.com bubble of the late 1990s, the U.S. housing bubble of the early 2000s, and the housing and stock market financial crisis of 2008.

Asset bubbles are seen as an example of herd behavior in which one makes a decision to buy or sell simply on the basis of what one perceives other to be doing. Economists have concluded that within a bubble, buying while prices are rising is a rational response to given information, even if the larger markets indicate an anomaly. In turn, it has been thought that contingent market pricing, notably the use of option price and credit default swap contracts, could help investors to hedge against risk. Yet these derivative contracts often depend on valuations of stand-alone and portfolio assets that do not reveal sufficient transparency regarding underlying risks. As a result, in the presence of asymmetric information, prices can fail to achieve an efficient level, thus making it possible for asset bubbles to appear periodically.

When the financial crisis of 2008 drove down equity and housing market valuations in the U.S., Congress passed the Dodd-Frank Wall Street Reform and Consumer Protection Act. Its key provisions were the creation of the Office of Financial Research, the Financial Stability Oversight Council, and the Consumer Financial Protection Bureau. The Office of Financial Research was charged with identifying significant risks in bank and non-bank lending and to recommend to the Federal Reserve actions to mitigate these risks, including a mechanism for an orderly winding down of derivative positions and a framework for the orderly dissolution of failing firms. The thrust of Dodd-Frank was to have government not serve as the ultimate risk bearer for firms and markets.

Many of the Dodd-Frank reforms were challenged after the 2016 election, on grounds that the regulatory burden was too great. In 2018, Congress passed the Economic Growth, Regulatory Relief, and Consumer Protection Act. It reduced capital requirement for smaller and large custodial banks. It also provided additional requirements on Fannie Mae and Freddie Mac regarding alternative credit scoring systems in their reporting to the Federal Housing Finance Agency.

Fannie Mae and Freddie Mac continue to subsidize the housing market by purchasing mortgages from financial institutions. The 2018 legislation kept in place elements of the Volker Rule, which restricts banks from propriety trading in institutions to whom banks offer lending services, and which had been considered as a conflict of interest when banking reforms were enacted that reduced the barriers between commercial and investment banking back in 2000.

The problem with expanding regulations over an industry is that they often created the illusion that some institutions would be too big to fail. Andrew Ross Sorkin wrote a book under this title, and which became a best seller that helped to inspire the Dodd-Frank legislation.[83] The issue raised in "too big to fail" is moral hazard. An institution may perceive itself to be too big to fail and thus it takes on excess risk by assuming that in the event of a downturn, government will bail it out. That happened to the hedge fund firm, LTCM (Long-Term Capital Management), in 1999, but it did not happen in the case of Lehman Brothers, which went bankrupt on September 15, 2008.[84]

How does any of this related to our insights from neuroscience and risk? The short answer is that individuals respond to signals that drive emotions and decisions. People tend to discount the significance of past events on future conditions, and likewise, they discount the future are bearing little consequence for today. To take a longer view of events and decide how significant they are on the present requires that we rely on our frontal cortex more than the amygdala to make decisions. It is a difficult task to do, and becomes problematic when public officials are faced with monumental economic decisions, be they heads of private firms, or of government agencies charged with oversight responsibilities.

Regulation of Product Quality

Government regulation has evolved over time in response to the severity of events, the tendency to discount the past and future notwithstanding. While some regulation has been crafted to oversee financial institutions and firms, other examples can be found in terms of workplace conditions. In the early twentieth century, the United States was in the midst of an industrial revolution. Factory work was replacing craft work. Mass production became the new norm. As this transformation went forward, it would take a crisis to alert the public to the dangers of newly industrializing industries, and whose responsibility it would be to oversee the attendant risks. Few at the time thought government should be performing the role of regulating workplace and product safety, but the seeds of change were there.

Two examples serve to illustrate the point. One being on worker safety conditions, while the other focused on product safety. In the early years of the 20th century, the Chicago meatpacking industry was wracked by scandal involving unsafe and unsanitary working conditions, and by serious risks to worker health. Upton Sinclair published *The Jungle* in 1906, a journalistic exposé of these conditions. When Sinclair published his book, the U.S. population had a low literacy rate, no radio or television communication, and information on product safety was acquired through newspaper and book sales. Sales of Sinclair's book led to a Congressional investigation and the adoption of legislation that led to the creation of the U.S. Food and Drug Administration in 1906.[85]

The FDA is charged with the responsibility of examining food and drug production standards, thereby providing protection to the consuming public for goods. In the early twentieth century, consumers in one part of the country typically were unaware of the working conditions of meat preparation in Chicago, a major production for freshly slaughtered and canned meat. Buying a can of tinned meat, or fresh meat offered no guarantee of quality, and consumers made their purchases on the reputation of a brand. A food health outbreak was the only known way that unhealthy and unsafe conditions may have been in the preparation and distribution of a given product.

What the FDA has had to contend with is how much risk is safe enough for consumers. There simply is no way to ensure that any given product is

Figure 4.3 Book Cover Image of *The Jungle*, by Upton Sinclair.

Source: Cover of the original edition of Upton Sinclair's *The Jungle*, published by Doubleday, Page and Company in 1906.

one hundred percent safe to consume. Yet, producers and consumers can arrive at a satisfactory decision with little regulatory oversight as long as there is informational clarity and transparency.

In contrast, two recent cases illustrate that an oversight function can be redundant in the presence of a high level of information available to all. The two cases involved Tylenol, a popular over the counter aspirin substitute, and Pepsi Cola, a popular soft drink. In the former case, a disgruntled employee tampered with a few packages of Tylenol and placed arsenic in them, thereby causing what seemed to be random fatalities to a few unsuspecting consumers.

Within the space of a week of this autumn 1982 story, not only was this event broadcast on all major radio and television stations throughout the United States. Johnson and Johnson, parent company of Tylenol manufacturer McNeil, took out an expensive recall campaign in the media, asking consumers to return their supplies free of charge in exchange for either a cash exchange or a tamper-proof replacement, which the company soon put on the market.

The second case involved the apparent discovery a syringes in Pepsi Cola cans, which again was broadcast on national radio and television within a short space of time. The company undertook an investigation and discovered that a hoax had been perpetrated, after which the issue evaporated in a matter of days. In both instances, the reputations of major brand name producers were at stake, and consumers were informed rapidly of the threat to product integrity.

Congress in general, and the FDA in particular, did not undertake any oversight measures in either instance, thus pointing up the importance of how improved information can enhance the role of markets in matching supply and demand. What these examples do not resolve is just what kinds of products are likely to function best within such market driven circumstances, especially in developing countries where the quality and quantity of information can be substantially different. As a counterexample, infant milk formula has been sold in many developing countries to mothers who for various reasons have not followed the full prescribed dosage allowances, with the result that many children have been a greater risk of malnutrition than where infant formula has not been used.

Manufacturers such as Abbott Laboratories and Nestlé, both producers of infant formula products, have tried to combine commercial self-interest with an evident need to provide more extensive consumer information and orientation than would be the case in developed countries. Having made this comparison, however, it does not follow that just because a commercial product is available on a local market, that extensive regulation by a public sector entity is warranted. Were Abbott and Nestlé to continue to experience malnourished children in the markets in which they sold their products, parents in general, and mothers in particular with either modify their use of infant formula to the prescribed directions on each can, or revert to nursing as a traditional method.

For mothers with problems of lactation, and where wet nurses are not generally available, this leaves open the question of to what extent can commercial infant formula products satisfy both consumers and the producers of these products in a mutually satisfactory way. What these examples illustrate is that where commercially available information exists, then the need for public sector intervention is diminished. While it leaves open how such information is generated, how much it costs, and how it is distributed between producers and consumers, before one calls for public sector intervention, the relevant test should be to what extent is the equivalent amount of information essential to a prudent economic decision less costly when generated through market processes than when generated through public sector institutions.

When government exercises oversight over institutions, it may either over or under-regulate. In the case of Tylenol, we have seen that government did not have to exercise regulatory oversight because market signals were sufficient to provide self-correcting action to the benefit of consumers. In other instances, markets may work less well, as in the Chicago meat packing case.

One recent example highlights the problem of asymmetric information, namely, the conduct of Enron Corporation beginning in 2004.[86] Enron, a Houston-based natural gas firm began expansion of operations in 1994 just as the stock market began to rise with the dot.com tech bubble. By using shadow corporations to cover losing operations, Enron leveraged its assets to unsustainable levels and then began to collapse.

By December 2001, Enron filed for bankruptcy. With assets of $25 billion, it was one of the largest bankruptcy filings in U.S. history.

What a subsequent investigation and court trials of principals revealed was that Enron had used shadow corporate entities to hide growing losses from its energy futures trading. In the end, Enron is still engaged in a series of legal actions beyond prosecution of managers in an effort to recover losses of shareholders. As with any instance of asymmetric information, reported statements on earnings may fail to convey an accurate picture of a firm's net worth and performance, with the result that true earnings, and stock market prices may be inaccurate. It was the bankruptcy of not just Enron, but also Tyco International, WorldCom, and other firms that led Congress to adopt the Sarbanes-Oxley Act of 2002 in an effort to hold management to a higher standard of accountability than in the past.

In all of these examples, regulation of manufacturing and financial markets, and food, drug, and health products, government is setting standards for the management of the associated risks. In some cases, regulation may seem too limited, while in others it may be excessive. The problem with government regulations is that by adopting a one-size-fits all approach, it fails to take into account the variation in attitudes toward risk that we examined in the previous chapter. For this reason, while regulation can reduce some risks, in other cases, it may not, which is why the pricing of risk through market instruments may work ultimately to reduce the inefficiencies that government regulations inherently create.

Neuroscience Redux

When thinking about the FDA, or any other regulatory agency today, most examples that are invoked to change the level of public intervention are driven by the severity and time-distance of historical events. No one today argues in support of the FDA based on the Chicago meatpacking industry, or of quack medicinal practices from long ago. As our brain responds to various stimuli, it goes almost without saying that this makes it problematic to arrive at some optimal degree of regulation. When government regulates too little, arguments fly about how markets are failing to deliver essential services. When it regulates too much, the opposite is true, and where comparisons with other countries often are invoked to justify a reduction in regulations, based on prevailing perceptions of risk.

Seat belt regulation serves to illustrate the problem of risk perception and management. During the early 1960's studies on highway fatality rates showed that seat belts could save lives by as much as 90 percent. Seat belt regulation did not control for the state of roads, nor of the physical condition of drivers, nor of existing traffic enforcement, but was designed to reduce highway fatalities as population grew and highway vehicle travel density increased.[87] As a result, Congress mandated that starting with the 1968 model year, manufacturers must include seat belts as standard equipment on vehicles. States then adopted standards that drivers, and later passengers, must use seat belts while driving or face fines, difficult though that has been difficult to detect.

In terms of highway seat belt standards, we find a divergence between mandatory seat-belt legislation and driver behavior. While seat belts have been proven to save lives, drivers have responded by driving faster, and in buying larger vehicles such as SUV's. As a result, highway traffic fatalities have come down as compliance has expanded, but offset to some extent by the shift in driver buying and driving habits.

Drivers thus display a tolerance for risk beyond what the seatbelt legislation alone could provide, as illustrated below. When we see larger and larger vehicles on the road, we adopt herd behavior in imitating what others are doing. It is the illusion that we are better drivers than others, even at higher speeds of travel with ever heavier vehicles. Whether it is the Environmental Protection Agency or some other institution, it is difficult to design and enforce a uniform standard that varies not only by region, but over time, as perceptions of risk change in response to new data.

A similar standard evolved regarding the mandatory installation of catalytic converters on vehicles, the objective of which has been to reduce exhaust emissions, beginning with the 1975 model year. Enforcement standards on catalytic converters and replacements have been set by the

Figure 4.4 Heterogeneous Perceptions of Risk can alter the Validity of Laboratory Tests.

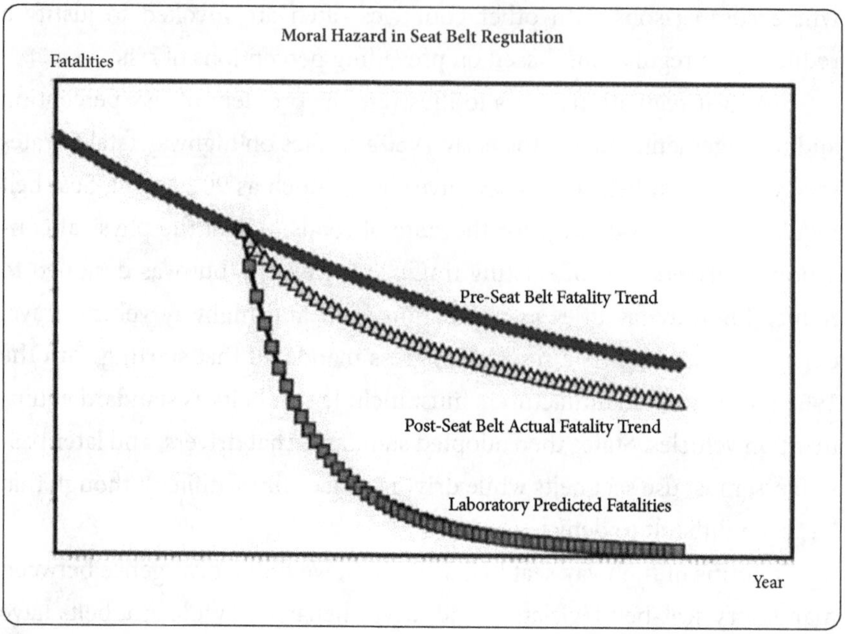

Environmental Protection Agency, and now includes after-market replacement and installation.[88]

When Donald Trump was elected in 2016, he promised to reduce the regulatory burden on business, and set about dismantling many of the agencies and standards that had evolved in recent decades.[89] Not everyone agreed that these reductions would lead to everyone being better off without them than keeping them in place. California, a state with some of the highest emissions control standards in the U.S., challenged the federal government by asserting the ability to set standards above what the government has otherwise defined under the 1963 Clean Air Act, and in this case, reduced. These measures stand counter to evidence of the impact of emissions on climate change, as already noted, and pits scientific evidence against a tendency to deny or discount longer term consequences of today's decisions.

Coronavirus and Institutional Resilience

Perhaps nothing these days illustrates the question of risk and institutional governance better than the coronavirus pandemic. Although knowledge of the human coronavirus was first known as far back at the 1960s, the current COVID-19 variant traces back to just late 2019 when first discovered in Wuhan province in China.[90] Because symptoms are not necessarily obvious at first when infected, the coronavirus has spread at exponential rates now worldwide, with the United States now at the epicenter of infections.

As with any phenomenon, the first evidence of an event does not claim priority on one's attitudes toward the underlying risks. This was certainly true in China when the government dismissed and ignored medical reports of the outbreak in Wuhan. As tracking of cases, followed by fatalities began to take place, different governments responded in differing ways. At first, China led in the total number of cases and fatalities. Then for countries with fewer restrictions in place, the virus quickly became an epidemic. Italy would soon displace China with the total number of cases and fatalities, only to be replaced more recently by the United States.

Key to all of this has been the timing of precautionary measures. Absent a suitable vaccine, countries underwent panic buying of household goods. Basic items soon were not to be found in many stores. In addition, facial masks, ventilators, prophylactic gloves, and hospital treatment facilities all were inadequate. Eventually, governments adopted alerts and varying degrees of mandatory precautionary measures, even as data showed that the coronavirus had yet to show a universal slowdown in expansion.

How can one determine the gravity of the coronavirus? Thus far, data area becoming available on reported cases and fatalities, from which a crude fatality rate can be computed. These data are being compiled and made available at the international country level, and, for the United States at least, at the state level, as well as at the county and local level.

One problem with the data compilation is that testing standards are far from uniform and inclusive, with the result that any trend could

Figure 4.5 International Coronavirus Cases.

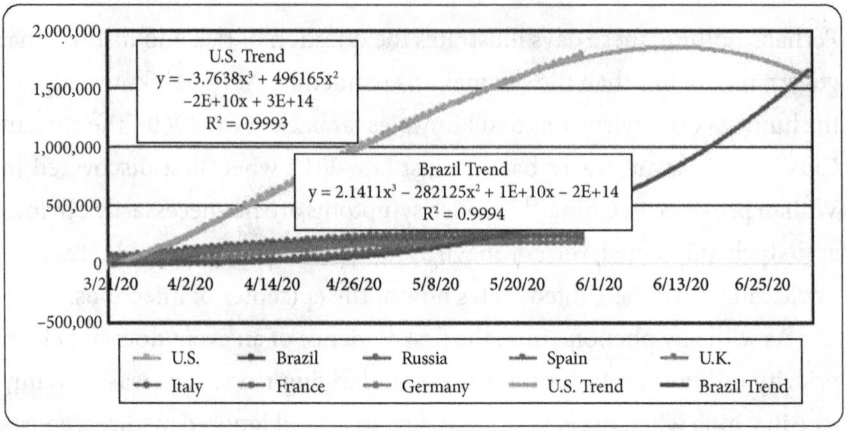

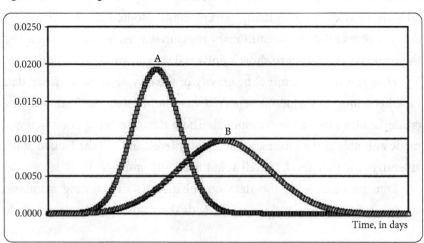

2,000,000
1,500,000
1,000,000
500,000
0
-500,000
U.S. Trend
y = -3.7638x³ + 496165x²
-2E+10x + 3E+14
R² = 0.9993
Brazil Trend
y = 2.1411x³ - 282125x² + 1E+10x - 2E+14
R² = 0.9994
3/21/20
4/2/20
4/14/20
4/26/20
5/8/20
5/20/20
6/1/20
6/13/20
6/25/20
U.S.
Brazil
Russia
Spain
U.K.
Italy
France
Germany
U.S. Trend
Brazil Trend

Source: https://www.worldometers.info/coronavirus/

be misleading. As a result, in the U.S., tracking is being done on the basis of hospital admissions and recovery rates, but even this indicator does not capture those who may not need hospitalization and may yet still be undetected carriers because of inadequate levels of testing.

Against these caveats, simply reporting on case and fatality levels also can be misleading in that it does not consider frequency levels in

Figure 4.6 Flattening the Coronavirus Curve.

0.0250
0.0200
0.0150
0.0100
0.0050
0.0000
A
B
Time, in days

a population. As a result, when looking only at the number of cases or fatalities, one does not have a sufficient picture from which to judge the severity of an outbreak. Our reactions become driven by emotional responses to images of overburdened medical facilities and personal tragedies when arriving at an assessment of the magnitude of the problem.

Despite the tendency to magnify the coronavirus pandemic through imagery, what also is clear is that the economy is falling into a deep recession, if not a depression. At some point, a shift in precautionary measures would be reasonable to consider, though not before then. In the United States, when the stock market dropped valuations by an order of 20 percent, this led Congress to intervene with a mix of regulatory and fiscal measures. The idea is to flatten the expansion of cases and fatalities over time. The question is how soon one should relax precautionary measures as efforts to contain the virus are just building up.

Intervention in the economy to counter the coronavirus involves a combination of regulatory and fiscal actions. The U.S. has been waking up to the magnitude of the crisis and has combined precautionary health measures with a $2.2 trillion fiscal stimulus package. Whether that will flatten the coronavirus curve and keep the economy on a full employment level remains to be seen.

Timing is critical in responding to the coronavirus. Acting too late or too soon may not help to optimally manage the outbreak. Italy has recently imposed a total lockdown to contain the expansion of the virus. The United States is not at this point, but has been slow to recognize the gravity of the virus. What this leaves us with is how to people process information? As we have noted, a seemingly small event today may have significant repercussions in the future. Yet the natural inclination is to discount future consequences, just as today's behavior tends to discount the past.

Reaching a consensus on recognizing the gravity of the problem requires generating data in as transparent a manner as possible, and which includes inclusive testing so that appropriate measures may be implemented. What is clear from the coronavirus pandemic is that markets alone have not been in a position to adapt to changing conditions, and instead have become victims of a major health crisis. Government regulation in a timely manner and at an optimal level that can balance physical and economic health of a country is not simple, but a necessary step if markets are to perform at an efficient level.

In countries such as China, South Korea, and Germany, mandatory testing and precautionary steps to limited social spreading appear to be making a difference in the coronavirus cycle in those countries. The U.S. has been slow to adopt more stringent measures, in part because the public has not been convinced of the severity of the pandemic until its spread has already gotten under way. That may change in time, and government leaders bear a particular responsibility in conveying credible information on the coronavirus so that attitudes may adapt to the new realities.

CHAPTER FIVE

DEFINING AND ACHIEVING DISTRIBUTIVE JUSTICE

The Search for Distributive Justice

The second economic function of the public sector is both well-known and widespread, namely, distributive justice. The key here is whether the market generates a distributive outcome that is viewed as fair. If markets are seen as unfair, then calls for redistribution look to government intervention to bring about a change.

There are two kinds of fairness: procedural fairness, and distributive fairness. Public discourse on distributive justice often fails to make a clear distinction between the two, particularly when pressure is placed on governments to undertake a change. Procedural fairness means that no one is treated differently before the law on the basis of one's race, ethnicity, gender, religion, or any other arbitrary criterion. As long as citizens of a diverse community trust that they will be treated equally before the law, this reinforces adhesion to the social contract, and thus political legitimacy.

As elsewhere, the United States has a mixed history of procedural fairness. The Constitution incorporated slavery as a legal institution, a state that was not changed until the Civil war and the adoption of the 14th, and 15th amendments. Women did not have the right to vote until the adoption of the 19th amendment in 1920. The struggle to achieve procedural fairness is far from complete, as the recent police killing of George Floyd by the

Minneapolis police attests. Such unequal justice conditions are echoed in the Myanmar treatment of its Rohingya Moslem minority as well as the Indian government decision to remove equal justice protections from its own Moslem community.

While procedural fairness is a foundational element of political legitimacy, our focus here is on distributive justice. Defining distributive economic justice is a complex task, requiring that one take into account both process and outcomes. If one holds to a standard of rationality in decisions, then decisions regarding distributive justice must include the time over which a given change should take place.

Economics is not well suited as a discipline to provide an answer to the question of what constitutes the optimal distribution of income and wealth. Years ago, Nobel economist Paul Samuelson (1915–2009) said that society should first determine what is a fair distribution of income or wealth. Economists should then find the least costly way of achieving it. What he was asserting is that insofar as economics is a social science, it should not impose *a priori* subjective value judgments on a given distribution.

Samuelson's advice has not always been upheld by his fellow economists. Today, we find some advocating for a particular distribution of income even though economics does not provide an objective way to evaluate an *a priori* set of subjective values. If one believes in democratic principles, then the voice of an economist should stand alongside that of a worker, a business executive, a religious leader, or anyone else who participates in making such choices.

A simple way of illustrating the question of an optimal distribution of income can be seen in the following example. Consider three individuals each with an initial level of income (or wealth). Each attaches an underlying value to a change in income, as expressed in terms of a simple exponential coefficient, expressed here initially as one in which each individual attaches an identical value of 1.

Now consider the effects of a program of government taxation, which we define here initially as a proportional tax, that is one that is applied at the same rate to each individual, in this case at 10 percent. One can now calculate the impact of the imposition of a proportional tax.

First, total satisfaction over the three individuals is computed using the exponential coefficient times the initial level of income, from which the sum may be thought of as an initial level of total social welfare. Then, one can compute tax revenues collected from each individual to compute the level of tax revenues overall and the post-tax net income of each individual. From that position, one can then calculate the new level of total social welfare using the same procedure applied to pretax income. Individual satisfaction, or utility, for each individual has been reduced by the extraction of tax revenues, as is the level of total social welfare.

Now we come to what government may do with regard to income distribution. In one scenario, government decides to divide and allocate tax revenues based on the total population. Once we allocate equal amounts to the three individuals, we can then note the post-tax redistribution of income, and from which we re-calculate the new level of total social welfare. The results can be seen in Table 5.1, from which we also compute a measure of the level of inequality.[91]

In our comparisons we simplify all calculations by assuming that government redistribution is costless. Under costless redistribution leaves the total level of income in each stage remains unchanged, while the level of total social welfare, or social utility, and the degree of inequality can be changed.

In our initial scenario, it should be noted that while income and utility of the two lower income individuals has increased, the wealthier individual's income and utility are reduced. The question is who should make a judgment regarding whether distributive justice is achieved under such a scenario.

If this were a democracy, and individuals A and B voted to redistribute income through a proportional tax regime, individual C would have to agree to a reduction in his (or her) income and utility.

Consider next the imposition of a progressive tax rate. In this case, tax revenues are increased, while overall post-tax redistribution restores total

Table 5.1 Income Distribution and Social Welfare.

					Scenario 1				
	Income Function	Pre-Tax Total Utility	Tax Rate	Taxes Collected	Net Income Before Tax Redistribution	Pre-Distribution Total Utility	Allocation of Tax Revenues	Net Income After Tax Redistribution	Post-Tax Distribution Total Utility
A.	$U_A =$ ($200.00) 1.00	200.00	10.00%	$20.00	$180.00	180.00	33.33%	$226.67	226.67
B.	$U_B =$ ($400.00) 1.00	400.00	10.00%	$40.00	$360.00	360.00	33.33%	$406.67	406.67
C.	$U_C =$ ($800.00) 1.00	800.00	10.00%	$80.00	$720.00	720.00	33.33%	$766.67	766.67
Totals:	Income: $1,400.00	Utility: 1400.00		Taxes: $140.00	Income: $1,260.00	Utility: 1260.00		Income: $1,400.00	Utility: 1400.00
Inequality:	0.1429	0.1429			0.1429	0.1429		0.1141	0.1141

Table 5.2 Income Distribution and Social Welfare.

	Income Function	Pre-Tax Total Utility	Tax Rate	Taxes Collected	Net Income Before Tax Redistribution	Pre-Distribution Total Utility	Allocation of Tax Revenues	Net Income After Tax Redistribution	Post-Tax Distribution Total Utility
						Scenario 2			
A.	U_A = ($200.00)$^{1.00}$	200.00	5.00%	$10.00	$190.00	190.00	33.33%	$246.67	246.67
B.	U_B = ($400.00)$^{1.00}$	400.00	10.00%	$40.00	$360.00	360.00	33.33%	$416.67	416.67
C.	U_C = ($800.00)$^{1.00}$	800.00	15.00%	$120.00	$680.00	680.00	33.33%	$736.67	736.67
Totals:	**Income:** $1,400.00	**Utility:** 1400.00		**Taxes:** $170.00	**Income:** $1,230.00	**Utility:** 1230.00		**Income:** $1,400.00	**Utility:** 1400.00
Inequality:	0.1429	0.1429			0.1229	0.1229		0.0935	0.0935

income and utility, but income inequality is further reduced. Once again, if individuals A and B voted in favor of a progressive tax while individual C opposed, under a democratic regime, individual C would presumably have to accept the outcome.

At some point, you might ask to what extent is individual C willing to accept a concentrated reduction in income in exchange for a greater degree of social equality. Democratic institutions may then be subject to challenge as elites oppose at some point carrying additional economic burdens in exchange for greater social equality. They may choose to undermine or overturn democratic foundations, or seek to evade higher taxes through shelters, be they within the country or by an export of income to more favorable locations.

Now consider a third alternative. A regressive tax system is applied for which revenues are again equally distributed. In this case, initial inequality is considerably lower than in the previous scenarios because the valuation each individual attaches to an extra dollar's worth of income is inversely proportional to the level of income. But while the post-tax pre-redistribution level of income is reduced as is the degree of inequality, the post-distribution level of income and utility es more equally distributed in comparison to the initial distribution.

What this suggests is that when considering the use of government taxation and spending to purely redistribute income, whether inequality of income and social welfare is increased or decreased depends on two considerations: 1. The value each individual attaches to an extra dollar's worth of income, and 2. the formula used to redistribute tax resources. In practice, politicians engaged in redistributive taxation often make assumptions about the marginal value of an extra dollar's worth of income without an empirical basis linked to social welfare changes of the kind we are examining here.

It may be possible to design a redistribution program that maintains adherence to a democratic system via the choice of the level and rate of taxation, as well as in terms of the proportional distribution of tax resources.

Table 5.3 Income Distribution and Social Welfare.

	Income Function	Pre-Tax Total Utility	Tax Rate	Taxes Collected	Net Income Before Tax Redistribution	Pre-Distribution Total Utility	Allocation of Tax Revenues	Net Income After Tax Redistribution	Post-Tax Distribution Total Utility
A.	$U_A = (\$200.00)^{1.00}$	200.00	15.00%	$30.00	$170.00	170.00	33.33%	$206.67	206.67
B.	$U_B = (\$400.00)^{0.90}$	219.71	10.00%	$40.00	$360.00	199.84	33.33%	$396.67	218.06
C.	$U_C = (\$800.00)^{0.80}$	210.12	5.00%	$40.00	$760.00	201.67	33.33%	$796.67	209.42
Totals:	Income: $1,400.00	Utility: 629.83		Taxes: $110.00	Income: $1,290.00	Utility: 571.51		Income: $1,400.00	Utility: 634.15
Inequality:	0.1429	0.0007			0.1637	0.0030		0.1371	0.0003

In all three scenarios illustrated here, we have used the same redistribution formula, namely an equal per capita distribution while varying the tax rate and the marginal utility of income.

As the above illustrations suggest, it is as important to know what individual valuations are with regard to an additional dollar's worth of income as in knowing what level and kind of tax and redistribution formula under consideration. For several years the Charitable Giving Foundation has tracked giving in the U.S. based on tax returns.[92]

In ranking charitable giving by state, data show that there is an inverse relationship between the share of income devoted to charity and the level of income. While states with a higher level of income may give more to charity in absolute dollars, the share of income allocated to charity is lower than for states with a lower level of income. This also holds true for individual giving.

What does this picture tell us about the value of an extra dollar's worth of income? The short answer is that there is not an inverse relationship between an extra dollar's worth of income and the level of income, and that, if anything, the marginal, or extra, value is closer to 1 or possibly even increasing with the level of income, as some have observed in relationship to some individuals in public life.

To the extent that the charitable giving data are consistent, then, a progressive tax rate would not only fall on higher income individuals. So too would they bear the greatest burden in the redistribution of tax resources collected. The exception to this would be that one could still have a degree of regressivity in the tax system while at the same time reducing inequality through a more pro-poor allocation of tax resources.

In terms of political discourse and the type of governance regime, even in a democratic system we find that there is far too little coherence in advocating a particular structure to support some majoritarian system of fairness market dynamics. Conservatives usually focus primarily on tax cuts and with an aversion to measures that allocate more tax resources to those less well off. In contrast, those on the Left advocate a more progressive tax regime while calling for greater transfers of resources to those less well off.

Table 5.4 Income Distribution and Social Welfare.

	Income Function	Pre-Tax Total Utility	Tax Rate	Taxes Collected	Net Income Before Tax Redistribution	Pre-Distribution Total Utility	Allocation of Tax Revenues	Net Income After Tax Redistribution	Post-Tax Distribution Total Utility
	1.00								
A. $U_A =$	($200.00)	200.00	15.00%	$30.00	$170.00	170.00	60.00%	$236.00	236.00
	1.00								
B. $U_B =$	($400.00)	400.00	10.00%	$40.00	$360.00	360.00	20.00%	$382.00	382.00
	1.00								
C. $U_C =$	($800.00)	800.00	5.00%	$40.00	$760.00	760.00	20.00%	$782.00	782.00
Totals:	**Income:** $1,400.00	**Utility:** 1400.00		**Taxes:** $110.00	**Income:** $1,290.00	**Utility:** 1290.00		**Income:** $1,400.00	1400.00
Inequality:	0.1429	0.1429			0.1637	0.1637		0.1148	0.1148

Scenario 4

Making sense of differences in perspectives requires first as to whether a coherent system of fairness is embodied in any given piece of legislation, and whether that reflects majoritarian preferences of the population. We simply do not rise to that level of inclusiveness in most discussions of what constitutes a fair distribution of income. And we often make such decisions in which the time consequences are driven as much by the next election as it is over the full impact of such legislation.

Inclusiveness requires looking at distributive justice through various socio-economic groupings, for which racial, ethnic, and gender provide a reference. Achieving distributive justice begins in the first instance with a system in which the prevailing degree of global inequality is also true for any socio-economic sub-grouping. To the extent that it does not is evidence of distortions based on discriminatory considerations that may be practiced.

If a society declares its legitimacy as based on equality of opportunity, then such degrees of inequality for any sub-group should be no different than for the population as a whole. This said, one can then address the degree of global inequality as to whether it also conforms to a socially desirable state of affairs. In reality, differences in inequality for any sub-group often are entangled with the degree of inequality for the population as a whole. Measures to eliminate such social discrimination thus form a key element in achieving distributive justice just as one looks to achieving a global degree of distributive justice.

None of the comparisons we are illustrating here take into consideration the longer-term consequences of a given redistribution regime. What, for example, are the consequences of any given program of social justice on the rate of savings and investment in the economy? And what are the consequences of any given program on the level and rate of innovation, and growth in per capita income over time?

Few legislative debates consider these longer-term consequences. Politicians tend to frame their proposals in terms of the likelihood of being returned to office in the next election. This is not an argument against terms of service for elected officials, though there are arguments for term limits that are worthy of consideration even outside the current discussion. Rather, it is that framing a system of distributive justice out of given market dynamics typically takes place under limited information. Self-interest may be guided more by emotional signals than by rational conduct, as is evident in many of the ways in which political discourse informs our choice of fairness to pursue a degree of social welfare satisfaction.

Government Size and Distributive Justice

If anything could convince us as to the incoherence of arguments over distributive justice, let us look again at measures of inequality in comparison to the size of government. Back in our introductory discussion, we pointed out that inequality within states has recently been on the increase, after decades in which government intervention seems to have brought a measure of reduction. Taking a more comparative look, we see how different the United States has evolved in comparison to a number of other countries.

As we have noted previously, beyond some point, rising inequality undermines the degree of political legitimacy. Either rules involving access to opportunity are skewed by government policy or by default, a population

Figure 5.1 Top Ten Percent Share of Pre-Tax Income.

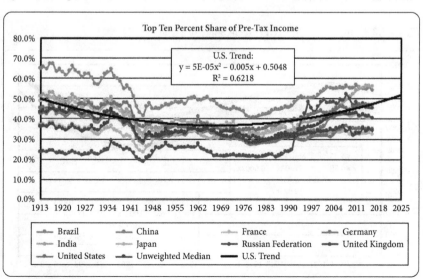

whose fortunes are determined by a narrow few become alienated from the state, and an overthrow of the existing order becomes more likely. In between extreme inequality and perfect equality is the contested terrain on which a search for distributive justice plays out.

Inequality in wealth is mirrored in inequality in income. Again, taking a longer view we note this trend for the United States when looking as far back as the early part of the twentieth century. Whether from the New Deal or the Great Society, the United States did go through a period in which rising incomes were accompanied by a reduction in wealth inequality. In recent years, this is no longer the case, and which has generated rising criticism of government policies.

The United States adopted an income tax in 1913, followed by estate taxation in 1916, as have a number of other high-income countries.[93] The introduction of income and wealth taxation, along with rising social welfare spending gradually reduced levels of inequality. Then, starting in the 1980s, changes in legislation resulted in a reversal of inequality. Today we see inequality trending back to conditions that prevailed earlier in the last century, even as real per capita incomes have grown.

Why do we see this inverted relationship? Years ago, Nobel economist Simon Kuznets (1901–1985) noted that in very poor countries

Figure 5.2 Comparative Top Ten Percent Share of Wealth.

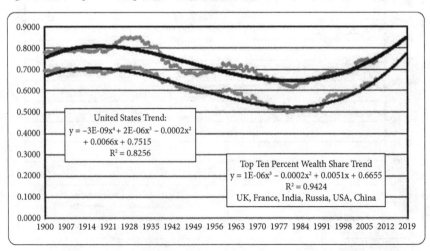

United States Trend:
$$y = -3\text{E-}09x^4 + 2\text{E-}06x^3 - 0.0002x^2 + 0.0066x + 0.7515$$
$$R^2 = 0.8256$$

Top Ten Percent Wealth Share Trend
$$y = 1\text{E-}06x^3 - 0.0002x^2 + 0.0051x + 0.6655$$
$$R^2 = 0.9424$$
UK, France, India, Russia, USA, China

Figure 5.3 Per Capita Income and the Kuznets Curve.

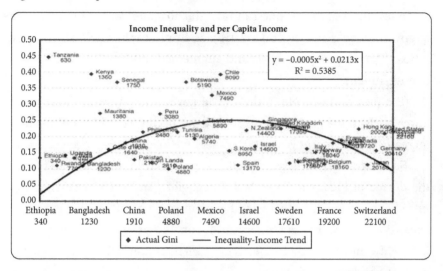

Source: *World Development Report* 1994 (Washington, D.C.: The World Bank, 1994).

the degree of inequality is relatively high. Then, as economies begin to undergo a period of development, inequality tends to increase, and as higher levels are reached, then begins to fall. This is completely opposite of what we are finding here among advanced countries. It is taking place at a time when government size is trending upward, as has the growth in real per capita income.

How can we take stock of government size and inequality? Governments perform a variety of functions, of which some standard of distributive justice is exercised through taxation and spending. Among advanced economies today, a rising share of expenditures is devoted to transfer payments, that is, payments based on criteria of past conditions, as in social security for retired individuals, or pensions for military service, for example. Now short of a more detailed examination of government budgets here, let us construct an index of government size and which we may use to compare with prevailing measures of inequality.

Using the United States as an example, we can derive an index of government size through a series of relative measures. First, one can compute the ratio of government spending to the Gross Domestic Product, or GDP. One can then do the same for the ratio of government tax revenues to GDP. Third, one can take the absolute value of the balance of government spending and taxation as a ratio to the GDP. These three ratios together provide a basic and augmented index of the relative size of government.[94]

The paradox we note is that while government intervention was at lower levels in the past when inequality was declining, it has continued to increase in more recent years at the same time inequality has been growing.

Such a pattern suggests that government transfer programs to reduce the degree of inequality have had a negligible, and even negative, effect in reducing inequality. This would explain some of the opposition to an expansion of government intervention on the grounds that it reduces inequality, and that other objectives of intervention have dominated the choice of budgetary priorities.

Figure 5.4 Augmented Government Weight Index.

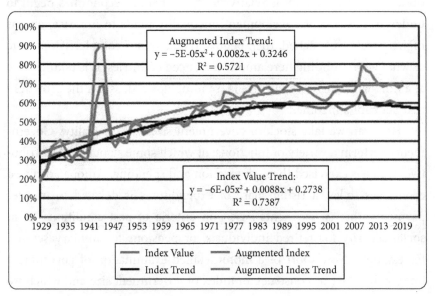

Note: The basic index consists only of the sum of the tax and spending ratios, while the augmented index includes the budget balance ratio.
Source: Federal Reserve Bank of St. Louis, FRED https://fred.stlouisfed.org/

Social Welfare Standards and Distributive Justice

As Paul Samuelson argued years ago, deciding what is the optimal level of income and wealth distribution is a socio-political judgment, after which economists can tackle the least costly way of achieving the objective. This criterion has come to be known as the Bergson-Samuelson welfare criterion, after fellow economist Abram Bergson came to the same conclusion at about the same time.[95] Yet economics, which has looked to a scientific foundation for its precepts, has traditionally held to an even more stringent standard known as Pareto optimality, after the Italian Vilfredo Pareto (1848–1923), who first wrote on the subject back in 1909.[96]

The Pareto optimality standard states that one has achieved an optimal state of affairs when any further re-allocation of resources designed to help an individual can only come about through a reduction in the welfare of someone else. In our previous distributive scenarios, none would satisfy the Pareto criterion because at least one individual's well-being has been reduced in the effort to achieve greater equality for the population as a whole. It is a powerful status-quo argument that ignores how an existing distribution came about in the first place, but serves as a reference for various proposals for redistribution.

Variants of the Pareto social welfare standard, including the Bergson-Samuelson criterion, have been put forth over the years, notably the Kaldor criterion and the Rawls criterion. Nicholas Kaldor (1908–1986) suggested a criterion in which one has an improvement in social welfare as long as the gains to the gainers exceed the losses to the losers.[97] In our distributive scenarios, using a money metric, none would satisfy the Kaldor criterion, though using a utility criterion, the second scenario in which individuals display a declining marginal utility of income would result in an improvement.

More rigorous work has been done to demonstrate the conditions under which a reallocation of resources can result in an improvement in social welfare. Nobel economist Kenneth Arrow (1921–2017), along with

Gérard Debreu (1921–2004) demonstrated that under a set of rational assumptions regarding consumer and producer choice, achieving a level of optimal social welfare would violate one or more conditions of a democratic society.[98] The Arrow "Impossibility Theorem", first put forth in 1951, would govern arguments over distributive justice for decades.

Only in more recent years has the argument been re-stated by some outside economics, such as the philosophers John Rawls (1921–2002) and Robert Nozick (1938–2002).[99] Both taught philosophy at Harvard University when following Rawls' *Theory of Justice*, Nozick offered a libertarian alternative, in *Anarchy, State, and Utopia*. Rawls considered prevailing economists' arguments and offered an explicit distributive criterion for improvements in social welfare: Any change in the allocation of resources that benefits the least advantaged member of society can be considered an improvement. In taking this position, he argued that a society's ethical foundations depend on such an explicit principle, and that it may well fall to government agency to intervene to bring about reductions in inequality to achieve the standard he put forth. In terms of our previous scenarios, all four would satisfy the Rawlsian criterion in that the least advantaged member of society winds up in an improved position after redistributive intervention has taken place.

Robert Nozick viewed Rawls' position as violating individual liberty through government intervention. He viewed taxation to achieve a more egalitarian distribution as confiscatory and contrary to democratic principles. Given any initial distribution, only under individual autonomy and freedom of choice can any action to redistribute income or wealth can be viewed as social justified. In stating this position, Nozick drew on English philosopher John Locke (1632–1704), who argued that natural law is the only ethical basis of society.

In Locke's view, natural law predates the existence of government institutions. When a government intervenes in ways that violate individual natural rights, then a regime can be considered as politically illegitimate. Locke's *Second Treatise on Government*, published in 1689 following the deposing of English King James II in the 1688 "Glorious Revolution", was an effort to anchor government responsibility to the security of its population, and to the protection of property rights as a foundation of natural law.

Locke was inspired by the beheading of King Charles I in 1649, by the civil war that ensued through the Commonwealth government of Oliver Cromwell, and then through the restoration of Kings Charles II (1660–1685) and James II (1685–1688). He also argued in contrast to philosopher Thomas Hobbes (1588–1679), who offered a defense of political absolutism in his 1651 essay, *Leviathan*.

Leviathan was a call for political absolutism to avoid the violence wrought about by the beheading of Charles I and the ensuing English civil war. He viewed an omnipotent state as the necessary alternative to chaos and disorder, from which he concluded that in the absence of a strong central government, life is "solitary, nasty, brutish, and short".

While Hobbes' views offered a defense of political absolutism, Locke's ideas prevailed, not just in England, but also were foundational in the crafting of the American Declaration of Independence and the framing of the Constitution. Through a separation of power inspired by the French writer Montesquieu (1689–1755) in his 1748 treatise, *The Spirit of the Laws*, the United States has evolved a system of shared governance based on the notion that checks and balances are essential to the preservation of individual liberty.

Political devolution in the United States has also been seen as a bulwark of democracy, as Alexis de Tocqueville wrote in his 1835 book, *Democracy in America*. The separation and sharing of powers is embodied in a long body of writings where government is viewed as a necessary evil insofar as some basic notions involving security and order are satisfied, and in which efforts by government to intervene in the social and economic institutions is viewed with concern as a reduction in individual liberty.

Former Texas Representative Ron Paul (1935–) went so far in the libertarian direction to call for the elimination of the Federal Reserve Bank, in his 2009 book, *End the Fed*.[100] His libertarian views are echoed by his son Rand Paul (1963–), U.S. Senator from Kentucky, and whose first name suggests a parallel to the conservative writer Ayn Rand (1905–1982).[101] In short, conservatives view any attempt to redistribute income and/or wealth as confiscatory. They assume that the existing social and economic order has come about through fair means, and that social welfare programs are incompatible with the freedom of choice which is at the heart of the conservative concept of the social contract.

Measures of Political and Economic Freedom

Can we measure political and economic freedom? We enshrine certain notions in both constitutions and through legislation, yet do not often have a clear notion of what constitutes a measure by which they could be judged. Short of a widely accepted standard, we do have some proxy measures that can provide some idea of where a country is moving in terms of inequality, the size of government, and economic growth.

In each case, an index of political and economic freedom is not a tradable good, and thus, the assignment of values to such indices depends on the gathering of indicators via surveys that are not immune to bias. Given this possibility, such indices can provide at least a first order of magnitude of some of the drivers of divisions that translate into voter preferences, and thus underlying notions of political legitimacy.

For some time, Freedom House, a government-funded private agency based in the United States, has been compiling scoring numbers to measure the extent of political rights and civil liberties for a range of countries.[102] Founded in 1941, its honorary chairpersons included Republican Wendell Willkie, and Democrat Eleanor Roosevelt. Through regular surveys, research teams assign values to political rights and civil liberties on a scale ranging from 1 to 7. A higher number implies a lower level of political rights or civil liberties, while a lower number implies a higher value of these indicators.

So presented, these scales seem counterintuitive, so inverting them provides a more accessible basis of understanding them when making historical and geographic comparisons. For our present purposes, we track these inverted values for a sample of 103 countries representing North America, Central and Latin America, Western Europe, Central Europe, East Asia, Sub-Saharan Africa, and the Middle East and North Africa. Where necessary, we use current political units such as the Russian Federation, Germany (once East and West Germany), and Czechia and Slovakia instead of Czechoslovakia.

Political Freedom

Using data from Freedom House, we can compile a profile of political rights and civil liberties. We can then derive a proxy index of democracy as a combination of the two instead of tracking the number, frequency, and participation rates in elections.[103] Our proxy index of democracy comprises the sum of the inverted scales for political rights and civil liberties, with a maximum value of 14 and a low of 1.

While economic growth in world per capita income expanded in proportion to increases in political rights and civil liberties, there has recently been a downturn as countries have embraced more authoritarian forms

Figure 5.5 World Civil Liberties, Political Rights, and Democracy.

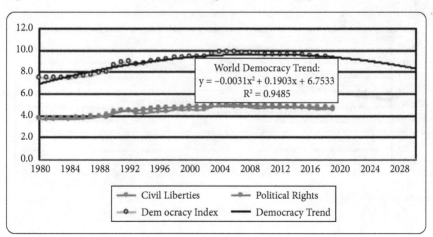

Source: Freedom House, with re-scaled indicators.

of government. This is evidence of the trend which we observed at this outset of this inquiry, namely, a tendency to discard fundamental democratic institutions, even in the presence of economic prosperity.

The rise of authoritarian government also is bringing about a reduction in economic freedom through measures to curtail the expansion of global trade and investment, among other indicators. As we have noted, restrictions on trade and investment often have foreclosed a window of economic opportunity that some now seem blind to its consequences.

Economic Freedom

As already noted, reductions in political rights and civil liberties is bringing about a contraction in international trade and investment. To track this trend, we draw on two measures of economic freedom, namely, property rights and judicial independence, which are lynchpins of democratic institutions. Drawing on the *Wall Street Journal* and Heritage Foundation Index of Economic Freedom, we extract an overall score for economic freedom, along with separate displays of property rights and judicial independence.

Figure 5.6 Property Rights, Judicial Independence and Economic Freedom.

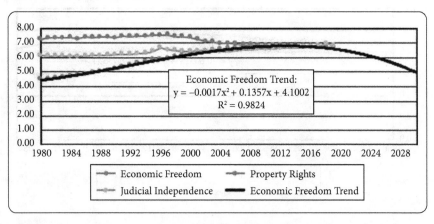

Economic Freedom Trend:
$y = -0.0017x^2 + 0.1357x + 4.1002$
$R^2 = 0.9824$

Source: *Index of Economic Freedom*, The Wall Street Journal and the Heritage Foundation.

The Index of Economic Freedom, which contains several components beyond property rights and judicial independence, demonstrated a steady increase from the 1980s to the early 2000's, and then has recently begun a downward turn. Although judicial independence has steady increased, it has been accompanied by a slow decline in property rights, among other indicators.

Where, then, does this leave us with this second function of the public sector as fulfilling a measure of distributive justice? First, we note that recent increases in inequality have been accompanied by a steady expansion of the size of government. This expansion of government intervention has not taken place in tandem with the level of democracy.

Both civil liberties and political rights, which expanded for much of the last 40 years, now are facing decline as more authoritarian governments come to power. At the same time, economic freedom, which expanded for most of the same time period, is also facing reductions. This can be traced to a decline in property rights in general, but also to international property rights as international trade and investment agreements have been under retrenchment.

Even if one has a socially agreed upon value as to what constitutes distributive justice, it does not follow that one then can ascribe all or part of the responsibility for achieving some standard through government intervention. Prior to the expansion of the welfare state in the twentieth century, there was little expectation that the question of income distribution was a proper function of government. That clearly has changed mostly in response to the Great Depression of the 1930's and to subsequent economic upheavals in the decades that have followed.

Then, and still now to varying degrees, the notion of a just distribution was a question that was considered an individual responsibility. If one were wealthy, then it is incumbent on such an individual to engage in philanthropic acts to those less fortunate. This indeed was the message of such gilded entrepreneurs as Andrew Carnegie and John D. Rockefeller. And we see it today in the philanthropic acts of the Bill and Melinda Gates Foundation, the John D. and Catherine T. MacArthur Foundation, the Ford Foundation, and a host of others.

However, even though well-off individuals may engage in acts of charity, there is no obligation for them to do so. This is what lay behind efforts
to use progressive income taxes and welfare programs by government over
the years. The assumption was that even if one takes into consideration the
philanthropy of the well-to-do, there is no guarantee that it will result in a
gain in welfare for the less well off.

One should be cautious about recommending an expansion of government intervention in the economy to reduce levels of inequality in income
and wealth. Overall, there has been a decline in global inequality in income
while intra-country inequality has expanded. The significance of this is
that notions of fairness do not guarantee reductions in inequality, as the
Kuznets curve suggested. What is clear is that when inequality in incomes
and wealth grows ever larger, it calls into question the political legitimacy
of the state.

How much has government intervened to affect the level of social welfare? If we look at industrialized countries over time, we see that the vast
majority of social welfare spending has taken place in the period following

Figure 5.7 Social Welfare Spending Ratio to GDP.

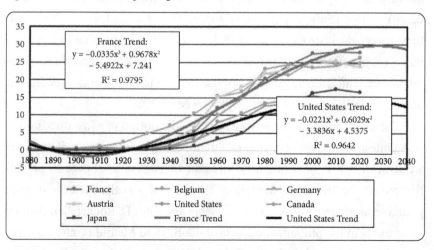

Source: https://www.oecd-ilibrary.org/economics/data/oecd-stat/data-warehouse_data-
00900-en

the Second World War. The United States stands at the lower boundary on the spectrum, but its social welfare spending does account for a significant share of public spending and economic activity overall.

We currently are living in an age of rising inequality as per capita incomes and wealth have increased. This divergence translates into political divisions over both the rules and outcomes of market institutions, and in which notions of fairness hang in the balance.

What is called for is a closer examination of how government incentives affect levels of inequality over time, and it should be an explicit performance indicator in budgetary accounting. Hopefully, that means a fairly elected democratic government that is representative of the priorities of the population at large and not just a funding source for the next election.

CHAPTER SIX

COMPETITION AND ECONOMIC EFFICIENCY

Tools for Promoting Competition

Governments intervene in an economy to achieve various goals. Already we have seen how government intervenes to achieve a measure of distributive justice. Another area of government intervention is to promote economic efficiency. The instruments used by government to do so are antitrust, regulation, public ownership, and the use of taxes and subsidies to achieve a given end. As in the case of distributive justice, if individuals determine that industries are behaving in such a way as to not serve the public interest, they pursue government intervention to bring about change. Public perceptions of industry and firm size in the economy drive much of these government decisions, and to the extent that government responds to them, it serves to affirm the political legitimacy of the state. We thus need to account for these perceptions, and on what basis government intervention responds to them.

In the seventeenth century, the Dutch were pioneers in the creation of a functioning stock exchange through which the corporate form of business could flourish. These institutions were foundational to Dutch prosperity and in setting the stage for the emergence of modern capitalism. It was an extraordinary achievement and a key innovation to manage risk.

A century later, when the English were setting up their own stock exchange, the prevailing mode of commerce at the time was mercantilism, that is, a system of private enterprise in which government relied on taxes and regulation to favor not just the national interest but also those of particular monopoly firms such as the East and West Indies Companies. The idea of public ownership of industry would come later in the 19th century, when Karl Marx (1818–1883) wrote critically of industrial capitalism in which monopoly was seen as an inevitable outcome until revolution could change direction.

Under mercantilism, state-sanctioned monopolies faced few restraints regarding the allocation of production and in the setting of prices.[104] Moreover, the prevailing residue of the medieval guild system tended to foster cooperation among those of a given trade, and thus to establish control over markets. This is what led Adam Smith (1723–1790) to rail against mercantilism as state-sanctioned private trading monopolies that served only themselves and not the public interest.

In his 1776 treatise, *The Wealth of Nations*, Smith wrote: "People of the same trade seldom meet together, even for merriment and diversion, but the conversation ends in a conspiracy against the public, or in some contrivance to raise prices".[105] Herein lies the heart of an argument regarding whether the state should intervene in the structure and conduct of markets in order to achieve a maximum level of social welfare, and to thus affirm the political legitimacy of government.

Considerations Regarding Competition and Economic Efficiency

What do we mean by a "maximum level of social welfare?" We already have provided a basic framework in our discussion of distributive justice. Smith just used the "wealth of nations", which today we would think of in terms of a country's Gross Domestic Product, or GDP. What economists have done is to provide measures linked more directly to components of an economy, as in individual satisfaction used in our discussion of distributive justice, or in the present context, how the performance of a sector of the economy contributes to its overall Gross Domestic Product.

In Smith's time, monopoly was viewed as a key weakness of mercantilism. By removing government sanctioned monopoly, he argued, firms would enter into competition to serve consumer interests. Competition, as Smith saw it, implied an infinite number of firms looking to serve the consumer and when firms did not do so, others would take their place as if an "invisible hand" were guiding production decisions.

Since Smith's time, much of economics writing has been devoted to understanding the market conditions under which consumer's social welfare could be satisfied. How many firms are needed, and how can we measure what is meant by efficiency under a given number of firms competing to meet consumer demand? When does competition fail to do so, and under what circumstances does this warrant government intervention?

What do we mean by efficiency? Competition in economics is seen as a continuous process, not as a winner-take-all outcome of a game. When firms enter a market, they face two kinds of decisions, namely, how to produce a given level of output and how much output to produce. Economics provides a set of rules by which these conditions can be met, and under which circumstances do they fail, and thus provide a *prima facie* basis for government intervention.

Deciding how to produce a given level of output can be thought of as a condition of technical efficiency. That means, whether firms can find the least costly way of producing a given level of output in terms of the level and mix of resources at a given moment.[106] What compels firms to seek this technical efficiency is competition—if your costs exceed those of other firms, you will not be able to compete, and either you adapt, go out of production, or redeploy resources elsewhere.[107]

Competition, both actual and potential, provides an incentive for firms to choose the least costly way of producing a given level of output, and can change in response to technological innovation, resource discoveries, and changes in the range and scope of both input and output sales markets. Barriers to entry constrain this process, as has been noted by many in analyzing market competition. In taking a perspective on consumers, Albert Hirschman

(1915–2012) characterized this as exit, voice, and loyalty. His analysis helped to lay bare questions of transactions costs in the presence of risk.[108]

In turn, allocative efficiency is the choice of the optimal level of output. In a market setting, the optimal level of output is one that maximizes profit, from which a corresponding rate of return can be derived. A rate of return can be measured in terms of sales, invested capital, or equity, and publicly listed firms routinely shared published variants of these measures to stockholders and to public entities. When firms see higher rates of return in an industry beyond their own, they look to enter those markets, the result of which the rates of return tend to be equalized over time, given differences in the level of risk.

Producers and consumers each act out of individual self-interest to achieve, respectively, maximum profits and maximum consumer satisfaction, wind out through market prices in allocating resources in such a way that best meets their respective interests, and thus achieve a level of social welfare as though an "invisible hand", rather than a government agency, were guiding the decision. Whether that holds true depends to no small degree on the level of information transparency and symmetry, a question we will take up later.

How, then, does a competitive market wind up with the best number of firms? Rather than Adam Smith's infinite number of firms, it turns out that one can achieve a relatively high degree of efficiency with a relatively small number of firms. The signal for firms to enter, stay, or leave a market depends on the firm's rate of return in comparison to the opportunity cost of capital. What does this mean?

The opportunity cost of capital is that rate which a firm would have to satisfy when replacing its existing stock of capital equipment. The opportunity cost of capital would obviously vary with the type of industry in question, and which also would vary over time, given changes in the technology of production and market conditions. Where do we find such rates from which to draw inferences about the decision to stay, leave, or enter a market?

Firms routinely publish results to shareholders that include various measures of a rate of return, key among them being the rate of return on sales, the rate of return on equity (for corporations listed on a stock exchange), and the rate of return on invested capital. If a firm is obtaining a rate of return equal to the opportunity cost of capital, there is no incentive for firms to either enter or leave the market, given transparency in the level of information available to investors and managers. Such a rate is considered to be a normal rate of return, equivalent to a zero rate of economic return. When a firm's reported rate of return exceeds the opportunity cost of capital, its economic rate of return is positive, and this serves to attract other firms to enter the market.

Any rate above the opportunity cost of capital is considered to be a positive economic rate of return. This difference serves as a signal for other firms as to whether they should enter a market in which the economic rate of return is positive. Under competitive dynamics, the number of firms in a market thus is determined by the combined level of output that through a reduction in market prices from greater competition, reduces the average market rate of return to the opportunity cost of capital. The number of firms so realized will vary from one industry to another, even under conditions of zero innovation or any other kind of change.

Given the above characterization of market conditions, we can now proceed to address the question of how many firms are needed to achieve a relatively efficient level of competitive output, that is one in which the accounting rate of return approximates the opportunity cost of capital, and thus a zero economic rate of return? In the early 19th century, a French economist, Antoine Augustin Cournot (1801–1877), came up with a way to provide an answer.[109]

In a purely competitive world, maximum efficiency is achieved with an infinite number of buyers and sellers, much as Adam Smith suggested. In the real world, no such configuration ever exists. Instead, as the number of firms becomes smaller and smaller to a limit of a single monopoly, Cournot demonstrated how much efficiency could be obtained. He did so by formulating a duopoly model, that is, a market in which there are not one but two firms. Under the assumption that each firm seeks to maximize profit by setting output to a point where the marginal, or extra, cost of the last unit produced is equal to the marginal revenue.

Assuming that the two firms did not collude and were of equal size and the same technology, the total level of output under duopoly is greater while the price and economic profit levels are lower than under monopoly. If we compare the level of social welfare under monopoly in comparison to a perfectly competitive market, we have a measure of the relative efficiency of a given market structure.[110] If one then does a sequential calculation when the number of firms is allowed to increase, we can obtain a discrete measure of how relative efficiency increases as the number of firms increases. This parametric comparison is known as a Cournot conjecture.

As shown in Table 6.1, a relatively high level of efficiency can be obtained through a remarkably small number of firms. At what point, then, does government intervention to achieve a competitive level of output justified? This question has rarely been so posed in practice, in part because industry concentration changes over time and because different

Table 6.1 A Cournot Conjecture to Assess Monopoly and Competition.

Number of Firms	Relative Efficiency	Relative Losses
1	75.00%	25.00%
2	88.89%	11.11%
3	93.75%	6.25%
4	96.01%	3.99%
5	97.21%	2.79%
6	97.94%	2.06%
7	98.42%	1.58%
8	98.74%	1.26%
9	98.98%	1.02%
10	99.16%	0.84%

Source: https://msuweb.montclair.edu/~lebelp/ApplicationModules.html.

displace existing firms and industries as innovation takes place. Yet it is worth pointing out, if for no other reason than it challenges our perception of how we perceive and define imperfect competition.

The Cournot conjecture provides a conceptual basis from which to weigh the costs of corrective action against the economic efficiency gains to be achieved. As long as the costs of corrective action are less than the gains in consumer welfare, government intervention can be seen as warranted.

As appealing as Cournot's framework is, it leaves aside the question of collusion. As Adam Smith pointed out, and as can now be seen from the Cournot framework, it may pay a group of firms to collude to reduce collective output to the level of a single monopolists. Such collusion is a cartel, and whether a cartel makes sense to its members depends on the value of setting collective output equivalent to a monopolist in comparison to the existing number of firms. And is also forms the *prima facie* case for applying a key tool to correct for imperfect competition, namely, antitrust.

A classic case regarding collusion involves the international market for crude oil. As the early twentieth century got under way, industrialization was producing a dramatic shift from coal to crude oil production to fuel the economy. Wildcat explorers and major firms might come across a productive field only after a number of wells had been dug.

While property rights on the surface conveyed title to extraction, oil reservoirs could extend well beyond surface rights, thus leading firms to maximize extraction once a reserve had been discovered Given the state of geological knowledge at the time, an initial discovery would quickly lead to a rush of producers seeking to discover and extract crude oil from adjacent fields. The result was wild shifts in proven reserves and production, with a comparable impact on prices.

Against fluctuations in crude oil prices, a group of European and American oil firms met at Achnacarry castle, Scotland in 1928, to set rules on production.[111] Their efforts to control the price of oil would later inspire the creation of OPEC, the Organization of Petroleum Exporting Countries, in 1960. While cartels are considered illegal in many countries, international petroleum firms in general have complied with OPEC production quotas, even though this has not resulted in a stabilization of revenues.

The reason for cartel instability is that marginal players seek higher shares of revenues and tend to cheat on quotas. And then there is the impact of technological innovation on discoveries, namely, the spawning of shale oil production in recent years, along with improved methods of extraction and new reserve discoveries.

While OPEC still exists, its share of crude oil production has been falling relative to production of other countries, notably Russia and the United States. And while some claim adherence to a purely free and competitive market, we now have politicians such as Donald Trump seeking to set production quotas for OPEC member and non-OPEC countries to restore profitability to crude oil production in light of a fall in demand due to the coronavirus pandemic. But let us now turn to a classic case that defined antitrust early in the 20th century, namely, the Standard Oil Company decision of the U.S. Supreme Court in 1911.

John D. Rockefeller (1839–1937) symbolized the rise of extraordinary wealth in America. Born into humble circumstances in Elmira, New York, his parents moved to Cleveland, Ohio at an early age prior to the American Civil war. There, he apprenticed himself to a local accounting firm where he learned about the nascent petroleum industry.

In the 1850's, when Rockefeller was learning accounting, refined petroleum was used primarily as a lubricant for steam engines, for commercial waxes, and later for medicine, of which one product, Vaseline, is still on the market today.[112] In 1859, wildcat developer Edwin L. Drake struck oil by digging the first successful well in Titusville, Pennsylvania, thereby setting the stage for oil exploration and extraction on a large scale.

It was only after the Civil War, that the demand for petroleum grew quickly, and John D. Rockefeller established the Standard Oil Company in 1870 to take advantage of exploration, extraction and refining, along with distribution to achieve almost unimaginable wealth. Development of the internal combustion engine and then commercial aviation would drive much of the demand for oil.

Standard Oil's operations enabled John D. Rockefeller to become by 1916 the country's first billionaire. His net worth in today's dollars was equivalent to U.S. $418 billion dollars, well in excess of today's wealthiest individuals Jeff Bezos ($114 billion), Bill Gates ($99.1 billion), or Warren Buffett ($80.8 billion).[113]

At a time when average per capita income was U.S. $1,300, such astounding wealth produces two kinds of reactions. One is, "How can I get a piece of the action?" The second is "This could only have happened through cheating and lawbreaking". Such sentiments have prevailed ever since all the way down to Bernie Sanders' lament of Wall Street: "... we will no longer tolerate the greed of Wall Street, corporate America and the billionaire class—greed which has resulted in this country having more income and wealth inequality than any other major country on earth."[144] John D. Rockefeller emerged at a time of rapid industrialization in the United States and when the demand for oil was far from certain. He succeeded through a combination of shrewd business tactics and luck to generate his wealth.[115] Interestingly, the preoccupation with concentration and economic size changes over time, and the dominant firms today have emerged largely only in the last 30 years. Few today lament the power

Figure 6.1 Size Matters.

Standard Oil Company	Microsoft Corporation	Amazon.com
John D. Rockefeller (1839–1937)	Bill Gates (1955–)	Jeff Bezos (1964–)

of Standard Oil and its successors, and instead focus on Amazon, Google, Microsoft, and Apple.

Rockefeller's success was accompanied by substantial philanthropy that has continued through generations of his successors. But despite such gifts as the founding of the University of Chicago, the restoration of the Palace of Versailles at the end of the First World War, and other contributions, wealth alone aroused suspicion and envy not unlike what we see today. Although the U.S. had used regulation to address monopoly power, it was the rise of the petroleum industry and John D. Rockefeller's role as head of the Standard Oil Company that brought one of the first choices regarding government intervention to affect the level of efficiency.

In 1904, Ida M. Tarbell (1857–1944), a journalist working at *McClure's* magazine, wrote a history of the Standard Oil Company in which she portrayed Rockefeller as a ruthless capitalist bent on destroying all in his path, including her father, a small time wildcat explorer who went bankrupt when Rockefeller's railroad oil transport offered prices too low for him to survive.[116] Tarbell's account riveted public attention to the Standard Oil company. It helped shape hostility to Standard Oil in general and against John D. Rockefeller in particular. Lawsuits were brought regarding alleged violations of antitrust statutes. They eventually reached the U.S. Supreme Court in 1911.

The key founding statute of antitrust in the U.S. is the Sherman Act of 1890. Named after Senator John Sherman of Ohio, a key provision outlaws "all combinations that restrain trade between states or with foreign nations.[117] This prohibition applies not only to formal cartels but also to any agreement to fix prices, limit industrial output, share markets, or exclude competition".

In addition, the Sherman Act makes illegal all attempts to monopolize any part of trade or commerce in the United States. Later statutes such as the Clayton Act of 1914, the Federal Trade Commission Act of 1914, the Robinson-Patman Act of 1936, and the Cellar-Kefauver Act of 1950. The Clayton Act forbade interlocking directorates, the Robinson-Patman Act outlawed price discrimination, while the Cellar-Kefauver Act of 1950 set restrictions on vertical mergers.

In an 8 to 1 majority decision, the 1911 Supreme Court found Standard Oil guilty of violating the Sherman Antitrust Act of 1890. Moreover, it ordered the dissolution of Standard Oil, based on the asset valuation of the company's divisions operating in each U.S. state. The result was the creation of 33 separate companies, while those who held stock were given a percent of stock in each of the companies equal to their holdings in Standard Oil.

Instead of impoverishing John D. Rockefeller, the Supreme Court decision resulted in his holding assets worth three times what they had been worth under the old Standard Oil Company. This is not the outcome that many had envisioned when they first sought to file antitrust cases against Standard Oil. But it raises the question of whether antitrust legislation is intended solely to achieve greater economic efficiency or to affect the distribution of income.

Since the 1911 decision, economists sought to answer the question of whether a vertically integrated company such as Standard Oil could be more efficient than separately created number of firms. In the 1920's Paul Douglas and mathematician Charles Cobb produced a formula from which one could test for the presence or absence of economies of scale. Their formulation and findings were published in a 1928 article in the *American Economic Review*. If economies of scale can be demonstrated to exist, then it may be cheaper, and thus more efficient, for a smaller number of firms to produce a given level of output than a larger number producing the same level.[118]

Although production functions could be used to test for the presence or absence of economies of scale, economists have gone through several variations of production functions to test not just for economies of scale, but also economies of scope. An economy of scope is said to exist when it is cheaper for a smaller number of firms to produce a variety of outputs rather than each producing separate and distinctive products. Given the difficulties of defining how to capture market power through empirical tests, while the U.S. still has antitrust statutes that are used to prosecute cases against firms, there has been a declining reliance on its use for two basic reasons, namely, the pace of technological innovation, and globalization of markets.

In the 1960's, some 30 years after the Great Depression, only a smaller number of firms in such industries as steel and automobiles survived. Some called for breaking up these firms using existing antitrust statutes, but no legislative action took place. Then in the late 1960s, then Attorney General Ramsey Clark filed two antitrust lawsuits, one against AT&T and the other against IBM that would demonstrate the difficulty in deciding how and under what circumstances remedial action is justified.

The case against IBM was based on the fact that computing in the 1960s had evolved around mainframe technology and in which IBM held a dominant position of some 60 percent of the market in 1970. What was not then evident was that technology would change the nature of computing in such a way that antitrust no longer made sense. Few, if any, could foresee the rise of desktop computing, and later, laptop computing, and portable devices such as iPods and iPhones that could handle tasks once limited to mainframe computers.

With the introduction of the Apple II, then college dropout Steve Jobs redefined computing for his Apple Corporation as a decentralized work and personal technology, out of which came the Macintosh. Looking for a way to compete with the new desktop publishing industry, IBM created a separate division to start manufacturing and needed an operating system for its software. Bill Gates, a college dropout from Harvard University, landed the contract to develop IBM's operating system, then known only as DOS, and which evolved into the Windows operating system we know today.

The story of Steve Jobs and Bill Gates is not a morality lesson on why not obtain a college education. Rather, it is an indication of the role of creative entrepreneurship, something that few educational experiences can convey, for reasons noted by any number of observers.[119] Austrian economist Joseph Schumpeter wrote presciently of the role of the entrepreneur in his book, *The Theory of Economic Development*, first published in German in 1911, and translated into English in 1934, and which it has been in print ever since. Schumpeter described the qualities of an entrepreneur as grounded in psychology, from which a creative and rebellious spirit challenges the existing way of doing business.[120]

Despite the launch of an IBM personal computer line, it failed to recapture the market it had once dominated. By 1980, IBM's mainframe market share fell to 32 percent and, in January 1982, Attorney General William Baxter dropped the suit against IBM.[121] Today, IBM no longer even markets its own PC brand. It was sold to Chinese investors in 2005, who re-christened the line under the Lenovo brand, even though it still uses Microsoft's Windows operating software.

The rise of personal computing also held lessons for telecommunications technology. The internet was first developed to coordinate missile strike launches by the military. Few then foresaw a commercial application, yet the internet that evolved has fundamentally changed modes of communication, from email to online business. Out of this have come two of the largest firms today, namely, Google and Amazon, which along with Apple and Microsoft, are among the most valuable companies in the world. In 1970, none existed. In 1980, Apple and Microsoft emerged. In 2020 Amazon and Google joined with Apple and Microsoft to form the top third and fourth position on the list.[122] This points to the difficulty in targeting a firm or an industry as the object of an antitrust action.

As already indicated, technological change can upset the existing industry structure. Moreover, state-drive efforts to direct the flow of technology do not always succeed. A good example is the case of Minitel, one of the first internet communications technology to emerge in France. Begun in 1980 as a videotext online service operating via telephone lines, Minitel was operated by the French telecom government firm from 1982 to 2012.

At the time, Minitel had the ability to transmit text, but did not have video imaging capacity. What it did provide was the ability to make online purchase, acquire financial services information, reserve scheduled trains, and email. Although it reached some 10 million subscribers in France, it was abandoned in face of the overwhelming popularity of the internet and personal computers that perform even greater functions. Understanding how this came to be requires looking at what happened to the antitrust case against AT&T that was filed back in 1969.

What happened to AT&T tells a different path for antitrust. Prior to the internet, voice and data communication technology was driven primarily by the telephone, using an extensive network of land-lines connected by copper wiring. AT&T was an early winner in achieving a near monopoly in this technology, and was subject to a second instrument of government intervention in promotion of competition, namely, regulation.

Telecommunications over fixed land-lines was considered as an example of economies of scale. It made little sense for competing firms to duplicate the number of lines over a given space to develop a network of communications. In 1887, Congress faced a similar dilemma when railroads were transforming the country's ground transportation network.

Recognizing that railroads were faster than horse-driven transport, or the vast canal network that preceded them, government faced the problem of transport monopoly when a railroad established a line through a given area. Not only could it control fares and revenues for passenger and freight. Railroad companies often bought up rights of way of land on both sides of a rail line and through which they could control local businesses seeking to serve rail line customers.

Recognizing that railroads were a cheaper way of transport than the alternatives, Congress passed the Interstate Commerce Act of 1887, which established the Interstate Commerce Commission, and which exists down to this day. It also spawned the creation of the Federal Communications Commission decades later, in 1934, to allocate band-with to radio stations, and later television, and internet providers. And it also served as precedent in the creation of the Civil Aeronautics Board, or CAB, which operated from 1938 to 1985, when it was disbanded per the Airline Deregulation Act of 1978. In all three cases, the purposes was to set "fair prices", that is, fares that could enable a firm to earn a "fair rate of return", which meant equivalent to the prevailing opportunity cost of capital, the rate at which a firm could replace and expand its existing stock of capital.

As with the internet, price regulation of the railroads, and later aviation, failed to take into account the impact of technological change. In the case of the ICC, though railroads did hold an early monopoly in terms of passenger and freight transport, it operated with a fixed and limited perspective. The fixed perspective is that railroads were not the only way to transport passenger and freight. Congressional approval of the Federal-Aid Highway Act of 1956 would greatly reduce travel costs for passenger vehicles as well as freight trucking.[123] And though still largely under the jurisdiction of CAB regulation, airline passenger and freight travel also would reduce revenues from railroads.

By 1970, regulation and technological change had reduced railroads to ruin. The Penn Central Railroad, the then sixth largest corporation in the United States, declared bankruptcy. This prompted Congress to adopt to pieces of counter-legislation, namely the Railway Passenger Act of 1971, which created Amtrak, and the Consolidated Railway Act that became known as Conrail. Amtrak and Conrail are quasi-public railway corporations that enable private rail companies to acquire engines to carry passengers and freight throughout 46 states.

Today, Amtrak requires continuing subsidies to offset insufficient passenger service, and Conrail has witnessed a continuing consolidation of freight systems in the country. Although the Surface Transportation Act of 1995 replaced the ICC, distortions in transportation pricing still exist.

So what happened to the AT&T antitrust case? What undermined the logic of AT&T's position as a low-cost producer was the rise of wireless technology. As far back as the Second World War, companies such as Motorola had developed wireless communications for use in military equipment such as tanks and airplanes. At the time, few saw the commercial advantages of wireless communications. Then came innovations through space exploration.

When NASA was developing a rocket system to land astronauts on the moon, it required miniaturization of computer equipment and telecommunications.[124] Satellites were developed to improve wireless communications, and it spawned a number of competitors to traditional land-based telecommunications such as AT&T.

Instead of breaking up the firm, as in the case of Standard Oil, or walking away from the suit, as in the case of IBM, in 1984, the Second District Court in Washington, D.C. adopted a third approach, namely, the use of a consent decree. In a consent decree, a firm is not found guilty of violating existing antitrust statutes but promises to alter its behavior in the future. As a result, AT&T was broken up with the idea that a more competitive market structure would emerge.

AT&T could keep its long-distance services, Bell Labs, and the Yellow Pages, while divesting itself of local telephone service through the creation of what came to be known as the nine "Baby Bells": Bell Atlantic, NYNEX, Bell South, Southwestern Bell, Ameritech, US West, Pacific Telesis, Southern New England Telephone, and Cincinnati Bell.

As figure 6.2 illustrates, AT&T first acquired permission to compete with the regional Bell companies for local service. Then it began to pursue acquisition of several of these companies while it sought to bring greater geographic integration.

Figure 6.2 The Restructuring of AT&T.

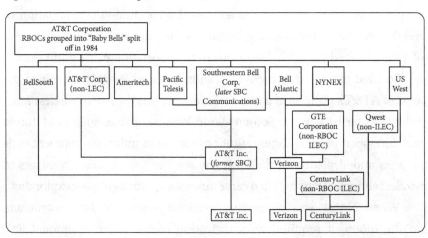

AT&T also entered the laptop personal computer business, though it has since abandoned the effort. As the parent company AT&T engaged in mergers and acquisitions, it also faced growing competition from one of the newly created regional Bell companies, namely, Bell Atlantic. Bell Atlantic recognized the growing importance of wireless telecommunications, and then started to offer both fixed and wireless service to customers.

Along the way, Bell Atlantic merged with NYNEX and with its wireless services, rebranded itself Verizon. The expansion of the internet engaged both companies in competing for internet services, including AT&T's decision to buy a DirectTV and Time Warner to deliver packaged entertainment along with basic internet connectivity.

Today, AT&T has sales of $159 billion in comparison with Verizon's $128 billion. Yet these two companies now operate on a global scale and face competition with China Mobile's sales of $109 billion, SoftBank's $83 billion, Nippon Telegraph and Telephone at $105 billion, among other firms. Under globalization, these firms are competing more directly than ever before conceived, raising the question of what entity, if any, could possibly apply some version of antitrust in the face of industrial consolidation. Huawei, a Chinese manufacturing firm, is offering 5G internet service on a world scale. The U.S. has opposed the expansion of Huawei on the grounds of security concerns, a charge that Huawei has contested.[125] Many see this as a form of protectionism consistent with the Trump administration's efforts to promote domestic industry.

What then, should we make of the 1984 AT&T consent decree? One could argue that a major result of that decision was to spawn the rise of internet services and the creation of a whole new range of support industries that today display dominance of a few major U.S.-based firms, namely, Apple, Google, Amazon, and Microsoft. Leaving to private firms the direction of telecommunications accelerated a trend toward innovation that may well not have taken place were the pre-1984 AT&T firm to have been left in place. But that result may be thought of as an unintended consequence, and certainly not the view of observers when the consent decree was handed down.

Beyond antitrust and regulation, a third tool to promote competition and economic efficiency is taxes and subsidies. Here the perspective is not to restructure or regulate prices and production as much as to contain the potential economic rates of return that might otherwise arise in the presence of industrial concentration. The most prominent recent example was the Windfall Profits Tax Act of 1980.

During the 1970s, as far back as 1971, the United States adopted a system of price controls to counter the inflationary impact of the Vietnam War. When the Middle East War of 1973 erupted, the price of crude oil jumped from an average of $2.50 a barrel to $12.00, a dramatic increase at the time, and one that precipitated a national debate on how best to provide security of oil supplies when primary producers in the Middle East were engaged in warfare.

One proposal was that the United States should adopt an oil import tax that would reduce dependence on foreign oil imports, and thus increase national security. It was not adopted, in part because one key result would be an accelerated pace of consumption from domestic reserves.

The United States adopted this position when it chose to deregulate the oil industry in 1980 with the passage of the Windfall Profits Tax Act. The deregulation of the industry was expected to create windfall profits in the industry, based on the chronic shortages in energy demand during the 1970's. Instead of industry reaping the benefits of deregulation, an excise tax would be used to capture some of that gain and increase the number of competitors in alternative energy technologies.

Few developing countries have opted for this approach, partly because the distorting effects of price controls have made it difficult to anticipate such an adjustment, partly because the institutional and economic environment for competing industries is so thin, and partly because governments have had so little experience with nurturing such alternatives. It is, however, a central element in the international debate over industrial policy, and matches some of the practices of MITI, Japan's Ministry of International Trade and Industry, which has tried to increase domestic market capacity in the face of international competitors. Such variations are also what clearly amount to mercantilism, and which is at odds with the underlying principle of economic efficiency based on increased market competition.

A third option is one well known in a number of developing countries, namely, nationalization of private enterprises as well as creation of a number of state-owned and parastatal enterprises. Many African countries opted for this approach in the early decades of the 1960's. African socialism, as espoused by Julius Nyerere, Leopold Senghor, and other African political leaders, was based on the notion that the colonial experience had retarded the growth and diversification of African economies, and that in the absence of a viable private sector, the only solution was for African governments to intervene directly in transforming existing industries while creating new ones in an effort to accelerate industrial development and economic growth of the continent. Because state owned enterprises were supposed to be serving national goals and not narrow profit-maximizing ones on behalf of private shareholders, they would, as a matter of national pride, focus on achieving technical efficiency in operations, and in setting output and pricing patterns consistent with a competitive-equivalent market structure.

The difficulty with public enterprises is that many of them have never experienced any competitive pressures, domestic or foreign. They did not experience domestic competition because government policy was driven by the notion that a publicly owned local enterprise would function automatically on behalf of the public interest, and that this would be sufficient. They did not experience much international competition because governments also tended to set automatically high tariff and import quota restrictions from abroad as a way of helping to ensure the success of local public enterprises.

The result is that many such state-owned and parastatal enterprises never earned any profits, did little by way of product and market innovation, and became chronic drains on hard-pressed local government subsidies just to stay afloat. Because losses from these enterprises because so significant, they reduced funding opportunities for other priority public sector activities such as physical infrastructure, health, and education. It is partly from this context that structural adjustment programs, begun in the early 1980's, were born, and why privatization was given the emphasis that it has.

Critics argue that state-owned monopolies are not responsive to the public interest, and that as guaranteed public entities, they tend to display moral hazard in terms of failing to minimize costs the way that a privately-owned entity facing competition would have to do. Opposition in the U.S. to Amtrak and, to a lesser extent, Conrail, is fueled by a high reliance on private automobile and truck transport, and critics regularly call for an end to any effort to build a high-speed rail network in the U.S.

The U.S. high-speed rail network stands in contrast to many other countries with which the U.S. is engaged in commerce, notably Japan, the U.K., France, Germany, and India. In those countries, public ownership ranges from a low 25 percent in Japan to 51 percent in France and in the U.K., all the way to 100 percent in other countries. What makes these public rail systems solvent is that these countries place relatively high taxes on fuel consumption, thus increasing the demand for public transport. And, it should be noted that France developed the first high-speed rail system as far back as 1981, and today, has the second largest railway network after China.

Choices for Promoting Competition to Achieve Economic Efficiency

Where does all of this leave the role of government in promoting competition? For a time, the United States was willing to use antitrust to prevent mergers and thus, in principle, to increase competition. Today, there is less willingness to use it to restructure industries, and instead to rely more on market forces to decide how many firms could efficiently support a market. This still leaves open the possibility of collusion and through such agencies as the Federal Trade Commission, some actions still are adopted. What has compounded the choice of government intervention is whether, in the presence of economies of scale, even a regulated industry should be embraced.

When the AT&T case was still in litigation, some went so far as to develop a theory of unregulated concentrated industries. This came to be known as contestable markets, an argument put forth in 1982 by William Baumol, John C. Panzar, and Robert Willig.[126] A contestable market is one in which an otherwise quasi-monopoly industry must adhere to a competitive market pricing structure because firms outside the industry could choose to enter. The threat of entry would be sufficient to maintain competitive practices.

One can ask why has antitrust lost its appeal as a means of promoting competition. It may be that promoting competition has been intertwined with the pursuit of distributive justice. When Karl Marx was writing on capitalism and exploitation in industrial England in the 19th century, he concentrated on industrial organization rather than on the personal distribution of income, even though his writing was intended to focus on income and wealth inequality.

Marx's prediction that capitalism would be replaced by socialism in England, then the most developed country in the world, he could not have been more wrong. Instead, it was the Russian Revolution of 1917 that created the first Communist regime in the world, and in a country considered to be one of the most backward of the time. Yet, the concern with capitalism's effects on income and wealth inequality have not gone away, as we noted in our observations on distributive justice. We see an echo of this concern in the writings of French economist, Thomas Piketty, who wrote extensively on the rise of inequality in the 20th century that would be checked only by war, pestilence, or some other form of social upheaval.

Setting aside the question of inequality in income and wealth, industrial concentration remains a continuing source of concern in many countries. Ironically, to the extent that one sees a need to apply antitrust to achieve economic efficiency, one is in at least implicit agreement with the Marxian theory of economic development. Yet evidence has pointed to something quite different, namely the impact of expanding international trade and competition on reducing the degree of industrial concentration in the global economy. In this context, all too often, critics of industrial concentration have failed to note the subversive role of technological innovation.

Marx, and other critics since then, often have failed to see how innovation would create different forms of industrial concentration, only to be displaced by yet another innovation. This was an insight put forth by economist Joseph Schumpeter (1882–1950), from which we have the phrase "creative destruction".[127] "Creative destruction" is more evident when we observe the "killer app" of some computer program or system that is designed to destroy the existing industrial order. But the story does not discard the notion of antitrust or other forms of government intervention. Instead, we need to account for why antitrust, the most favored form of intervention, has generally lost favor as an instrument to promote competition.

One thing that checked rising industrial concentration in the U.S. was the expansion of international trade and investment. Globalization served as a substitute for antitrust, especially in the automobile and aviation industries. In 1960, the share of U.S. GDP involved in international trade was under 5 percent. In 2017, it was 27 percent. In the case of the auto industry, imports in 1960 accounted for under 10 percent of domestic vehicle sales in the United States.[128] In 2018 they represented 60 percent of sales. If one looks at the degree of concentration in the U.S. vehicle industry, it is less than half the degree in the 1960's. And it displays an ability for newcomers such as South African entrepreneur Elon Musk, who founded Tesla to enter the vehicle market with all-electric models and which is compelling domestic and imported firms to develop their own versions.[129]

Globalization, it turns out, has served as a substitute means of promoting competition to reliance on antitrust, pricing regulation, taxes and subsidies, or public ownership. The motor vehicle industry is still one of the most important sectors of US manufacturing, much as it is for other industrial and industrializing countries. To the extent that countries turn inward and protectionist, this may lead to more government intervention to promote competition and economic efficiency, a direction that few now seem to be anticipating, and one in which greater economic efficiency is far from certain.

How can we reconcile the reduced emphasis on government intervention to promote competition with the current drift inward? Much has to do with perceptions of size as much as the degree of concentration. In the case of the Standard Oil Company, its size alone was viewed as a threat to individual freedom at the time, and it certainly was concentrated. Yet few saw how innovation would displace some of the concern over size. If we look at industrial concentration in the U.S. there are some industries far more concentrated than petroleum or motor vehicles.[130]

Consider, for example, the motor vehicle industry, once a target of antitrust. At the turn of the 20th century, motor vehicles were the new frontier technology, just as railroads had been viewed in the late 19th century. During the 1920's, the number of firms producing internal combustion engine vehicles grew rapidly, only to face bankruptcy and consolidation during the Great Depression of the 1930's. In the postwar era, the number of domestic surviving firms were concentrated around General Motors, Ford, and Chrysler, with smaller shares held by American Motors and Studebaker-Packard.

Concentration ratios for the number of domestic vehicle manufacturers stood around 90 percent by the late 1950's. What was not anticipated at the time was the energy crisis of the 1970's and the rise of imported vehicles in the U.S. domestic market. When crude oil prices skyrocketed from $2.50 a barrel to then then unprecedented $12.00 a barrel as the Middle East entered yet another war between Arab states and Israel, American consumers looked to fuel efficient vehicles. Few domestic firms could meet demand, and imports, largely made in Japan, began to fill the void. From that time on, imports would claim a growing share of vehicle sales in the

U.S. And concentration was thus reduced by the impact of an oil crisis from abroad, not the application of antitrust.

One thing that propelled a rising share of imported vehicles was that the U.S. also was engaged in a series of tariff negotiations under GATT, the General Agreement on Tariffs and Trade, which had been founded in 1947, and then replaced by the World Trade Organization, or WTO, in 1994. Overall, the share of international trade in the U.S. Gross Domestic Product grew from approximately 5 percent in 1960 to its current size at 27 percent. Interestingly, as tariffs on automobiles declined to their current average of 2.5 percent, tariffs on trucks reached 25 percent.

The current shift away from passenger vehicles to trucks and SUV's may be explained to some extent by the benefits domestic manufacturers receive from these tariff differentials. Domestic vehicle manufacturers are all too willing to promote these vehicles to higher margin trucks away from passenger vehicles, even though passenger cars still provide higher average fuel economy.[131]

And as foreign vehicles took a growing share of the market, concentration in the domestic market began to decline. Whereas imports accounted for a little under 10 percent in the early 1960's, by 2018 imports have grown to just under 60 percent. If we take the aggregate number of vehicle firms in the U.S. market, including domestic branches of overseas firms, the degree of concentration has dropped by 50 percent. U.S. vehicle manufacturers now face even new entrants such as Tesla, in the all-electric vehicle market, and domestic firms are scrambling to re-align their product lines to compete in this new arena.

In short, antitrust did not reduce concentration in the motor vehicle industry. International trade competition did. Although this has worked to the benefit of consumer choice, the rise of protectionism in the current age of nationalism threatens to undermine how markets can work on behalf of consumers. That was the message of Adam Smith over two centuries ago.

Smith's insight on competition now is being undermined by the new protectionism and the weakening of international governance institutions such as the WTO. And it has echoes in populist politicians ranging from Donald Trump to Bernie Sanders. Thus, of the role of government to promote competition, in a protectionist world that we see returning, antitrust may yet be revived as a tool. Experience suggests that antitrust is probably not as effective as international trade and investment on increasing the level of total social welfare. And it is problematic in terms of political legitimacy when individuals once again face the risks of rising concentration as the doors to international trade are closed.

CHAPTER SEVEN

GETTING THE RIGHT MIX OF GOODS AND SERVICES

Do Markets Satisfy What We Want to Consume?

If markets were efficient and equitable, one might be tempted to set aside whether government intervention lends itself to political legitimacy. Yet prices may fail to achieve an efficient outcome, even if markets somehow prove equitable. The problem, quite simply, is that prices may fail to incorporate all of the consequences of a given market transaction.

In some cases, markets may under-produce a good that is beneficial to society while in other cases, they may produce too much. The question, then, is how to get prices "right", and in order to do so, public intervention may be essential. And it may help to explain why we have government expenditures on national defense, education, and health and why we have taxes and regulation on congestion and environmental pollution.

One issue in which there is widespread agreement regarding government intervention is public expenditures on national security. There is a simple explanation for this agreement: we cannot go to our local market and purchase discrete quantities of national security. Economists call this a pure public good, even if the limits to national security may seem at times unbounded, and thus dangerous to a democratic society.

Market fundamentalists generally view government intervention as a reduction in individual choice, though paradoxically may view spending on national security as justifiable on the indivisibility of benefits. Market critics note that because benefits of national security may be indivisible, the level of spending must be definition be subject to non-market criteria. Striking a balance between states and markets that best satisfies social welfare in terms of national security is thus a matter of perceptions of national security risks, not market prices.[132]

National security is bounded to some extent by clarity in a region's borders, that is, expenditures on national defense, or state expenditures on state police, even down to a local level, are defined by a geographic jurisdiction. That sounds simple enough, but in an interdependent global world, even national borders become complicated by international trade and investment. Thus, we find national security expenditures that involve international commitments such as fighting in local wars, peacekeeping, and related functions that are incorporated into a definition of national defense.

A global security argument was used in the decision by the George W. Bush administration to invade Iraq in 2003: Overthrowing Saddam Hussein would reduce an expansion of Al Qaeda militants determined to strike again against the United States as they had done on September 11, 2001. It turns out that Saddam was more interested in preserving his regime than in providing cover to Al Qaeda. Saddam's motivations were ignored while a search for weapons of mass destruction was pursued following his overthrow. Weapons were found, but were never in the hands of Al Qaeda.

How can we measure efforts to provide national security? One way is in terms of the geographic deployment of forces. In the case of the United States, currently just under 85 percent of all military service personnel are deployed within its contiguous borders.[133] Outside the United States, 10 percent are engaged in theater conflicts in Afghanistan and Iraq, and the remaining forces are deployed in Western Europe and in other regions.

The significance of these geographic deployments is that they reflect security agreements decided over time in response to regional conflicts. They also reflect efforts to secure greater movement of trade and investment as the world economy has embraced globalization.

Having noted these historical patterns, as states turn inward, protectionist, and become less open to democratic accountability, international security agreements are being cast aside, and the share of military service personnel serving abroad is likely to dwindle. That trend has carried appeal both to conservative nationalists as well as to leftist critics of the role of the United States as a kind of policeman in global trade relations.

Another way to view national security measures is in terms of the share of a country's Gross Domestic Product devoted to military spending. Most, but not all, security spending is done by the military agencies. While perceptions of national and even international security have varied over time,

Figure 7.1 Military Spending as Share of GDP.

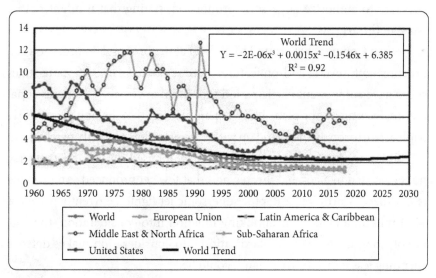

Source: World Bank Indicators: https://databank.worldbank.org/reports.aspx?source=world-development-indicators

as globalization has expanded, the share of GDP devoted to military spending has been until recently on a downward trend.

Given the difficulty in deciding the level of national security, reliance on spending as a measure is inadequate. It relies on an input measure and not an output one. What would be better is a cost-effectiveness measure, even though this is often declared to be the standard. A good example is the production of new weapons systems that demonstrate differences in effectiveness in peacetime versus wartime.

In peacetime, regardless of the budget, defense contractors face uncertain prospects for the demand for their wares. They wind up producing low volume high unit cost items to recover their costs. In wartime, the opposite holds true, when standardization prevails. The following serves to illustrate.

Years ago, James Fallows wrote *National Defense*, a study published in 1981 in which he illustrated the problem of cost-effectiveness in terms of then Northrop's F-5 Tiger supersonic jet fighter plane.[134] The company said that through standardization, they could produce fighters with specific capabilities at less than $U.S. 5 million per plane.[135] Defense officials were reluctant to authorize large-scale production, stating that it might not be "state of the art".

When Congress got around to looking at the proposal, in order to get a procurement, several add-on features were suggested in which more states could have component participation that could guarantee a Congressional buy-in. Eventually, the plane had so many features that the unit price nearly tripled. Northrop did not wind up with enough orders to justify production.

Today, we find military hardware today focused on features that may not be needed in a combat theater, and that few get produced. An example is Lockheed Martin's F22 Raptor supersonic jet fighter, currently priced at $152 million a plane.[136] Even taking inflation into consideration, the failure of Congress to take standardization into consideration makes defense spending less cost-effective than it could be.[137]

One other brief comparison, namely, civilian firearms ownership as an indicator of political legitimacy. The United States has the highest number of civilian firearms ownership in the world. As of 2017, with 393,347,000 estimated firearms in civilian possession, the ratio of civilian firearms per 100 persons, at 120.5, is twice that of the next highest ratio, Saudi Arabia, with its 53.7 per 100 persons. Debates over civilian gun ownership are often heated though not entirely partisan. Advocates for gun regulation point to ownership as a source of domestic and social violence, while defenders of gun rights view them as a constitutional right as framed in the Second Amendment.

Though the Second Amendment defines ownership as falling under the aegis of a well-regulated militia, only in 2008 did the Supreme Court issue a ruling in the case of the *District of Columbia v. Heller* that ownership is an individual's right unconnected with service in a militia. That decision may reflect as much as anything that the U.S. has had a gun culture ever since its War of Independence from Great Britain in 1776. While the Second Amendment was directed at protecting individuals against predations of English forces, it also embodies a deeper sense of mistrust in government intervention.

The irony of this perspective is that while traditional conservatives may favor greater military spending, Second Amendment advocates may also favor greater federal military spending. What evidence do we have on firearms ownership? Although the United States has the highest ratio of civilian firearms ownership, it ranks 39th in the world in terms of homicide rates.[138] In addition, one fear of gun ownership advocates is a need to provide personal protection against criminal behavior. Put somewhat differently, they argue that more gun rights means less gun violence, even if homicide rates have been in decline.[139]

In the United States, both property and personal crime rates have been in decline since the 1980's, and are now at levels comparable to those in the early 1960's. These trends suggest that gun ownership rights provide less of a standard for political legitimacy than other criteria involving government intervention. This said, debates over gun ownership rights are not likely to disappear from public discourse—they serve to animate partisan divisions when election cycles come up for renewal. And, none of the above takes away from the need for sensible gun legislation.

If national security expenditures are the logical province of government spending, is it as true for all public spending to affect the composition of goods and services? The answer is "no", examples of which are education and health, where both public and private expenditures determine the overall level of services provided.

We can think of education as providing two kinds of benefits. One is personal and private, while the other is social. If one were to adopt a purely private, and presumably rational, decision regarding how much education to pursue, one would equate the level with the corresponding private rate of return in comparison to the next best use of funds, including the time spent in schooling and foregone income while doing so. For some, such as college dropouts Bill Gates and Steve Jobs, it made economic sense to stop pursuing a college education and devote efforts to creating wealth and income in computing technology. For others, such a private calculus points to the higher level of lifetime income one would expect from a higher level of education than at the previous lower level. Although today one finds examples where higher education does not always translate into higher income, or in correspondingly higher rates of return, the principle has largely held true for the most part.[140]

Studies on rates of return to education indicate that if left to purely private individual decisions, the investment in education would be less than what is optimal for social welfare. The explanation for this is that in addition to the private benefits of education, e.g., income, intrinsic satisfaction from a greater variety of occupations, greater occupational mobility, educated individual also produce benefits to other members of society.

Positive Externalities

These benefits to other members of society are known as positive externalities, that is, positive outcomes that are unintended benefits that the individual creates but for which is uncompensated. If one adds these external benefits of education to the private ones, one can then derive a social rate of return to investment in education. If the social rate of return exceeds the opportunity cost of capital, then government should spend resources on education. How much government should spend on education should be determined by the costs of government funding in comparison to the external benefits that are generated.

How does this argument play in the hands of politicians? In democratic societies, politicians usually justify government spending on education as expanding opportunity for those unable to otherwise attend a given level of schooling. This is illustrated by current efforts in the U.S to expand access to higher education, to make it "free" to students seeking a two-year, or in more recent iterations, a four-year education. To do so would add significantly to federal government expenditures, even though government spending on education is largely a state-level responsibility.

As some have argued, if the principal reason why government should support education is to expand access and affordability, then why not tax the wealthy and provide income transfers directly to those less well-off so that they could make the choice for themselves. This argument was first put forth by libertarian economist Milton Friedman when he proposed adoption of a negative income tax instead of a complex set of government programs designed to help the poor.[141] Friedman's original proposal for a negative income tax has never replaced existing programs for the poor, be it in the case of education, or for other purposes.

One byproduct of the debate over government expenditures on education is the charter school movement. Charter schools are privately owned and managed but follow state-level curriculum standards, and receive government appropriations for part of their operating costs.[142] The argument for charter schools is that graduation rates in public schools are falling and reforms to improve performance have been too few and far between.

Critics of charter schools point out that such private schools are able to cherry-pick better performing students, and that they may be pursuing

goals such as a religious vocation, or a re-segregation of schooling following the landmark *Brown v. Topeka* 1954 Supreme Court decision that
outlawed racially segregated schools. Regardless of the reason, evidence
thus far shows that graduation rates from charter schools are no better
than for public schools, even if charter schools do provide the possibility of
improved school performance.[143]

So where does this leave the argument for government support of
education? When Adam Smith wrote the *Wealth of Nations* in 1776, even
he recognized the public benefit of education and suggested that government play a role in its provision. Yet government spending on education
has become significant only in the last 100 years.

Two trends for the United States stand out: One is that the share of GDP
accounted for by government spending on education has been increasing.
The second is that the share of government spending devoted to education has
been declining. This apparent contradiction is that the size of government in
the economy has been increasing, but that government spending on services
other than education has expanded at a faster rather than for education alone.

Figure 7.2 Education Share of Government Expenditures.

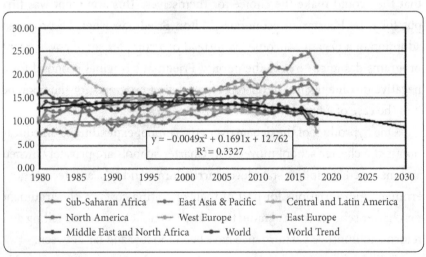

Source: World Bank Indicators: https://databank.worldbank.org/reports.aspx?source=
world-development-indicators

What also is clear is that while elementary and secondary schools have not been doing well on international standard tests, higher education in the United States still draws interest from around the world.[144] The appeal of U.S. higher education institutions is that they often are on the cutting edge of scientific research and it is through such institutions that highly innovative business-education partnerships have evolved.[145] Regardless of these rankings, support for public expenditures on education is one measure of our standard of political legitimacy. What remains is how much, how, and whether it is efficient.

We noted the both education and health qualify as goods that benefit from public support. As with education, because benefits are both private and social, we call such goods quasi-public, to distinguish them from a pure public good such as national security. In the case of health, the private self-interested dimension of investing in health is clear: the benefit of good health to the individual. At the same time, health benefits also redound to others in society. What is at issue here, as in the cases of national security and education, is whether expenditures on health yield an optimal outcome, and thus are considered preferable to alternatives.

Drawing on World Bank data, if we plot life expectancy against per capita expenditures on health, we find the U.S. to be less efficient than a group of other countries as shown in the above figure. Extrapolating from the trend, if we look at the estimated maximum life expectancy of around 81.2 years, we find that per capita expenditures are approximately $3,500. Life expectancy in the United States weighs in at just over 78 years, with per capita health expenditures at $7,410. The United States thus stands at 96 percent of the top life expectancy level but pays more than twice the amount for what it achieves. In this sense, health care in the United States can be considered relatively inefficient.

A higher life expectancy always is preferable to a lower one. Measures to achieve higher life expectancy involve both the supply and resources devoted to health care as well as the demand. Since 1960, the United States has allocated an increasing share of Gross Domestic Product to heath care,

Figure 7.3 Life Expectancy and Per Capita Health Expenditures.

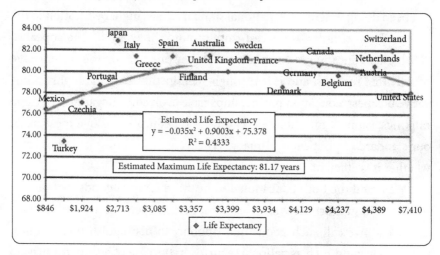

Source: World Bank Indicators: https://databank.worldbank.org/reports.aspx?source=world-development-indicators

even as life expectancy has moved higher in other countries with a lower claim on the GDP. Tracking trends in the U.S., we find that the greatest share of health care is on direct service delivery.

Administrative and public sector health account for a relatively small share of total health care expenditures, pointing to inefficiencies on the supply side in terms of hospital and medical service providers. In 1965, the federal government expanded its commitment to health care services through the creation of Medicare for the elderly, and Medicaid for lower income individuals.[146] Further expansion of government in health care took place with the Medicare Drug Prescription Act of 2003 as amended in 2006, and with the Affordable Care Act of 2010, otherwise known as Obamacare as it was passed during the administration of President Barack Obama.

The Affordable Care Act was designed to extend health insurance coverage to a larger share of the population, and it succeeded in doing so. Between 2010 and 2018, the number of uninsured went from 48.1 million to 30.7 million, a 36.2 percent decrease. The ACA was not designed to replace existing health care coverage but to provide a series of health exchange

Figure 7.4 U.S. Health Care Expenditures as a Percent of GDP.

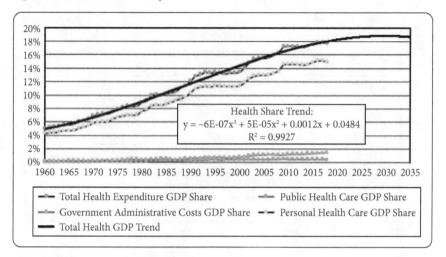

Health Share Trend:
$$y = -6E\text{-}07x^3 + 5E\text{-}05x^2 + 0.0012x + 0.0484$$
$$R^2 = 0.9927$$

- Total Health Expenditure GDP Share
- Public Health Care GDP Share
- Government Administrative Costs GDP Share
- Personal Health Care GDP Share
- Total Health GDP Trend

Source: https://www.cms.gov/Research-Statistics-Data-and-Systems/Statistics-Trends-and-Reports/NationalHealthExpendData/NationalHealthAccountsHistorical

markets that would provide policy coverage options not regularly available through existing markets.

What the ACA and previous health care legislation was to extend both insurance and service coverage but did little to address the question of costs and efficiency. As a result, while U.S. life expectancy has increased, it has done so at a slower rate and at a higher cost than among peer countries with whom U.S. health care is typically compared. And it is this gap that conservatives have used to oppose not just the ACA but also to repeal and replace insurance coverage though higher deductible private plans. That also does little to resolve the question of service efficiency, and remains so to this day.

Externalities can be good or bad, but they share the characteristic that they are unintended consequences of a transaction between buyer and seller. Most countries, regardless of their political orientation, have considered that market prices may fail to account for external effects in the production of goods and services. Such market failure would thus warrant corrective government intervention, either in the form of taxation or in the

Figure 7.5 Health Care Uninsured Percentage of the U.S. Population.

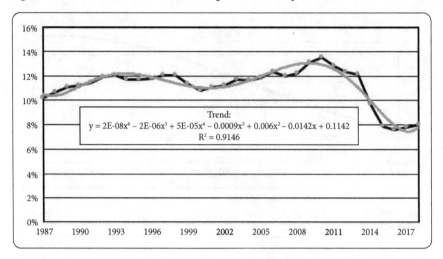

Trend:
$$y = 2E\text{-}08x^6 - 2E\text{-}06x^5 + 5E\text{-}05x^4 - 0.0009x^3 + 0.006x^2 - 0.0142x + 0.1142$$
$$R^2 = 0.9146$$

Source: https://www.cms.gov/Research-Statistics-Data-and-Systems/Statistics-Trends-and-Reports/NationalHealthExpendData/NationalHealthAccountsHistorical

form of subsidies. Let us now look at some other examples of how government intervention can affect the composition of goods and services.

Negative Externalities

On the negative side, environmental pollution is one of the most commonly cited examples, while traffic congestion is another. When someone buys a car, the agreed upon price does not embody the cost to third parties, and they may be adversely affected by the pollution that the vehicle will generate. Moreover, if the car is a used one, the buyer may know less than the seller, in which case the market price may be inefficient. This was noted by economist Gary Akerlof some time ago and has provided a basis for regulation to promote information symmetry between buyers and sellers.[147] This very asymmetry guided the passage of the Consumer Financial Protection Board Act in 2010 as an amendment to the Dodd-Frank Act of the same year in response to the financial crisis of 2008, an issue we will take up later.[148] But for now, let us continue with the automobile purchase decision.

If a vehicle, new or used, produces pollution emissions, this constitutes a negative externality. Unless otherwise corrected and accounted for,
the pollution will reduce someone's physical health and generate associated
economic costs. Under such circumstances, there are two possible solutions. One is to mandate the installation of pollution filters such as catalytic
converters on vehicles.[149] The other is to impose pollution control taxes on
the vehicle, in addition to imposing taxes on the fossil fuels that may be
used by the vehicle.[150] In our preceding discussion of distributive justice,
the idea behind such pollution taxes is that victims may be compensated by
the damage caused by operation of the vehicle.

It should be noted that the laws of physics preclude complete elimination of environmental pollution through either regulation or taxation. That
is the significance of the Second Law of Thermodynamics.[151] So the choice
of regulation or taxation can only operate on a relatively efficiency basis.
The key point is that in the absence of any regulation or taxation, the harm
to the environment will be greater for any given level of economic activity.

Figure 7.6 U.S. CAFE Fuel Standards.

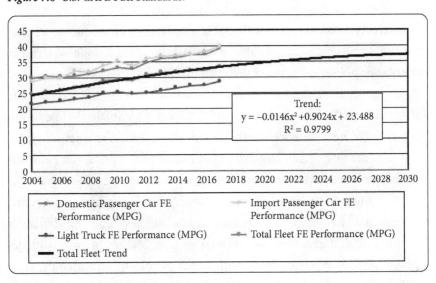

Source: https://one.nhtsa.gov/cafe_pic/CAFE_PIC_fleet_LIVE.html

In the United States, not only have there been mandates to install catalytic converters, but also inspection stations to test for emissions. In addition, since 1975, Congress has established Corporate Average Fuel Economy, or CAFE, standards for vehicles produced in the United States. These are set by NHTSA, the National Highway Traffic Safety Administration and administered by the Secretary of Transportation.

The question is whether these performance standards are sufficient to ward off major climate change originating with carbon dioxide and particulate emissions into the atmosphere. And it is a question that applies not just to the United States but to other countries as well.

Collective Negative Externalities and Global Public Goods

While some negative externalities have a partial local or regional character, others are more generalized, even up to the international level. Two examples illustrate the challenge of global negative externalities, namely, global warming, and the recent coronavirus pandemic. In each case, the scale of these externalities typically lies beyond state and national boundaries. Corrective actions to create sustainable and healthy economic conditions thus transcends national boundaries, even if the current populist trend in governance points in the other direction.

Environmental change has been noted by the scientific community for some time. We already have noted evidence on climate change in our discussion of neuroscience. At this point, the question is whether global economic activity driven largely by fossil fuel consumption can be a sustainable path for development. Critics point out that temperatures on the earth, in the oceans, and in the atmosphere are rising and are creating fundamental changes in the environment in which population dynamics are being altered at a possible irreversible rate. Market pricing is inadequate to provide efficient signals with which to adjust, and which thus sets the basis for government intervention to alter the composition of what is produced, and even how it is produced.

Putting aside the fact that millions of people face a permanent loss of habitat as sea levels rise from melting of the polar ice caps, the challenge we face is how to preserve a sustainable biodiverse environment. We already have seen measures to control emissions. But against what should we measure success? Should all species be preserved, and if not, which should be saved and which not. This Noah's Ark question lies squarely in the realm of ethics, but we can at least provide a way to take stock of biodiversity.

Sustainable Biodiversity

As environmental biologist Edward O. Wilson wrote in *The Diversity of Life*, "The stewardship of environment is a domain on the near side of metaphysics where all reflective persons can surely find common ground.... An enduring environmental ethic will air to preserve not only the health and freedom of our species, but access to the world in which the human spirit was born."[152] Here the question is whether well-defined property rights would forestall or completely prevent a loss of biodiversity.

Figure 7.7 Renewable Resource Biodiversity Growth Profile.

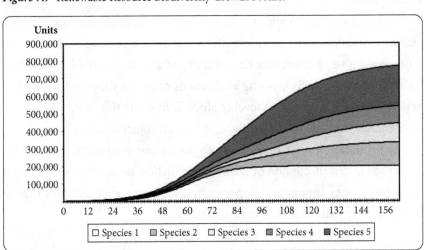

Figure 7.8 Relative Biodiversity Index.

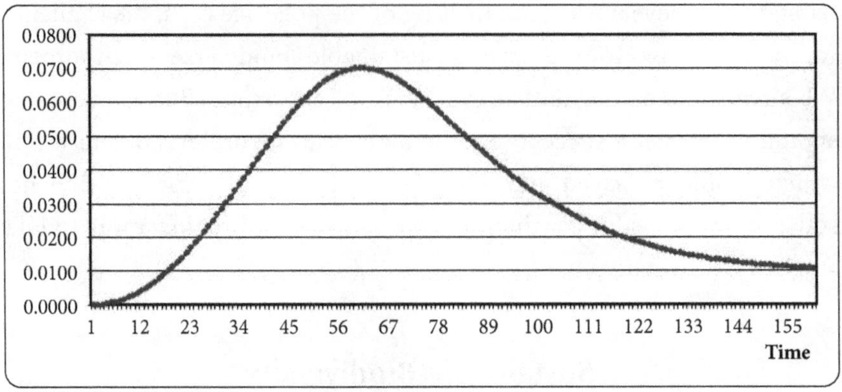

Source: Phillip LeBel, "Optimal Pricing of Biodiverse Natural Resources", *Journal of Development Alternatives* 24:1–2 (March–June, 2005), 5–38.

Economic theory says "yes" in principle, but because there are trans-actions costs in reality, we are likely to fall short, and thus we risk the loss not just of species but the scientific knowledge that such species affords to today's generation and into the future. Given that markets may work only imperfectly in the presence of incomplete property rights, governments may apply regulatory rules to achieve what incomplete property rights fail to accomplish, and thus move the economy and the environment toward a more sustainable future.

Without going into specific resource pricing models, we can illustrate our sustainability concern in terms of a measure of relative biodiversity.[153] Consider a given habitat that has a variety of species (it could be plant, or animal, or both), each growing at different rates. As they do in a natural setting, they wind up with a level of stock defined by the carrying capacity of the environment. In the absence of human intervention, one can then define an index of relative biodiversity using our inequality measure we presented in our discussion of Distributive Justice. Because species grow at differential rates, inequality of species first increases then settles in time at a steady-state pattern based on birth and decay.

Harvesting species at differential rates can preserve a given degree of biodiversity, and for this to succeed, property rights must be clearly defined. Unfortunately, in many countries, property rights may not be clearly defined, or enforced, in which case the pricing of a resource may not reflect the sustainable level, in which case overharvesting takes place.

As one notable example, ocean fish species have been harvested to extinction in some cases because no agency had authority to enforce a property rights regime consistent with a pattern of sustainable biodiversity.[154] This is why international agreements such as the Law of the Sea Treaty are important. Such agreements become undermined, however, when protectionist regimes choose to withdraw from them in the pursuit of narrow self-interest, but in which the global commons are at stake.

Perhaps nothing better illustrates a global negative externality than a disease pandemic. The coronavirus pandemic, which began in Wuhan province in China back in the fall of 2019, has since spread throughout the world, bringing health care resources close to the breaking point and causing economic havoc worth trillions of dollars. The problem with the coronavirus is that it is highly contagious and that short of a vaccine which pharmaceutical companies and government agencies now are scrambling to produce, the only effective short-term remedy is to impose social distancing, extra hygiene, and use of personal protective equipment.

Countries have thus far responded in varying degrees to the pandemic in terms of these measures. Diagnostic testing has been woefully inadequate, and in addition to not knowing what kind of vaccine may be effective, governments in many cases simply do not have an infrastructure in place to identify and coordinate suitable measures while vaccine research is under way. Millions have lost their jobs with unemployment rates soaring quickly to double-digit levels as manufacturing and retail commerce slow to a crawl. Economic losses in the United States are put in the trillions of dollars, not just in terms of a contraction in the value of financial assets, but also in terms of economic output.

Faced with the health dangers and economic costs of the coronavirus, countries have moved quickly to implement interim containment measures and to provide fiscal stimulus packages to offset income losses. Some have been able to work from their residential confinement locations while others face either a loss of jobs or must work in essential services to which they are exposed to the ongoing pandemic.

When such a calamity takes place, production not only goes into contraction. It also goes through a transformation from which things may never be the same as they once were. In education, schools are quickly moving to all-online instruction, and recalibrate semesters and programs to meet the new reality. Online commerce is rapidly displacing physical site commerce, accelerating a trend already under way before the pandemic. Such dislocation means that asset valuations are difficult to make with certainty.

Under all of these circumstances, we already have countries turning to inward protectionist policies already under way while prosperity was on the rise. Now we see further withdrawals from international cooperation and agreements. The Trump administration has chosen to withdraw funding to the World Health Organization, WHO, while it investigates charges that the Chinese were responsible for withholding information on the magnitude of the pandemic in China. Evidence so far points to just the opposite condition. Researchers already were sending reports via WHO and national channels to home governments that a pandemic was about to erupt and that countries should adopt preventive measures.

When markets have limited information from which to price resources, they fall short of providing an efficient solution to a shift in the composition and level of production. Governments thus have a logical role to play in the short-term, even though over the longer term, a shift to market incentives may be efficient. For now, some countries are doing a much better job in containing the virus and in developing plans for a phased re-opening of their economies than others.

In Europe, as of April 21, 2020, Germany has the fifth highest number of cases, at 149,401, but ranks 25th in its fatality rate of 3.4 percent, well below the world average of 6.97 percent, with neighboring Belgium, the Netherlands, France, and Italy each experiencing double digit levels. Germany is a democracy, yet acted in a clear and comprehensive fashion in response to the crisis through all of the measures now being undertaken elsewhere. At a 5.5 percent fatality rate, the United States ranks 12th in international rankings, even though it is less than the world average.

How is it possible that the United States, with the largest economy in the world, and which spends by far more on health care than any other country, so ill-prepared to handle a pandemic such as the coronavirus? As we have noted earlier, putting political considerations aside, one explanation is that if one has not experienced such an event, there is a tendency to downplay the risk, and to forego preparations accordingly.

Even if warnings were coming in at a reasonable pace, the response was not, and this may simply be that public officials, and many in the public at large, simply could not grasp the significance of a pandemic. Although the United States did experience pandemics such as the AIDS, Swine flu, and Ebola epidemics in recent years, nothing on the potential scale of the coronavirus seems to have made much of an impact on decision-makers.

The closest one could come to the current pandemic is in reference to the 1918 influenza pandemic that broke out just at the end of the First World War. That conflict already had inflicted up to 40 million military and civilian fatalities, and left countries already weakened when the influenza pandemic broke out. It lasted from 1918 to the end of 1920, infecting as many as 500 million people worldwide, and causing fatalities estimated at between 17 and 50 million people, a figure already on top of the casualties of the First World War. Fatalities in the United States were estimated at 675,000, a figure well within reach of the parameters of the current coronavirus pandemic.[155]

As we noted in our discussion of neuroscience, individuals tend to discount the future just as they discount the past. The 1918 influenza

Figure 7.9 U.S. Public Health Share of Total Health Expenditures.

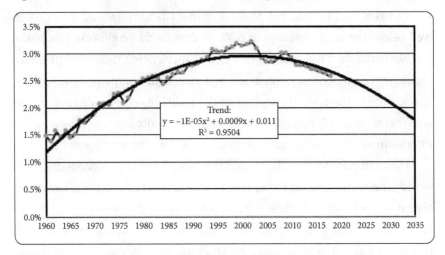

Source: https://www.cms.gov/Research-Statistics-Data-and-Systems/Statistics-Trends-and-Reports/NationalHealthExpendData/NationalHealthAccountsHistorical

pandemic took place over 100 years ago, and while it was contained, no one alive today is likely to be able to recall what it was like back then, let alone inform current thinking on the subject.

If there is an analogy to how we may think about remote events, it is in terms of a black swan, the title of a 2007 book on financial risk by Nassim Nicholas Taleb that came out just on the eve of the financial crisis of 2008.[156]

Noting that the Roman writer Juvenal may have first coined the term, Taleb demonstrates that thinking based on a normal distribution of events may not correspond to a given reality. As rare as a black swan may be, its appearance can be significant, even if one is tempted to discount its likelihood. So it has been with the coronavirus

If we tend to discount potentially significant but seemingly low probability events, then we are likely to avoid taking action. Years before the coronavirus was on anyone's topic list, science writer Laurie Garrett noted the decline in public health services in the United States.

Following the 1918 influenza pandemic, public health services did tackle some of the ongoing health risks, and helped to establish a public culture of health dynamics from chronic diseases to communicable ones. While considerable success was made, public attention began to dwindle as overall health improved. As a result, spending on public health services became neglected, and capacity in terms of diagnostics, staffing, and stocks of reserve equipment fell into short supply. The coronavirus has reminded us of the shortcomings of neglecting public health services, and for which public officials are now stepping up efforts to expand.

As the above figure illustrates, the decline in public health services was already under way before Donald Trump became President. Politics being what it is, he is getting blamed for inadequate stocks and deployment of medical equipment to states which themselves are scrambling to build up their capacity to handle the coronavirus pandemic.[157] Our point here is not to offer an evaluation of the Trump administration as it is to illustrate the circumstances under which government intervention may be warranted.

Let us take stock of the focus of this governmental role, namely, to intervene to affect the composition of goods and services produced in the economy. In the presence of externalities, markets provide an incomplete map of how to apply purely market prices to allocate resources that best serve the public interest. In the case of national defense, we have a pure public good that requires the collection of taxes to support spending to produce a level of service in proportion to public perceptions of the level of risk. In the case of a pandemic, the is a pure public bad in which market prices work imperfectly to provide an efficient solution. Beyond these two examples, we also have quasi-public goods, and quasi-public "bads" that may require government intervention to adjust the composition in a way that best satisfies society.

If one relies on purely market forces in the presence of quasi-public goods, too little investment will be made. In the case of environmental pollution, the opposite is true, and some combination of regulation and taxation may be needed to offset the negative externalities arising from production of a given good. In the context of purely private goods and quasi-public goods, markets may need a degree of regulation to compensate for imperfect information and which may be asymmetrically distributed between buyers and sellers.

We see examples of information asymmetry in terms of consumer protection laws, and in which we used the Consumer Financial Protection Board as an example. The key is that purely market pricing may fail to generate an optimal composition of goods and services and some measure of government intervention may be necessary. The question is how much is efficient, given the transactions costs of intervention that any economy faces when seeking to correct for distortions in market pricing. Deciding how much to affect the optimal composition is thus a logical role of government and is foundational to our notion of political legitimacy.

To sum up, we have seen various aspects over the significance of externalities in deciding the optimal composition of goods and services. Taken together, we find that the overall government share of GDP has risen gradually to around 20 percent.

Figure 7.10 Government Consumption Share of GDP.

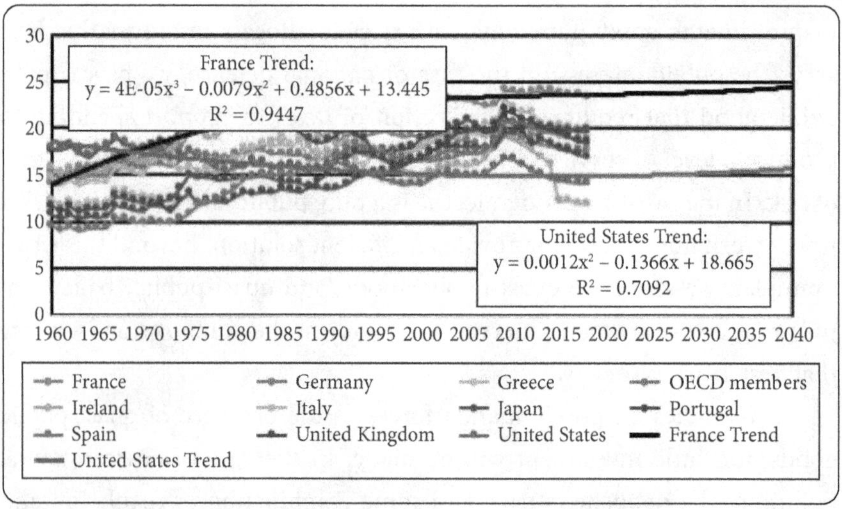
30
25
20
15
10
5
0
France Trend:
y = 4E-05x³ – 0.0079x² + 0.4856x + 13.445
R² = 0.9447
United States Trend:
y = 0.0012x² – 0.1366x + 18.665
R² = 0.7092
1960 1965 1970 1975 1980 1985 1990 1995 2000 2005 2010 2015 2020 2025 2030 2035 2040
France
Germany
Greece
OECD members
Ireland
Italy
Japan
Portugal
Spain
United Kingdom
United States
France Trend
United States Trend

Source: The World Bank, Development Indicators. https://databank.worldbank.org/reports.aspx?source=world-development-indicators

The government share of the U.S. GDP is lower than for comparable industrialized economies. Whether the public share will rise further depends in part on the choice of pricing and regulatory incentives that may be applied in responding to the various ways in which market prices have led to a mix of goods and services may not always have met the public interest. In any case, vigorous debates on this function will continue to inform our notions of political legitimacy in which well-being depends on some measure of adjustments to purely market forces. These debates will be driven fundamentally by perceptions of risk as opposed to size and concentration alone, or even rates of return.

CHAPTER EIGHT

CAN MARKETS ACHIEVE STABILIZATION AND GROWTH?

Defining Stabilization and Growth

Today, we often take for granted that in a major economic shock, government will automatically step in and bring about a correction. We see evidence of this when we look at the response to the financial crisis of 2008 and now, in response to the global coronavirus pandemic. Stepping back in time, it is worth noting that this was not always considered to be the case. It took a series of historic shocks to bring us where we are today. As the current role of government may face economic, not to mention political, limits, it is worth looking at how the present policy architecture came into being, whether it is relevant to current and future events, and thus to political legitimacy.

Going back over a century, the notion that government had any role much beyond raising money to pay for war was not on the minds of leaders of the day. Indeed, the origins of the nation-state in Europe lie largely in contests for power, between a landed aristocracy and a monarch, or between monarchs and the papacy, or between monarchs themselves. The idea of political rights and civil liberties we almost take for granted today simply did not exist except in periodic uprisings against a ruler.

The two instruments of economic stabilization are monetary and fiscal policy. Monetary policy evolved sooner than fiscal policy, but reliance on one or the other has varied since then by various events. The U.S. chartered its first national bank in 1791 and which was located in Philadelphia, Pennsylvania, and whose charter expired in 1811, just prior to the War of 1812. Following a hiatus, Congress issued a charter for the Second Bank of the United States, which lasted until 1836 when then President Andrew Jackson chose not to renew its mandate, shifting banking and currency responsibility to the states and local institutions.

The United States then went through a period of state-chartered banking, from 1837 to 1862, when the Civil War placed a strain on how to pay for military expenditures. Under President Abraham Lincoln, Congress approved a system of nationally chartered banks, with no particular one serving as the primary central institution.[158] This condition lasted through several financial panics, in 1873, 1893, and in 1907, when Congress looked at reforms, resulting in the creation of the Federal Reserve Banking system in 1913.[159]

The panic of 1907 was a pivotal moment for central banking. In the face of a liquidity panic, New York financier J.P. Morgan (1837–1913), sequestered a group of major New York banks to agree to an infusion of credit to ward off a depression. It worked, and served as an example for the creation of the Federal Reserve System.[160]

Even with the creation of the Federal Reserve in 1913, Congress did not envision it as an active policy agent, only one to accommodate changes in liquidity. That all began to change with the Stock Market crash of October 1929. As Milton Friedman and Anna Schwartz would later write, having a central bank does not guarantee wisdom as to which actions to take.[161]

In their monetary history of the United States, Friedman and Schwartz pointed out that the correct course of action following the stock market crash should have been an easing of policy rather than the tightening the Fed then chose to pursue. And this was a lesson not lost on Ben Bernanke when during the financial crisis of 2008, he worked for a policy on monetary easing, and then quantitative easing that many today as having forestalled another Great Depression.

Tools of Economic Stabilization

Briefly, what are the tools of monetary policy today and how can they affect efforts to stabilize the economy? As any student in an introductory economics class learns, the Fed, as it is called, has five basic tools: 1. the discount and federal funds rate, 2. required reserve ratios, 3. open market operations, 4. interest on excess reserves, and 5. moral suasion. The discount rate is that which member banks must pay to borrow from the Fed to meet their required reserve ratio. The Federal Funds Rate is the rate member banks charge each other to do the same, but undergo less scrutiny by the Fed, and thus there is an interest rate premium. Required reserve ratios are a bank's cash and treasury securities balances as a fraction of its demand and time deposit liabilities. When a bank has excess reserves, it can either lend them, buy US Treasury securities, or hold balances with the Federal Reserve on which it can earn interest (function number 4).

Open market operations, the most frequently used, is the buying and selling of U.S. Treasury securities by the Federal Reserves. When it sells securities, if offers them at a discount, thus increasing interest rates at which banks will in turn make loans, and by which banks that purchase them are decreasing their excess reserves, thus tightening credit, and vice versa.

Moral suasion is when in making periodic public appearances both mandatory and discretionary, the chair of the Federal Reserve can provide signals as to future intentions on policy even if nothing is actually undertaken. The idea is to persuade banks and the public to alter their expectations and behavior in a way that otherwise would require the Fed to intervene more concretely to achieve its objective. In all of this, very little money is actually printed. Most changes in the supply of money take place via changes in current and time deposits of the banking public.

When the Great Recession of 2008 unfolded, the Fed deployed its arsenal of tools to offset withdrawals and a general decline in lending. Interest rates went down as the Fed bought Treasury securities, while the Treasury was in the process of selling them to finance to expansion of spending designed to offset a decline in consumer and investment spending.

As banks became hesitant to lend, the Fed adopted quantitative easing, which meant that in addition to buying Treasury securities, it would buy assets of financial institutions and provide them with credit with which they could pursue lending. All of this worked to offset the downside risks of the Great Recession of 2008. It illustrates how monetary policy can affect the direction of economic activity.

How does monetary policy go beyond financial transactions to the rest of the economy? The Fed sets monetary and interest rate targets to enable the economy to expand in a non-inflationary way and in which excess unemployment is avoided. Put simply, there is a rough relationship between the supply of money in an economy in which a given supply will recycle through rounds of spending and thus affect the real level of output. If the rate of spending, or velocity, is relatively constant and predictable, then there is likely to be a rough proportional relationship between the supply of money and the level of output, or GDP.

If the supply of money expands too rapidly, output capacity will shrink, and inflation will result. On the other hand, if the supply of money expands too slowly, the economy will fall short of a full employment target level. This general relationship continues to guide Federal Reserve money supply and interest rate targets. One way of judging performance was put forth a number of years ago, namely, the misery index. It is simply the sum of the unemployment and inflation rates. Success is achieved when these rates are minimized, and the economy is able to expand in proportion to increases in productive capacity.

How fast the money supply expands and how rapidly it is spent is not just a function of monetary policy. Fiscal policy, as defined by the setting of taxation and spending rates of government, also bears consequences on the supply of money and interest rates.

When the U.S. stock market crashed in October 1929, many thought it would be but a temporary adjustment. At the time, economist Irving Fisher (1867–1947) proclaimed on October 16, that the stock market had "reached a permanently high plateau".[162] On October 24, the stock market dropped initially by 9 percent, then continued a downward spiral over the next several trading days for a loss of 24 percent by October 30.

At the time, companies selling stock on exchanges were not required to report earnings, and as a result, few seemed able to figure out why the crash took place or how to respond. What did take place was the Great Depression, and in response, the election of Franklin D. Roosevelt in 1932 led to a series of reforms in which government would come to play a much greater role in economic stabilization than it had done in the past.

FDR created a vast series of programs known as the New Deal: Unemployment insurance, Social Security, Civilian Conservation Corps, the Securities and Exchange Commission, among others, with the goal of creating greater transparency in market institutions while creating public spending programs on infrastructure development. When Franklin Roosevelt was inaugurated in March 1933, the unemployment rate was 25 percent. By 1941, it had declined to just under 10 percent. What finally brought the U.S. out of the Great Depression was the Second World War, when by 1945, it was under 2 percent.

How can we account for government's role in economic stabilization? Years ago, economist Arthur Okun proposed that one measure the performance of the economy through use of a misery index.[163] The basic formulation of the misery index is the simple sum of the unemployment and inflation rate. Since neither is to be desired, measures that reduce one or the other, or both in some combination, can be considered as a reflection of the effectiveness of stabilization policies.

Two things stand out as we note the misery index. First, it has been trending downward over time, an indication that government, through monetary and fiscal policy, has been increasingly successful in stabilizing the economy. Second, fluctuations around this downward trend have also been

Figure 8.1 The U.S. Basic Misery Index.

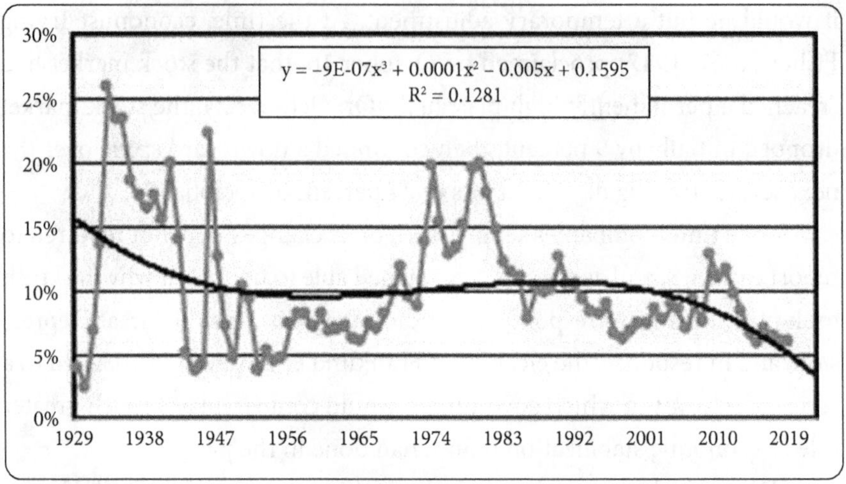

$$y = -9E\text{-}07x^3 + 0.0001x^2 - 0.005x + 0.1595$$
$$R^2 = 0.1281$$

Source: U.S. Bureau of Labor Statistics, https://www.bls.gov/data/

declining, meaning that addressing episodes of inflation and unemployment have produced shorter periods of adjustment than once was the case.

How has it been possible for government to improve economic stabilization? As already noted, monetary policy plays an active role in stabilization, in particular through use of open market operations. But stabilization has been achieved through both monetary and fiscal policy. We already have noted that government's role in affecting the composition of goods and services has been driven by a concern over externalities. Here our concern is the role of government spending and taxation to affect the level and stability in the production of goods and service.

Another Way of Viewing Size Matters

Looking at the United States, at the turn of the 20th century, the combined levels of Federal, State and Local spending represented less than 10 percent. World War I saw a jump in spending, but quickly settling back into a gradually increasing trend until the Great Depression and the Second World War.

To pay for such spending, government has several choices. One is to raise taxes. Another is to borrow through government bond sales. The third is to print money. Raising taxes to finance government spending can have an expansionary effect through a greater velocity of spending. Unless the Federal Reserve accommodates government borrowing by purchasing new Treasury issues, sales to the banking system and the public will have a contractionary effect. Finally, printing money, which many countries have used when trying to stimulate economic activity, almost inevitably will create inflationary pressure in the economy.

As the Great Depression got under way, FDR's New Deal served as a practical application of a debate economists were then engaged in over the role of the state in economic stabilization. The standard narrative of the time was that prices would automatically adjust to changes in market conditions and that bank lending would help restore investment to bring about a return to full employment.

The problem with this narrative is that prices and wages were "sticky" at the time, that is, slow to adapt to the reality of a depression, and as a result, even if an expansionary monetary policy were to be pursued, banking lending would not respond accordingly. This became known as the "liquidity

Figure 8.2 U.S. Federal, State and Local Government Spending Ratio to GDP.

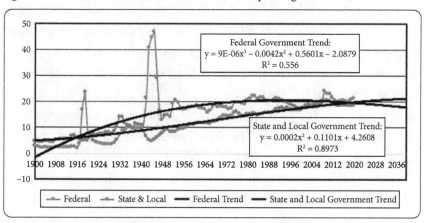

Source: Federal Reserve Bank of St. Louis, historical data https://fred.stlouisfed.org/searchresults/?st=government%20spending%20to%20gdp%20ratios

trap" in which monetary expansion is offset negatively by a reduction in the velocity of spending such that the level of GDP would be no higher.

A key figure in all of this was Cambridge University economist John Maynard Keynes (1883–1946), whose 1936 treatise, *The General Theory of Employment, Interest, and Money*, argued that relying solely on market forces to bring about a restoration of full employment was far from certain.[164] In his view, government should engage in deliberate discretionary deficit spending to stimulate the economy in bringing about full employment.

In summing his argument for government intervention, he said "In the long-run, we all are dead." What few have bothered to acknowledge in the meantime is that Keynes also argued that in prosperous time, government should run deliberate budget surpluses to ward off inflation, and that over time, deficits would be offset by surpluses such that government would remain solvent. And it certainly was not foremost in the minds of governments when they looked to ways to combat the Great Depression.

Keynes' argument was met with criticism by those who viewed such intervention in the name of stabilization as leading to authoritarian government rule. Chief among his critics was Friedrich Hayek (1899–1992), an Austrian economist who observed first-hand the role of Adolf Hitler in annexation of his country and whose economic policies he viewed as lending themselves to dictatorship. Hayek's classic response was *The Road to Serfdom*, published in 1944.[165]

Hayek did not tackle the issue of the liquidity trap as a reason for government spending. Rather, he grounded his argument in the threat he saw to democratic institutions of civil liberties and political rights. As such, his argument stood on libertarian grounds rather than on whether Keynes' position regarding deliberate deficit spending was necessary. As events turned out, the Second World War saw not only England but also the United States and other countries engaged in massive government borrowing and spending, and in which few could appreciate the libertarian basis of Hayek's critique.

Figure 8.3 U.S. government Size Relative to GDP.

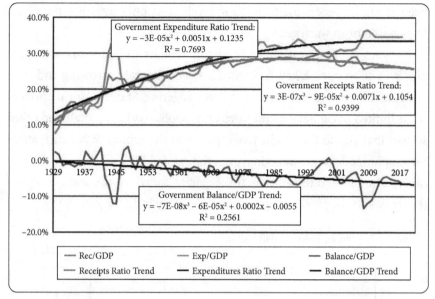

Source: Council of Economic Advisors, *Economic Report of the President*, historical tables.

If anyone could provide a critique of Keynesian economics, it was Milton Friedman (1912–2006), who taught at the University of Chicago and led a program of research on the determinants of monetary policy while at the same time invoking the libertarian principles put forth by Hayek and other economists of the time. Friedman's classic response was that monetary policy, properly defined, could provide better long-term stabilization than any fiscal policy alternative.[166]

Debates among economists have led to numerous efforts to find a balance in whether to rely primarily on monetary or fiscal policy to achieve stabilization. What has become clear in recent years is that fiscal policy has been very much in disarray, often incapable of adopting timely budgets, and in which continuing resolutions have served as a poor surrogate for budgetary discipline. At the federal government level, the result has been that neither Democrats nor Republicans seem able to agree on whether budget deficits are important to stabilization, let alone solvency of government. In the process, the level of debt relative to the GDP has been rising in peacetime to historic levels seen only in either the Great Depression or in wartime.

Keynes' admonition about balancing deficits in bad years with surpluses in good ones, a key difference between federal borrowing and state and local borrowing is the use of capital budgeting. State and local borrowing is limited to capital expenditures on schools, roads, hospitals and other sectors that add to the productive capacity of the economy. No such stricture applies to federal budgeting, even though federal expenditures do bear on investments and thus productive capacity, for which the space program that began in the 1960's is a good example. Why is this significant?

Figure 8.4 U.S. Public Debt to GDP Ratios.

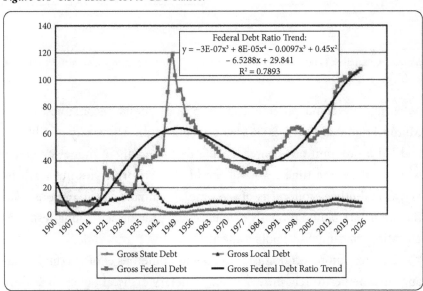

Federal Debt Ratio Trend:
$$y = -3E\text{-}07x^3 + 8E\text{-}05x^4 - 0.0097x^3 + 0.45x^2 - 6.5288x + 29.841$$
$$R^2 = 0.7893$$

Source: Council of Economic Advisors, Historical Tables.

As long as borrowing is used to increase productive capacity, it makes it logical to amortize that debt over the successive generations who benefit from such spending. When government borrows simply to support consumption expenditures, it is doing so to some extent to stimulate over-all economic activity with a given capacity, or to make efforts to affect the level of distributive justice, or both.

The United States differs from almost every other industrial country in terms of capital budgeting. In effect, the U.S. federal budget has no such accounting principle, which confounds the question of expenditures that result in greater productive capacity from those that focus essentially on current consumption. For years, economist Robert Eisner (1922–1998) advocated the adoption of capital budgeting principles for the U.S. government.[167] His recommendation has been largely ignored, with the result that federal government budgeting in particular does not provide a ready basis from which to make borrowing decisions.

Another question that arises is are there limits to government debt? We have examples of governments going into default when debt service payments are not made. Some historical examples go back to the Czarist regime in Russia, when after the Russian revolution of 1917, the Bolshevik government repudiated all of its debt obligations. That was not a technical inability to service the debt but simply a political revolutionary act, but which made it difficult for the new Soviet government to enter global capital markets. Similar challenges have arisen in more recent times, notably, defaults by Mexico (1982–2008), Thailand (1997–2007), Russia (1998), Greece (2012, 2015), among others.[168]

Why, one might ask, does the United States not face financial retribution in terms of higher interest rates, and thus borrowing costs, when its public debt to GDP ratio expands to wartime equivalent levels. A simple answer that the United States has no record of an historical default. But a more important reason is that the U.S. dollar serves as a principal reserve currency in most countries, and thus, through trade and investment, other countries rely on the dollar to facilitate transactions to balance their international accounts. Historically speaking, this was not always the case.

Going back to the 19th century, gold and the British pound sterling performed much of the role of a reserve currency. Then, following the First World War, when England became a debtor nation, primarily to the U.S. the dollar began to supplant sterling as the primary reserve currency.[169] Today, the dollar retains that role, alongside the euro and the Japanese yen. It accounts for 60 percent of global reserve currency, and accounts for 90 percent of international transactions, followed by 31 percent for the euro, 21 percent for the Japanese yen, and 12 percent for the British pound sterling.[170]

The convertibility and price stability of the dollar have been key to its role as a global reserve currency. The creation of the euro in 1992 facilitated transactions with the European Union, but did not result in its being used to a great extent as a reserve alternative to the dollar in part because the European Union, even with its central bank, does not have the same degree of fiscal integration as does the United States, and thus poses a problem for countries within the Union in terms of adhering to its monetary rules. Greece, and to a comparable extent, Italy, Spain, and France, illustrate the difficulties in adhering to the EU requirement that deficits account for no more than 3 percent of a country's GDP, and that its inflation rate not exceed this level.[171] Greece, Italy, Spain, and France each have debt to GDP ratios well in excess of the 60 percent standard, and have had government deficits in excess of the 3 percent rule.

Yet if we compare these standards to Japan, Great Britain, and the United States, three countries whose currency have provided a reserve standard, they also have exceeded these limits: Japan (240 percent), Great Britain (116.56), United States (135.12). One difference is the degree to which countries depend on external finance for government budgeting.

Because a number of countries rely on U.S. dollars for their reserve currency, they often buy U.S. Treasury securities, even if the U.S. pursues an expansionary policy in which yields may not be as high as domestic government securities. What all of this thus comes down to is credibility that the U.S. can manage its monetary and fiscal stabilization policies in such a way that neither inflation nor unemployment rates rise significantly. Under the current massive stimulus programs now being implemented to finance programs to respond to the global coronavirus pandemic, in the short-term, not only is there likely to be turbulence in the search to res-stabilize the economies thus affected.

Limits of Government Intervention

Historically, economic growth has been viewed as a spontaneous process reflecting resource discoveries, technological innovation, and human ingenuity. Within this framework, government's role would be to provide rules to promote socially efficient prices in a way that prudential investments could be taken that yield productive outcomes in terms of an economy's productive capacity. At the same time, monetary policy would not serve to guide an expansion of an economy's money supply consistent with a non-inflationary full-employment path, but also to provide sufficient incentives for capital formation through various types of saving. The idea that government should consciously craft policies to promote economic growth is a relatively recent phenomenon, arising out of the Great Depression of the 1930's and the postwar reconstruction era following World War II.

How did this perspective evolve and to what extent was government thought to play a more active role? During the Great Depression, not only did individual economies undergo a massive rise in unemployment. They also experienced a contraction in international trade and investment. One thing that exacerbated the great contraction was the rise of protectionism in which a country's problems were politically viewed always as someone else's fault.

Global protectionist policies were wrongheaded in the 1930's, of course, just as they are today. Nothing illustrated this protectionism better than the imposition of high tariff rates. Although the United States historically had used tariffs to promote domestic industries, in June 1930, Congress passed the Smoot-Hawley tariff which imposed rates up to 60 percent for some

20,000 imported goods.[172] Other countries responded in kind in escalating rounds of tariffs in what was little more than a beggar-thy-neighbor attitude designed to placate newly unemployed at home, only to discover that the collapse in trade would simply make matters worse.

Aware that the contraction of trade and investment was a major contributor to the Great Depression, toward the end of World War 2, leaders of major countries held meetings out of which not just the creation of the United Nations, but also two international finance and trade organizations, namely, the International Monetary Fund, and the World Bank, respectively. While the IMF concentrated on balance of payments issues, the World Bank served to stimulate economic reforms and international trade to countries devastated by the war.

Figure 8.5 U.S. Average Tariff Rates, 1820–2016.

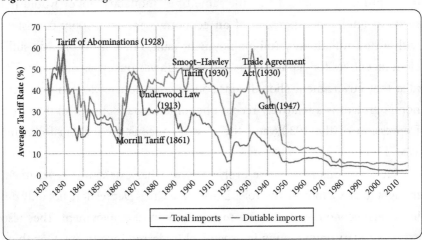

Source: US Department of Commerce, Bureau of the Census, Historical Statistics of the United States 1789–1945, U.S. International Trade Commission, dataweb.usitc.gov

To complement these organizations, countries agreed to a global system of trade negotiations, starting with the creation of the General Agreement on Tariffs and Trade (GATT) in 1947, and which was reformed to address services and issues not previously covered, the World Trade Organization in 1994. For many countries that had weakly developed capital markets, reliance on IMF and World Bank support was instrumental in attracting foreign investment. And in terms of trade, the principle of the most-favored nation clause meant that any agreement that was most favorable to some countries would apply to all, thus simplifying negotiations and creating a more level playing field.

Today, tariffs have been at nearly their lowest point in history. Various rounds of trade negotiations have produced substantial declines in rates where on average they are less than 5 percent for imported goods and services. At the same time, both under GATT and under the WTO, negotiations also have taken place to reduce non-tariff barriers, that is, systems of regulations and quantity controls that favor domestic production over foreign producers, particularly in industries that are seemed to be of critical national interest. What defines "national interest" often serves as a point of contention, particularly if a country winds up stockpiling or holding back trading stocks of goods as a principled effort to promote its national security.

This brings us to looking at five areas in which a country can look to higher rates of growth and development: Output specialization through international trade, increases in the stock of inputs, input specialization, and technological innovation that produces a more efficient allocation of resources. The significance of trade in a country's development was noted long ago by Adam Smith, but given a concrete formulation by David Ricardo (1772–1823). Ricardo, whose ancestors were from Portugal, grew up in England at the time when warfare was a constant factor in interrupting international trade.

Ricardo was pre-occupied with the impact of the Napoleon's trade embargo on England, which precipitated a shift in production into agriculture at a time when England was faced with food shortages. When Napoleon Bonaparte (1769–1821) rose to power in the chaos of the French revolution, he found himself engaged in a seemingly endless series of conflicts with England and with neighboring continental powers. As Napoleon's army reached Moscow in 1812, his power began to wane as losses increased. England developed alliances with Russia, Prussia, and Austria to help defeat Napoleon's army, culminating in the Battle of Waterloo in 1815, and Napoleon's exile to the South Atlantic island of St. Helena.

What European powers faced, not unlike the situation right after World Wars I and II was what kind of postwar arrangements should be adopted to avoid future conflicts. At the Congress of Vienna in 1815, few territorial adjustments were made while victorious powers looked to the restoration of traditional authority, which in the case of France meant the coming to power of King Louis XVIII (1815–1824).

In England, which had been forced to arrest the progress it had made in industrialization by turning to domestic foodstuff production while facing a continental embargo system that Napoleon had succeeded in erecting, a great debate unfolded. Thomas R. Malthus (1766–1834), perhaps best known for his *Essay on Population* (1798), wrote a *Principles of Political Economy* text in 1814 in which he argued that England should remain self-sufficient by not lowering its tariff levels to those prevailing prior to the Napoleonic continental system. He argued that even though this would benefit property owners, they would spend at a sufficiently high rate as to provide full employment to the enjoyment of the general population.

Ricardo, who had served briefly in Parliament and had become a successful stockbroker, was a personal friend of Malthus and therein began a stream of commerce in which Ricardo laid out his thinking in his own *Principles of Political Economy and Taxation* in 1817. Ricardo considered protectionism as something that reduced income in the economy because it was inefficient. Instead, he proposed the principle of comparative advantage in which each country should specialize in the kind of production in which the opportunity cost (that is, the next best use of resources) was lowest.

The very phrase 'comparative advantage' has been embedded in international trade negotiations ever since. As to Ricardo's argument in favor of free trade, England took action with the Repeal of the Corn Laws in 1846. Neither Ricardo nor Malthus lived to see the day, but in essence, the

1846 act would prove Ricardo's case. England went on for several decades to expand its international trade and re-industrialization, becoming the richest country in Europe until displaced by a newly industrializing Germany and the United States. In short, as noted in the introductory chapter here, trade and investment are an important source of economic growth. When governments engage in negotiations to reduce trade barriers, the benefit is a higher degree of real per capita income than in going down the route of protectionism.

Since the election of 2016, the United States has taken a step back from the march to growth through trade. The Trump administration took the position that the North America Free Trade Agreement (NAFTA) negotiated in 1993 and which went into effect on January 1, 1994. Outsourcing of production, notably first to Mexico, and later to China, cost many jobs in manufacturing in the United States, though many new jobs were created in other industries, with a net gain in employment as specialization took place within the United States and its trading partners.

In 2001, China was admitted to the World Trade Organization on condition that it engaged in market-oriented policy reforms. What China did was to welcome outsourcing investment from countries such as the United States, and in the process, wound up creating an export-led policy of economic growth. It wound up lifting millions out of poverty and the creation of a prosperous middle class that could enable China to resume its role as a significant world power.[173] Since then, China has displaced Japan as the world's second largest economy and has declared its intention to be the number one economy in the world in the 21st century, engaging in a series of trade agreements and foreign investment with a number of countries to realize its ambition.

The Trump administration has not only criticized the NAFTA agreement. It also has accused China of not living up to its obligations under the WTO. As to NAFTA, the Trump administration recently replaced that agreement with the United States Mexico, Canada Agreement (USMCA) in 2019, in which restrictions have been put into place that require greater

U.S. content for goods imported from Mexico and Canada, a clear move away from the more open agreement under NAFTA, but one that may provide short-term political benefits even if the longer-term effects may reduce economic growth.

On China, the Trump administration has moved to impose unilateral trade restrictions that are clearly intended to reduce U.S. outsourcing investment in China. The Trump administration has declared that tariff revenues collected from its current policy have been used to offset the losses felt by farmers in the mid-West, and in which the administration claims that overseas U.S. firms will be returning many of their operations back to the United States. The key provision in this is the relaxation of taxation on overseas income of U.S. corporations, coupled with specific trade restrictions on China.

For both Mexico and China, two vastly different countries, the impact of trade restrictions is already being felt. Already, China's economic growth was slowing even before the outbreak of the coronavirus pandemic. And while Mexico may receive some benefit from the realignment of trade and investment away from China, its growth is still adversely affected by the USMCA agreement that mandates more domestic content from outsourced production that it once enjoyed.[174]

Beyond trade, what of the other determinants of economic growth? Increases in the stock of resources also contributes to growth. This includes capital stocks as well as natural resources. As long as capital stocks are increasing faster than the rate of depreciation, the net stock can add to a country's rate of growth. Depreciation rules affect the rate of capital investment, as do interest rates.

When an economy pursues a monetary policy of low interest rates, it favors more capital investment as long as the economy's consumer spending warrants a change in capacity. For the U.S., declining interest rates favored an expansion in stock market prices, making equity cheaper to finance capital investment. Yet if consumption is largely being driven by credit, debt levels provide an upper limit on consumer spending. Thus, investment can be precariously balanced between depreciation levels and the level of consumer spending.

What about the significance of investment on environmental quality? In the United States, one recent source of growth has been the expansion of fracking of shale oil deposits, creating both jobs and income in states such as Pennsylvania, New York, and West Virginia that have exploited the Marcellus Shale deposits, followed by Texas and Louisiana with the Haynesville-Bossier shale deposit. In addition, efforts have been made to increase mining and logging permits inside federal lands and offshore.

As these measures have expanded, there have been adverse impacts on environmental pollution, leading some to argue that increases in the consumption of natural resources is not a viable long-term solution to economic growth. This has led to the formulation of green energy growth policies in which less polluting renewable resources can provide a source of more sustainable growth. This has not been the position of the Trump administration, which views domestically produced coal as a viable energy resource that can propel economic growth, and which again is driven by a more inward-looking economic policy than the trade-based policies of previous administrations.[175]

What about input specialization and innovation? Input specialization has been going on for some time, in which particular specialization has produced efficiencies that a more general trend might not achieve. We see evidence for this in robotic surgery, 3D printing, precision drilling, among others. Labor skills become specialized along with capital equipment specialization with a result that yields become higher per unit of effort.

Of all the contributing factors to growth, innovation ranks as among the most important. Innovation can create whole new industries, just as it can offset adverse effects of the consumption of natural resources. A classic example is when ENIAC, the first digital computer was developed in 1946, it relied on vacuum tubes, weighed more than a ton, and took up the equivalent of several rooms to operate. With 500,000 soldered connections, 70,000 resistors, and 10,000 capacitors, it had the capacity equivalent of 4 kilobytes.

A new Apple iPhone XS Max has 64 gigabytes of memory and costs something on the order of $400 in comparison with ENIAC's 1946 price of $400,000 ($5.65 million in 2020 dollars). Continuous innovation such as solid-state transistors, high density memory chips enabled both massive price reductions as well as reductions in the size of computer technology, thus avoiding levels of consumption of natural resources and the associated effects on the environment that would be the case were there no innovation.

Battery storage technology is a key to renewable energy technologies such as wind and solar. It also is critical to a transition from fossil fuel driven vehicles to electric ones. Rauch and Lang, based originally in Cleveland, Ohio began producing electric vehicles in 1905 and from 1922 to 1932 it produced models until 1932 when it folded under the weight of the Great Depression. Its vehicles had top speeds of between 32.2 and 40.2 kilometers per hour (20–25 miles per hour), and had a range of 48.2 kilometers (30 miles) before recharging was needed.

The Great Depression aside, electric vehicle market sales began to lose out to gasoline powered vehicles that could achieve much greater speeds and driving ranges. As a result, electric vehicles went largely ignored until exploratory efforts were revived by major companies such as General Motors. Between 1996 and 1999, General Motors produced the EV-1, an all-electric 2-seat car that had a highway range of 480 kilometers (300 miles), fuel economy of 28.3 kilometers per liter (80 miles per gallon), and highway speeds of 129 kilometers per hour (80 miles per hour).

Today, entrepreneur Elon Musk (1971–) has launched a new generation of electric vehicles with the Tesla brand. It has a range of 385 kilometers (240 miles), and speeds as high as 128.7 kilometers per hour (80 miles per hour), sufficient to compete with existing gasoline-powered vehicles. As a result, other major companies have been retooling production to meet both mandated fuel efficiency standards as well as to compete in this updated technology market. Carbon fiber materials also are reducing weight while maintaining tensile strength, thus reducing the demand for steel in vehicles.

This list could go on. The point is that much of this innovation is being introduced by private firms, working at times in tandem with government agencies, while at other ones, taking on the broader risks that market forces may present.

In terms of government intervention, drawing on our observations regarding externalities, private firms survive on the basis of a return to investment, while government may not be so constrained other than by its own cost of borrowing. Thus, when NASA first undertook space exploration in the late 1950's, the only role for private firms was in serving as contract manufacturers for components needed in the development of rocket and satellite technologies. In the period after the moon landing of July 1969, the United States began to shift production toward the construction of a space station that could be used for scientific experiments that would be largely paid for by private firms looking to develop new technologies.

NASA took the next step with the inauguration of the first space shuttle mission in 1981. It lasted until 2011 when NASA began work to develop new generations of rockets that could reach other planets in the solar system, notably the planet Mars. In this phase, NASA turned over rocket technology largely to private firms that could develop re-usable components as well as to explore new commercial opportunities such as space tourism. The same Elon Musk who developed the Tesla all-electric vehicle, also invested in the development of SpaceX starting in 2002 to produce both advanced rockets and spacecraft. Amazon CEO Jeff Bezos launched Blue Origin in 2000 with the goal of developing new space technologies, in particular rocket-powered vertical takeoff and vertical landing for sub-orbital and orbital space. Unlike the singular focus of NASA's original goal of placing an astronaut on the moon, these innovations are exploring new dimensions of how space technology may create new industries even as continuing reductions in natural resources moves in the direction of sustainable economic growth.

How does government intervention help promote economic growth beyond specific investments in such industries as space exploration?

One is the strengthening of property rights protection to firms undertaking new innovations. This is a process that transcends innovation and growth, and is basic to the efficient operation of markets. In all of this process, one key factor that shapes the rate of innovation is research and development, a process that governments do engage in funding. For the most part, government research and development, as in our discussion of space exploration, makes the most sense when the returns to investment are not yet feasible. Private investment steps in at an applied stage when applied research can yield commercial opportunities, whether in space, medicine, energy, or some other field.

Today, the United States ranks tenth, in terms of the GDP share of research and development expenditures, even though in absolute expenditures, it is second only to China, with 2018 outlays at $511.1 billion. In per capita terms, on a Purchasing Power Parity (PPP) basis, the United States ranks fourth, at $1,586, after Israel (at $1,973), Singapore (at $1,832), and Switzerland (at $1,648).[176] The significance of research and development is that, along with the other determinants we have mentioned, is a contributor to basic and applied innovation, and thus to growth in per capita Gross Domestic Product. For the benefits of research and development to be fully realized, however, countries need an institutional framework that recognizes comparative advantage, as well as takes into consideration the environmental impact of resource-driven policies.

As we have noted, while thermodynamics precludes a zero-growth in emissions universe, the United States and other countries have far from exhausted opportunities for environmentally-inclusive sustainable growth. To do so requires a recognition of interdependence in the global economy and of the institutions that make internationally agreed-upon standards a fundamental pillar of international economic and social well-being. The challenge is how to craft policies that address these mutually inter-related determinants of growth and to do so in a way that reduces global poverty, along with appropriate measures to sustain a socially acceptable level of distributive justice.

CHAPTER NINE

RISK AND UNCERTAINTY IN POLITICAL LEGITIMACY

Perceptions of Risk Affect Political Legitimacy

We already have noted that from neuroscience, the wiring of our brain may affect how we make decisions. Not only do individuals differ in their ways of making decisions. These differences also shape notions of political legitimacy. We now have looked at political legitimacy through the lens of economic functions of the public sector. To recapitulate these functions: Provide a legal and institutional framework for the efficient allocation of resources; Promote distributive justice; Promote competition in support of economic efficiency; Promote an efficient composition of production; and Promote economic stabilization for economic growth. In each category, we have noted the importance of basic government institutions in terms of a well-defined system of property rights and an independent judiciary that addresses the allocation of property rights, in addition to civil liberties and political rights. What each of these functions shares in common is how individuals and the governments they choose perceive risk and take actions accordingly.

At this point, we have considered risk only at a very general conceptual level. How risk is objectively measured and subjective perceived is central to the question of what size of government relative to an economy a country chooses to adopt. Until we come to grips with the presence and role of risk in the economy, notions of economic freedom and political legitimacy will remain largely unresolved to any degree of satisfaction.

Risk exists in many forms—political, economic, financial, and environmental. Risk is the probability that some event will take place. It differs from uncertainty where events are so unusual that no objective probability can be assigned. Additionally, it is central to how we behave in the context of political and economic decisions. How one chooses to understand how risks arise and how to respond to them is critical to how much we expect of states and markets.

How is risk measured, and how does it differ from uncertainty? For any asset or event, risk is the probability that some outcome or another will be realized. This probability is obtained through repeated observation of events, and forms the core of how insurance markets work. If one knows the various probabilities of a given event in the future, one can then multiply the various probabilities by the associated value of the outcome to derive the expected value of an event. As to uncertainty, here we do not have directly observable experience from which to derive empirical probabilities. Instead we rely on subjective estimates of probabilities to gauge the outcomes of an event, and act accordingly.

In the financial world, we rely on absolute and relative risk measures. Absolute risk can be measured by the standard deviation of a sample of observations, while relative risk can be derived by the coefficient of variation, which is the standard deviation divided by the mean of a sample. From these measures, one can then derive adjusted measures of the value of assets, and obtain estimates of a risk-adjusted rate of return to compensate for some underlying level of risk. Markets thus have instruments available to use to factor in a level of risk. The challenge is whether any sample we may be using is reflective of the larger universe that generates the kinds of risks that apply to individual assets.

Our attitudes toward risk vary with the magnitude of an outcome and how far into the future, or the past from which we assign a probability. Finding an explanation is a function of psychology, and more fundamentally, how one's attitude toward risk is ingrained in responses in the brain.

Consider a situation in which one faces a series of choices. Each curve above portrays the range of probabilities that characterize a given choice, with a probability of an event shown on the y-axis and the value of that event on the x-axis. Now suppose that you a faced with a choice of only between distribution A and distribution B. Which would you choose?

Each distribution has the same average value, as portrayed by where the peak probability corresponds to the given value on the x-axis. As the left and right tails are symmetric, the only basis on which you would logically make a decision is in terms of the spread of probabilities and events for each distribution. Given that distribution B has lower probabilities for values other than at the average, the rational decision would be to select it over distribution A.

Now consider distributions C and D. They each have the same average value, and this value is higher than for either distribution A or B. At the same time, C and D each have lower probabilities than for either distribution A

Figure 9.1 Alternative Symmetric Distributions.

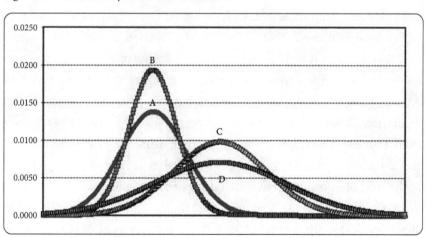

or B. If the choice is only between C and D, once again the logical decision would be to select the distribution with the higher expected value, which in this case is distribution C.

Finally, in a more complex world, consider where the decision now is between distribution B and distribution C, which would you choose? Here is where the answer is not obvious. Although distribution C has a higher expected value than distribution B, it also has a lower probability. If we were to take the relative risk measure and multiply it by the corresponding value to obtain an expected value, distribution C would still be higher than distribution B, but have a lower likelihood of its outcome.

The question is how much risk are you willing to take on the chance that you will be better off with distribution C in comparison to distribution B? There is no simple answer to this question in that it all depends on the attitude toward risk of an individual.

Risk is the opposite of a certain universe. It is based on the probability of various outcomes. These probabilities are based on experience, and the usual way that these probabilities are used in a market context is through insurance. Insurance markets function when the underlying probabilities are evenly understood among buyers and sellers in a market and enable decisions to be hedged through insurance. As we also have noted, when sellers have incomplete information about the universe of buyers, they may mis-price insurance if the insured have higher rates of accident claims than sellers have estimated. That is what we have noted is known as adverse selection. In turn, if a public agency offers implicit protection against perceived levels of risk, those who are covered by such insurance may take on excess risk beyond what they would have done in the absence of such insurance. That is what is known as moral hazard, and we already have cited numerous examples. Taken together, what adverse selection and moral hazard represent in the importance of transparency and symmetry in the level of information in which decisions are undertaken.

But our notion of risk does not stop at this point. Since we are concerned about political legitimacy, let us look at the measurement of risk, how it is perceived by those faced with a decision, and to which we can link our insights from neuroscience to gain a deeper perspective on political legitimacy.

The Measurement of Risk

Without getting too much into statistics, let us simply note some basic concepts that are used to measure risk. As students know from an introductory statistics course, probability is defined on the frequency of an event, as in tossing dice, or a coin. In the case of the coin, if enough tosses are undertaken, the probability of heads is .5, and the same for tails. From sampling, one can then assign the probability of an event. But probability doesn't capture all of our concern over risk. Instead, we are interested in knowing by how much from a given toss, or event, an outcome will differ from its probability over many trials.

In measuring risk, statisticians use the notion of the standard deviation of the mean, or average, as a starting point. Adding the sum of the squared absolute values of an event from its mean, or average, which is the variance of an event. The standard deviation is simply the square root of the variance. From experience, if we know the average, we can then compute the standard deviation, which is an absolute measure of the risk of an event.

Again, from the world of statistics, computed values of the standard deviation do not lend themselves to comparisons with other events because the sample size values may be different. To make useful comparisons, one then can use the coefficient of variation, which is simply the standard deviation divided by the mean, or average.

The coefficient of variation is a measure of relative risk of an event. When comparing the risk of one sample to another, the coefficient of variation can then enable one to draw meaningful conclusions as to which has greater or lesser risk. In managing financial portfolios, one can look at the relative risk of a portfolio and compare it to the broader risk in the market. What economists have long noted is that stocks are riskier than bonds or other comparable assets.

Figure 9.2 Annual Rates of Return to Stocks, Bonds, and Bills.

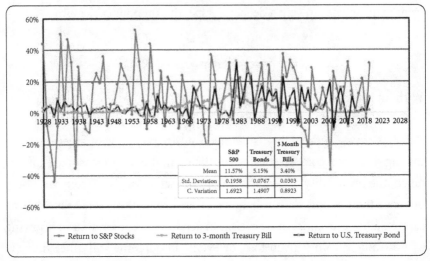

Source: Aswath Damodaran, NYU Stern School of Business: http://pages.stern.nyu.edu/ ~adamodar/New_Home_Page/datafile/histretSP.html

To compensate investors for the higher degree of risk, stocks on average have a risk premium rate of return. The greater the volatility in a portfolio, the greater the risk premium. The risk premium attached to a portfolio is not however a linear relationship. Beyond some point, a risk premium no longer holds and the implied rate of return may be negative, as in gambling in a casino. And when it comes to constructing a portfolio through an advisor, you often are asked what is your tolerance for risk, in which case the components are adjusted to an adjusted expected rate of return consistent with your tolerance for risk. Moreover, in terms of our discussion of cognitive bias in decision-making, how much importance should we attach to the long run trends we may observe to making a decision for the immediate future.

For over one hundred years, the annual rate of return to stocks has been greater than for bonds, and in turn the return to bonds has been greater than for short-term Treasury bills. If we look at the absolute and relative risk of these assets, stocks carry greater risk than bonds, which in turn have greater risk than Treasury bills. The higher rate of return on stocks compared to Treasury bonds embodies a risk premium, that is, by accepting a higher degree of risk, one is rewarded accordingly. The question is whether the risk premium rate of return accurately reflects the actual degree of risk, the answer to which is that it depends on the level of transparency in the available information regarding these asset transactions. And, given our psychological biases, how far back in time should we consider the degree of risk we face today in making a decision about the future.

Some time ago, economists argued that the U.S. economy is generally competitive, particularly in light of competition from expanding international trade.[177] This caused some economists to see if the same generalization were true in the case of financial markets. Finance economist Eugene Fama answered "yes", and set out to prove it through a series of studies. In a subsequent iteration, he qualified efficiency in terms of the amount of available information, which means that imperfect information can still determine asset prices.

Alongside the efficiency question, economists also have tried to come up with a way of determining just what should be the risk premium that should be embedded in the price of a stock. The Capital Asset Pricing Model, or CAPM, used a simple technique of comparing the returns to a stock, or portfolio of stocks, relative to a broader stock index such as the Dow-Jones or S&P 500 average.

Fama, and his colleague Kenneth French, looked to other variables that could best explain the risk premium, developing first a three-factor and then a five-factor model that included market risk, outperformance of small versus large capitalization companies, and the outperformance of high book to market values in comparison to those with a lower book to market value.

The issue still is subject to ongoing debate and research, but the main thrust of work in this area is that when new information becomes available, stocks and other assets are adjusted accordingly as to whether the news augurs well or not for a firm's earnings. One problem with these and other measures is that they do not account for individual attitudes toward risk.[178]

Derivatives and the Management of Risk

Can one eliminate risk in financial decisions? The question has intrigued economists for some time, and back in 1900, a French graduate student came up with a way of doing so. Louis Bachelier (1870–1946), submitted his doctoral thesis, "The Theory of Speculation", in which he developed an equation to price an option contract.

As far back as the Sumerians, contracts could be arranged on a spot price basis and on a future price basis. In a futures contract, one agrees now to buy or sell a stipulated quantity in the future at an agreed upon price today. In agriculture where weather and pestilence can greatly influence market conditions, a futures contract was one way to hedge against risk. Then, with Bachelier, an option contract provided a way to price the option to buy or sell an asset in the future at an agreed upon price today. The value of an option contract would decline as the execution date approached, but it provides a way to hedge against fluctuations in the underlying asset, in effect, a form of insurance.

Bachelier's thesis went un-noticed in part because one of his jurors was Henri Poincaré (1854–1912), the noted French mathematician who did not think that an application of mathematics to the pricing of an option contract was worthy of consideration. Bachelier, who did receive approval of his thesis, did not wind up at a prestigious university but instead spent his career at the University of Besançon. It was only in occasional mentions in the research literature that many had even heard of him. Then, in the mid-1950's, Paul Samuelson visited the library at the University of Paris and soon requested that Bachelier's thesis be translated into English. Paul Cootner published the translation in 1964 in a book, *The Random Character of Stock Market Prices*.[179]

The essence of Bachelier's argument is that stock prices vary in a purely random fashion but that an option contract could enable one to hedge against stock price fluctuations. Since being translated into English, other economists picked up where Bachelier had left off in looking for a way to provide a more accurate formula for an option price contract.

Fisher Black (1938–1995) and Myron Scholes (1941–), working independently in the 1960's each came up with improvements in the option price model, to which Robert Merton (1944–) at the Harvard Business School added a refinement using the technique of stochastic calculus. As Fisher Black had passed away in the mid-1960's, Scholes and Merton were co-winners of the Nobel Prize in Economics in 1973, but the model today is still referred to as the Black-Scholes model.[180]

The lure of option price contracts is that in theory, they could eliminate all risk in making a purchase or sale decision today on an asset at some point in the future. It was enough to draw both Merton and Sholes into the creation of a giant Wall Street hedge fund known as LTCM, or Long-Term Capital Management, led by John Meriwether, a former Vice-President at Salomon Brothers.

Looking at the behavior of financial markets around the world, using option price contracts to hedge against losses, starting in 1995, the fund was able to initially enjoy attractive rates of return above standard portfolio investments: 21 percent the first year, 43 percent in the second, 41 percent in the third year, but in 1998, it suffered a $4.6 billion loss in the first four months due to exposure to the 1997 Asian financial crisis and the 1998 Russian default on its debt. At that point, the Federal Reserve created a consortium of banks to take over LTCM to unwind its portfolio and liquidate the firm, which it did by early 2000.[181]

When LTCM faced bankruptcy in 1999, the total losses that were at risk were it to do so, amounted to as much as one trillion dollars, the size of the U.S. Federal government budget at the time. The fact that a government agency was involved in a bailout of LTCM led many to conclude that many Wall Street (and even Main Street) institutions were too big to fail and thus government would serve as a lender of last resort.

Although option pricing failed to reflect the true degree of risk in the LTCM episode, the derivatives market has continued to grow. Today, derivatives applied to interest rates alone are valued at $200 trillion dollars, while the value of these contracts in other areas is estimated to have a notional value of $1 quadrillion dollars, that is, $1 thousand trillion dollars. And they cover contracts for equities, commodities, interest rates, currencies, and even estimates of the GDP. And yet, there are unanticipated risks for which such insurance contracts may not have anticipated, as in much of the current coronavirus pandemic that erupted in early 2020.

The liquidation of LTCM was not the last time a financial crisis would hit Wall Street. In late 2007, both housing prices and the stock market were increasingly seen as unsustainable, and thus laden with risk. For some time, the U.S. has supported the notion that home ownership was a key goal. Over time, the Federal and state governments created various institutions and incentives in support the goal of home ownership, notably Fannie Mae in 1938 and Freddie Mac in 1970.

These institutions purchase mortgages, respectively from large financial and small savings institutions, respectively, to inject liquidity in the housing market with the objective of promoting home ownerships. This said, whenever the U.S. economy has undergone a recession, Fannie Mae and Freddie Mac typically have incurred deficits that have required bailouts from the U.S. Treasury. Some have argued that this implicit government commitment to cover housing losses causes investors to engage in moral hazard by driving up housing prices and ownership to rates that wind up being covered by the taxpayer.[182]

Over the 20th century, ownership of housing has risen gradually from just under 50 percent to just under 70 percent during the early 2000's. When the Great Recession, or the financial crisis of 2008 began to unfold, housing prices underwent a decline of just under 32 percent from August 2006 to February 2012. At the same time, home ownership rates fell by 8 percent, and as a result, Fannie Mae and Freddie Mac, along with many financial institutions with large size housing portfolios, started running significant losses.

Overall, the financial crisis of 2008 cost $30 billion in U.S. federal loan guarantees, $182 billion in a bailout of AIG, a multinational insurance firm, along with a series of fiscal stimulus programs. TARP, the Troubled

Figure 9.3 U.S. Home Ownership Rates.

Source: Federal Reserve Bank of St. Louis, https://fred.stlouisfed.org/series/USHOWN

Asset Relief Program in 2008 involved spending $440 billion to keep banks operating.

Following the November election, Congress passed ARRA, the 2009 American Relief and Recovery Act, which involved outlays of $830 billion to financial institutions and tax relief. Together, along with $187 billion spent to cover losses at Fannie Mae and Freddie Mac, the total cost amounted to $1.488 trillion, an unprecedented sum at the time. And as many have noted, moral hazard aside, it avoided what many thought was a downturn on the scale of the 1929 Great Depression.

New York Times writer Andrew Ross Sorkin (1977–) would later write *Too Big to Fail*, a 2009 account of how large Wall Street financial institutions took on excess risk with the notion that government would somehow bail them out in a crisis.[183] Having government take over failing enterprises harks back to the financial panic of 1907 when J.P. Morgan (1837–1913) orchestrated a coalition of banks to inject liquidity in the system, and which later led to the creation of the Federal Reserve.

The idea that government should manage risk is far from universally accepted, but in times of crises, private sector institutions often turn immediately to government to bring back a more normal state for markets to function. David Moss (1964–) wrote *When All Else Fails: Government as the Ultimate Risk Manager*, in 2002, to examine how government arbitrates risk in a variety of areas right down to product liability laws.[184] Congress did enact some reform legislation, notably the Dodd-Frank law of 2010 which established a Financial Stability Oversight Council and the granting of new powers to the Federal Reserve to regulate systemically important financial institutions.[185] It included an orderly liquidation authority to avoid the too big to fail problem. Under the Volcker Rule, banks were restricted from making speculative investments.[186]

Dodd-Frank required that credit-default swaps and other derivative-based contracts be cleared through either existing exchanges or clearinghouses. And, with the passage of time and the restoration of economic growth, in 2018, the Trump administration reduced some of the provisions of Dodd-Frank on grounds that it was imposing an unnecessary regulatory burden on financial institutions.[187]

Consider a key illustration of attitudes toward risk: pension funds. The Old Age and Survivor legislation of 1935 established the system of Social Security, and to which in 1965 were added Medicare and Medicaid. Putting aside the health legislation, the idea behind Social Security retirement funding was that individuals may not set aside sufficient funds during their working years to carry them through retirement. This idea was appealing when, following the stock market crash of October 1929 and the onset of the Great Depression, many individuals indeed had not set aside sufficient funds for retirement, let alone the lack of income when unemployed.

During the 1920's, rising stock market values led many to believe that this trend would continue, the result of which was a decline in the rate of personal saving relative to the growth in financial assets. Today, few would argue that Social Security retirement funds were intended to cover the equivalent of income earned during one's working years, but many have treated it as such.

Public and Private Pension Decisions

Facing a retirement decision, how much should one consider investing one's savings in the stock market as opposed to withholding funds that are paid into Social Security? Back in the Clinton administration of the 1990s, the question was raised but no legislation came of the working group tasked with investigating the question.

Here is a way to illustrate the question: the current system of Social Security relies on a pay as you go arrangement, that is, current retirees' Social Security payments are based on personal and employer contributions to the Social Security Fund, and to some extent by withholding funds supplied by the currently active working population. Because individuals are living longer than they were in the 1930's, there are periodic proposals to raise the retirement age so as to help keep the Social Security Trust Fund solvent. But that assumes that Social Security will remain as a principal source of retiree pensions. The principal alternative is to place some proportion of current withholding in financial market portfolios. But stock market returns carry a degree of risk, as we have seen. The question then is how much individuals are willing to risk in exchange for higher pension levels when they retire.

With a retirement age at 65, if an individual started out earning initial earnings at $15,000, and income grows at an average of 3.5 percent per year, with a withholding rate of 10 percent and retirement at 65, the current pay as you go system would produce an average Social Security benefit of $16,200 a year.[188] If on the other hand, those funds were invested in stocks, the benefit amount upon retirement at age 65 would be $29,725 a year, almost twice the amount as the current pay as you go Social Security system. Polls indicate that every time a proposal is made to invest Social Security funds in the stock market, there is strong political opposition. Given that Social Security Funds may not be able to fund all retirees at current rates of withholding and retirement age, it may require growing share of the Federal Government budget, foreclosing alternative uses of government spending.

In terms of psychological responses, those contemplating retirement tend to look at Social Security benefits as a secure base that permits them to invest in riskier assets in anticipation of retirement funding. It is a parallel to individual attitudes toward risk when considering ownership of a home and investing in financial assets. As long as home values are seen as an almost guaranteed increasing value asset, individuals are willing to take greater chances on financial assets than if home values were subject to downturns, as they were not just in 1929 but also in other financial crisis episodes.

As already noted, risk exists in many forms. Thus far, our discussion has been limited to economic and financial risk. In each instance, we have seen the problem of moral hazard, and in the tendency to discount past events while enacting legislation designed to respond to risk. With greater transparency in derivatives trading, some have argued that such contracts can be used to hedge against any number of risks, given that markets continue to display risk.[189]

Creating broader insurance contracts to hedge against risk is one way to help make market transactions more efficient. However, efficiency depends on the level of information pertaining to risks as well as on perceptions of those risks. As cognitive psychologists have demonstrated, our behavior often is driven by the kinds of biases we noted in our discussion of neuroscience. In 1981, Baruch Fischoff (1946–) summarized perceptions of risks by samples of groups of individuals in comparison to statistical evidence compiled by experts.[190] By computing the ratio of sample group perceptions of risk in comparison to expert statistical evidence, we have an idea of how our behavior may be driven by distorted understanding of human safety risks.

An example is perceptions of risks in smallpox vaccinations in comparison to strokes, tuberculosis, diabetes, and heart disease. Fears of contamination have led many to support an anti-vaccination movement, known as anti-vaxxers, while the actual risks are far lower by 80 percent. While smallpox is considered to have been eradicated since detection of the last case in 1977, school systems continue to promote vaccinations against

Figure 9.4 Ratio of Popular Judgment to Statistical Evidence of Risk Events.

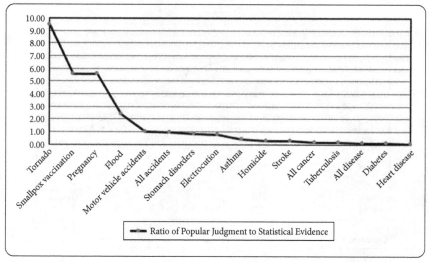

Source: Baruch Fischoff, et al. Acceptable Risk (Cambridge: Cambridge U. Press, 1981).

smallpox and other communicable diseases, but against which anti-vaxxers now argue pose risks for birth health conditions.[191]

Sample perceptions of risks of strokes and tuberculosis are lower than expert statistical evidence suggests. As a result, individuals are reluctant to adopt dietary and exercise practices to maintain good health. In the case of the United States, the divergence in perceptions regarding strokes may explain the prevalence of obesity among the general population, and despite medical evidence of the linkage between obesity and strokes.

Between 1960 and 2015, obesity rates for women in the United States increased from 42 percent to 77 percent.[192] Over the same period, obesity rates for men increased from 50 percent to just under 80 percent. While there are numerous health services at the Federal and State levels, providing effective health care depends on a congruence between sample perceptions of risk and expert statistical evidence, a task that depends on widespread public education about health risks.

What about gun ownership and crime? For several decades, the United States has expanded measures to allow individual gun ownership, driven to no small extent by the National Rifle Association and arguments

Figure 9.5 U.S. Crime Rates.

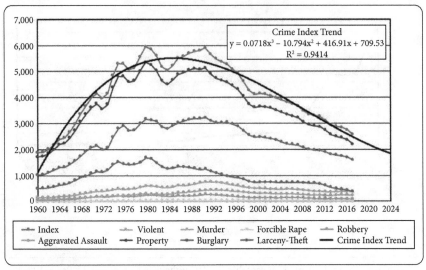

Source: https://www.ucrdatatool.gov/

arising from interpreting the Second Amendment of the U.S. Constitution. The United States has the highest rate of civilian arms ownership in the world, at 120.5 per 100 persons, in comparison to 34.7 in Canada, and 12.9 in Mexico. At the same time, crime rates in the United States have declined significantly since the 1970's to levels approaching those in 1960.

Despite this downward trend, the United States still ranks far above other countries in intentional homicide rates. As noted previously, gun control and the right to own firearms remains a flashpoint of public debate, but not one that confirms or rejects a clear-cut case of political legitimacy, in part because of perceptions of risk around firearms vary so substantially in the population.

The Coronavirus Pandemic and Uncertain Responses

Let us round out our discussion of risk in reference to the current coronavirus pandemic. Perceptions of the risks surrounding the coronavirus pandemic have varied in space and time such that managing the outbreak has produced substantial divergence in results.

Putting aside opinion polls, how should one respond to data on the pandemic—total cases, total fatalities, cases and/or fatalities per million population, fatality rates, rate of change in cases and/or fatalities? The public can seem bewildered when faced with such data, and it complicates the basis on which individuals and public agencies are likely to respond. In this sense, we face the same difficulty as with the gaps between risk perceptions among the general public and expert statistical evidence.

First, thus far, fatalities from the coronavirus are much greater than from the flu, and for which no known vaccine is presently available. In terms of the flu, in 2019, there were 35.5 million cases that included 490,600 hospitalizations and 34,200 fatalities. Starting in January, 2020, as of August 16, 2020, there were 5,573,475 cases of the coronavirus in the United States, but with 173,187 fatalities. Thus, a much higher fatality rate from the coronavirus in comparison to the flu: 5.89 percent versus .10 percent. Because there are effective vaccines against the flu, no quarantine measures have been needed during the winter flu season.

Looking back in time, during the 1918 influenza pandemic that killed some 50,000,000 people worldwide, there were approximately 675,000 who

Figure 9.6 International Coronavirus Fatality Rates.

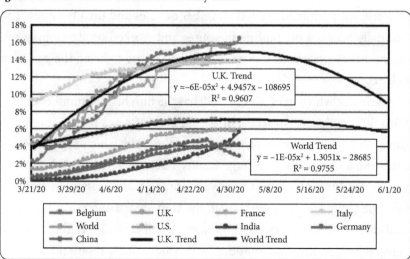

Source: https://www.worldometers.info/coronavirus/

died in the United States. At that time, less was known about communicable diseases than now, and while there were quarantine measures put into effect, the flu largely subsided in a few months. The coronavirus is thought to be at least as contagious as the 1918 flu. To keep the number of fatalities as low as possible, measures to shut down the economy have brought widespread economic damage today, with losses in the trillions of dollars. These losses have put pressure on states to re-open their economies as soon as possible while the cumulative health impacts of the coronavirus are still unfolding.

Under such circumstances, should states re-open to conditions that prevailed before the quarantine national emergency was declared on March 11, 2020 or should re-opening the economy be undertaken with many of the precautionary measures now in place be maintained? It is a question of how individuals perceive the risks of the coronavirus and whether they value a resumption of economic activity at the risk of additional lives lost. It reminds one of a joke once told by the comedian Jack Benny. A robber holds a gun to his head and demands money. There is a long pause with no answer from Benny. Finally, the robber says, "Well, what's your answer?" Benny answers, "I'm thinking".

At a more serious level, the public response by the United States has been to adopt practices observed in other countries. In Europe, Italy led the world for a while in the total number of cases and then fatalities. They eventually adopted quarantine measures and worked on developing testing and tracing methods that are slowly beginning to bring the pandemic under control.

Germany, which as of May 5, 2020 has the fifth highest number of cases at 167,007, ranks 16th in terms of the number of cases per million population, ranks 22nd in terms of the gross fatality rate, which at 4.19 percent is two-third of the world average fatality rate of 6.91 percent. From such comparisons, in which country do you face the highest risk of infection? It is not the United States, even though the United States accounts for a third of all cases worldwide, and over a quarter of all fatalities. Rather, you face a greater risk in tiny Luxembourg, which has over 6 thousand cases per million population in comparison to 3,740 in the United States. This stands in comparison to the world average of 480 cases per million.

Politics often consists of blaming others for whatever crisis prevails at the moment, especially if you are seen as not getting sufficient support for your policies. It could be the domestic opposition, or in today's nationalist and protectionist environment, blaming the government of some other country, in this case, China, from which the coronavirus is thought to have been the source in the province of Wuhan, and whose existence was detected as far back as December 2019.

Another target of blame has been WHO, the World Health Organization, for its alleged silence on reporting the dangers of the coronavirus to the world community. Based on this perception, the Trump administration has chosen to withhold funding from the organization until an investigation of unknown scope has been completed, undermining in the interim the ability of WHO to provide timely information on the spread of the virus and any countermeasures.

In a climate of protectionist fear, one theory circulating about is that the coronavirus has been a plot orchestrated by Chinese authorities to bring down Western countries in general and the United States in particular. This makes absolutely no sense in that economic growth in the United States and other industrialized countries is essential to the export-led growth model that the Chinese have been pursuing ever since the country began to open up its economy following the death of Mao Tse Tung in 1976.

China's extraordinary export-led growth has lifted millions out of poverty and created a middle class whose prosperity depends on a continuation of trade-based growth. That the slowdown in global trade and economic activity has led to a more than 6 percent contraction in the Chinese economy during the first quarter of 2020 carries at least as much risk to the Chinese system of governance as the coronavirus could have caused.

Allegations around the origins of the coronavirus call into question the political legitimacy of the Chinese Communist government, which has operated on an understanding that its political monopoly on power is based on the ability of the government to bring economic prosperity to the Chinese population. It is a social contract built on a different premise than in Western democratic countries but one that thus far has resisted change as long as economic success can take place.

Conspiracy theories are bred from ignorance. Not only does this apply in the case of why in Wuhan did the coronavirus originate, but also to what extent is there complicity at a governmental level for one country to inflict harm on another. What we do know thus far is that the coronavirus did originate in Wuhan as far back as the fall of 2019. A major virology laboratory know for work on infectious disease may have experienced an unanticipated release of the virus, but this should be considered in the context of the physical location of the lab just a few hundred meters from the principal animal market in the same city, where products sold could as well have been carriers of viruses unbeknownst to both merchants, laboratory professionals, as well as the government.

We know that there may be thousands of viruses carried by various animal populations, only some of which have a demonstrated capacity for transmission to the human population. It certainly has been the case with the AIDS pandemic, which has killed approximately 770,000 worldwide since being first detected in 1981, and which resulted in 16,350 HIV related fatalities in the United States in 2017.

The AIDS pandemic has since declined in frequency with both precautionary and remedial measures, but thus far, no known vaccine as effective as those developed for annual flu vaccinations has yet to be discovered. AIDS has not stood in the forefront of today's preoccupation with the coronavirus, primarily because it is not a contagious respiratory disease, dangerous though it is.

Where does our examination of risk, risk measurement, and risk perceptions leave us in terms of political legitimacy? When a respiratory pandemic such as the flu or now, the coronavirus, erupts, market institutions by themselves are largely incapable of providing adequate protections in proportion to a population's perception of the associated risks of contamination and fatality.

As with a major financial crisis, governments are called in to enact emergency measures to bring conditions as closely and as quickly as they can to a pre-crisis status. Once they are seen as succeeding, market institutions can resume their role in allocating scarce resources within a framework of traditional economic functions of the public sector.

In a closed society in which political power is concentrated and can control the flow of information, citizens may have an awareness of the dangers of a risk catastrophe but unable to exert sufficient influence on a government to respond in proportion to perceived levels of risk. Many have contended that China deliberately withheld information on the coronavirus outbreak in that it could create a crisis of confidence, even though the Chinese government was quick to enact strong quarantine measures throughout the country once the dangers of the outbreak became more widely known.

Official figures on the coronavirus in China point to a low rate of infection, as well as a low fatality rate.[193] They stand in contrast to India, the world's second most populous country, whose infection rate per million population of 2,853 is above China's 115, relative to the world average of 480. What is clear from current data is that variations in infection and fatality rates cannot be explained by the type of government in a country as by the precautionary and remediation efforts a country has chosen to implement.

This said, it is only in more democratic societies that voters have a direct say as to whether they view the public response to the coronavirus pandemic as politically legitimate. It is certainly a key in the United States for its November 2020 election, but equally valid in other countries when the next electoral cycle unfolds. And much will depend on public perceptions of risk that include the health risks weighed alongside the economic risks of losses of income as long as remedial and precautionary measures remain in place.

CHAPTER TEN

REFORMS TO STRENGTHEN POLITICAL LEGITIMACY

Governance and Political Legitimacy

We have thus far examined historical and contemporary dimensions of various economic functions of government, and have placed them in consideration as elements of political legitimacy. What we have not yet done is to examine the rules of governance and the extent to which they are key to political legitimacy.[194]

We stated at the outset that political legitimacy is a set of understandings by which a society either chooses or accepts a prevailing political order. We then have identified just what some of those understandings are and have identified criteria by which they could be judged. Now we look at the institutional structure of governance. In so doing, we look to integrate elements from neuroscience and economics to the framing of governance institutions. Individuals tend to discount both the past and the future when making decisions, but the proximity and severity of events shape the time horizon of decisions. When faced with immediate risk, individuals tend to look to government for direction and a solution instead of relying on markets alone. How, then, does this inform what kinds of governance institutions a society chooses in the presence of risk?

In an authoritarian society, press censorship and control over individual behavior begs the question of political legitimacy. Popular values count for less than those in power, and so, short of revolution, one has the illusion that the conduct of the regime is legitimate. In this West, this notion has gone through a series of challenges as more democratic institutions have emerged to provide a check on a given government. But what of the democratic institutions themselves?

In the West, and as pursued elsewhere, democracy has come to mean open elections for public office at regular intervals. Is this a sufficient definition? Many would say "no", since elections are no guarantee of democratic institutions and in fact, what may be as important as an open election is the institutions that sustain them. These institutions include a clear system of property rights and an objectively administered legal system that provides impartial judgments that uphold a system of laws in which a democracy can function.[195] And to the list of institutions, one should include the extent to which both civil liberties and political rights can be exercised freely.

To add to this framework, political legitimacy is best achieved when voting, citizenship, and civil rights and political liberties are based on a universal standard of inclusion. This means that governance shall not be based on race, religion, or ethnicity, and in which constitutional guarantees are placed and enforced to protect those minorities whose characteristics differ from a predominant majority. The U.S. Constitution, as amended, has moved to fulfill this standard, as have a number of other states, even if the results have been less than perfect. This said, what kinds of reforms for the United States could improve the level of trust in public governance?

Legitimacy Under Electoral College Majorities

In most democratically organized societies, elections are intended as a referendum on leadership based on popular vote majorities. This is mostly true for the United States as well, but the peculiarities of the Electoral

College can result in a Presidential election in which the winner receives a smaller share of the popular vote than the loser. Such was the case in the election of Donald Trump in the 2016 election, but it was not the first time. John Quincy Adams defeated Andrew Jackson in 1824, Rutherford B. Hayes defeated Samuel Tilden in 1876, Benjamin Harrison defeated Grover Cleveland in 1888, and George W. Bush defeated Al Gore in 2000. The idea behind the Electoral College as embodied in Article II, Section 1 of the U.S. Constitution of 1787 was that at a time when literacy rates were relatively low and communications were often delayed, the Electoral College would serve as a safeguard to ensure the integrity of an election. Article II was changed by the Twelfth Amendment of 1803, in which each member of the Electoral College must case distinct votes for President and Vice-President instead of the original two votes for President, with the runner-up in the voting become Vice-President.

The Electoral College consists of 538 electors and is formed every four years for the purpose of electing the President and Vice-President of the United States. Electoral College membership is determined by each state legislature, and is based on each state's membership in the U.S. Senate (two per state), and the number of members in the U.S. House of Representatives. The Twenty-Third Amendment of 1961 entitles the District of Columbia to the number of electors it would have were it a State, but no more than the least populated state.

Presidential elections are to take place on the first Tuesday after the first Monday in November of an election year. In forty-eight states, the winner of the plurality of the statewide vote receives all of the electors. Electors are pledged typically to vote for the winning candidate. State electors then meet in their respective state capitals on the first Monday after the second Wednesday of December to cast their votes, which are then counted by Congress, and then confirmed in the first week of January by a joint meeting of the Senate and House of Representatives.

Several factors drive electoral college victories without a popular vote majority. First is the rural weighting bias in which a low population state such as Vermont (623,989 in 2019), Wyoming (578,759 in 2019), Rhode Island (1,059,000 in 2019), or Delaware (973,764 in 2019), each have two Senate seat members in the Electoral College, the same number as in more populous states such as New York (19,450,000 in 2019), California (39,510,000 in 2019), or Florida (21,480,000 in 2019). The two-Senate seat per state bias is offset to some extent by the number of electors per members in the House of Representatives.

Even here, there is potential bias arising from several factors: 1. Reapportionment of the number of representatives occurs only once each decade, based on a census of the population as prescribed in the U.S. Constitution; 2. Gerrymandering of election districts by state legislatures to favor a particular party outcome, even if not directly affecting the Electoral College composition; 3. Voter eligibility rules set by each state; 4. Voter participation rates; 5. Elections contested by more than two parties ; and 6. Voter fraud.

The U.S. Supreme Court occasionally has ordered individual states to redraw their election districts on the basis of perceived unrepresentativeness of an existing system, thus providing a periodic check on Gerrymandering. Voter eligibility is determined by individual state legislatures, but rules have been challenged on the grounds of discrimination dating back to the days of slavery in the nineteenth century. The U.S. has embraced reforms starting with the 13th through the 15th amendments to the Constitution. In the twentieth century, the 19th amendment extended voting rights to women, and in the 1960's, Congress enacted voting rights reforms that were designed to counter voting restrictions in several states that had reduced voter participation rates by African-Americans. Native Americans were granted citizenship rights only in 1924, and the right to vote in every states was granted as recently at 1962, when Utah removed the last remaining barriers.

To this list we also should note that since 1910, Congress has adopted rules that effectively limit the size of Congress to 435 members in the House of Representatives.[196] With an ever-growing population, and the 1959 admission of Alaska and Hawaii, there has been a 340 percent increase in the average population per member of the House of Representatives. In 1913, one member of the House of Representatives had 223,506 constituents. In 2019, the number of constituents per member of the House stood at 760,928.

Where does this leave our focus on elections as a key to political legitimacy? Given the gradual expansion of voting rights, since 1824 almost half the number of Presidential elections have been decided by a candidate obtaining either a majority of electoral college votes, but less than a simple 51 percent majority of popular votes. Whenever a President has not received a popular vote majority, it has tended to produce more partisan challenges than when a popular vote majority has been won.

The U.S. Constitution defines a politically legitimate Presidential election is one in which a majority is required in the Electoral College. If we take a broader view that reflects the percentage of the population that is eligible to vote, the voter participation rate, the popular vote margin, and the Electoral College margin, and apply equal weights to these criteria for each election since 1824, 93 percent of the 45 Presidential elections would satisfy the simple 51 percent majority political legitimacy test. If we increase the majority percentage rule to 60 percent, only 30 percent would be legitimate. Similarly, if one increases the weight of voter eligibility and the turnout rate, the political legitimacy standard falls even under a simple majority rule.[197]

The default principle of elections as an instrument of political legitimacy is, in the first instance, the House of Representatives, in which case an Electoral College virtual tie or no majority in an election is adjudicated through a House vote. But that is not the only route. The Supreme Court has served as another, as evidenced in the 2000 election contest between Al Gore and George W. Bush. Arguments over whether hanging chads in Florida's vote should be subject to another recount, the Supreme Court

Table 10.1 Electoral versus Popular Voting Margins in U.S. Presidential Elections.

Year	President	Electoral Percent	Popular Percent
1824	John Q. Adams	31.8	29.8
1844	James K. Polk (D)	61.8	49.3
1848	Zachary Taylor (W)	56.2	47.3
1856	James Buchanan (D)	58.7	45.3
1860	Abraham Lincoln (R)	59.4	39.9
1876	Rutherford B. Hayes (R)	50.1	47.9
1880	James B. Garfield (R)	57.9	48.3
1884	Grover Cleveland (D)	54.6	48.8
1888	Benjamin Harrison (R)	58.1	47.8
1892	Grover Cleveland (D)	62.4	46.0
1912	Woodrow Wilson (D)	81.9	41.8
1916	Woodrow Wilson (D)	52.1	49.3
1948	Harry S. Truman (D)	57.1	49.5
1960	John F. Kennedy (D)	56.4	49.7
1968	Richard M. Nixon (R)	56.1	43.4
1992	William J. Clinton (D)	68.8	43.0
1996	William J. Clinton (D)	70.4	49.0
2000	George W. Bush (R)	50.3	47.8
2016	Donald J. Trump (R)	56.5	46.1

decided by one vote that the winner was George W. Bush, who then went on to win a less contested second term in 2004.

There are any number of reform proposals designed to update the U.S. election system.[198] Among them is a proposal to abolish the Electoral College, which comes up every time someone is chosen by the Electoral College without a popular vote majority. Americans by and large have supported the idea of federalism as embodied in the Electoral College in which power is shared between the Federal government and those of the 50 states.

Outsiders observing the U.S. correctly note that the United States proclamation of democratic elections is belied by the machinations of the Electoral College system. What can be said is that there is a movement not to abolish the Electoral College, which would require a Constitutional amendment, but to require that states pledge their Electoral College votes to the popularity majority in their state election. It is a proposal somewhat strongly advocated by contemporary Liberals and stoutly resisted by Conservatives who consider less populated rural states as essential to embodying a politically legitimate form of government. Under the present system, elections in the United States continue tolerate the selection of a President via the Electoral College against the prospect of a non-majority popular vote. Other democracies have come to view this as inconsistent with a declared upholding of democratic elections in the United States.

Electoral Considerations in Political Legitimacy

Other considerations also are worth raising in the voting system. As pointed out previously, one way to look at political legitimacy is through participation rates. In the United States, voter participation rates tend to be higher in Presidential election cycles than in other years. Even with this qualification, voter participation in parliamentary elections, which means

Figure 10.1 Participation Rates in National Parliamentary Elections.

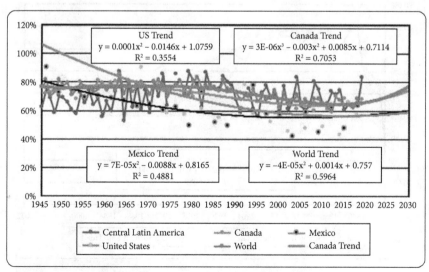

Congressional elections in the United States, show that Americans show less interest in those elections than in Presidential ones.

The U.S. displays a lower rate of voter participation in Congressional elections than for comparable parliamentary elections in other countries. As shown here, the United States voter participation rate in Congressional elections is lower than for Canada to the north but higher than for Mexico to the south, and yet still below the world average trend. And, it should be noted, it has been on a downward path in recent elections.

A similar pattern exists in European Union parliamentary elections, but voter participation rates remain higher than those for U.S. Congressional elections.[199] When voter participation rates fall to such levels, it raises the question at which point can an election no longer be considered politically legitimate.

As to Presidential elections, the United States has shown a downward trend in voter turnout over a long period. Where in the 19th century, voter participation rates often reached 80 percent, in recent 20th century elections, voter turnout rates have been hovering in the 50 percent range.[200]

Figure 10.2 U.S. Presidential Election Voter Turnout Rates.

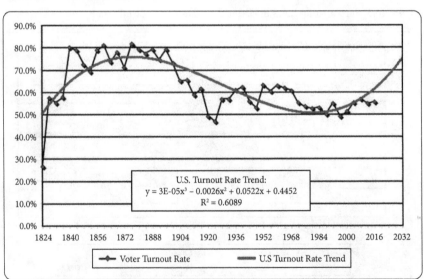

U.S. Turnout Rate Trend:
$y = 3E\text{-}05x^3 - 0.0026x^2 + 0.0522x + 0.4452$
$R^2 = 0.6089$

At one point, one has to ask, does a voter participation rate of 50 percent display a disregard for democratic governance, and more to the point, should voter participation rates fall below 50 percent, does this make Presidential elections illegitimate? The U.S. Constitution provides no guidance on this question, but when voters display such low levels of interest in elections, be they Congressional or Presidential, the prospects for malfeasance and corruption abound.

Trust in Public Institutions

One explanation for declining voter participation rates, be they in the United States, or elsewhere, is whether citizens place trust in the officials who seek public office. Some time ago, the sociologist Max Weber (1864–1920) noted that trust is a key element in delegating trust in governance to public officials.[201] Trust is created by consistency in the delivery of decisions that accord with the values a citizenry generally express. When governments resort to secrecy in the conduct of decisions, and the secrecy is revealed to be in a widening gap between the self-interest of those who govern and the public responsibilities the citizenry expect, cynicism arises. We have already noted this previously, but it is relevant here to our understanding of electoral systems of governance.

A source of trust findings is the series of public opinion polling undertaken by such institutions as the Gallup Organization and the Pew Charitable Trust Surveys of Public Opinion.[202] What they each have found in periodic opinion polls is that trust in public institutions has been in decline over time.

U.S. residents place the lowest level of trust in Congress, in the range of the low 20 percent, while placing the highest level of trust in the military, averaging in recent years between 70 and 80 percent. You might think this reflects a dictatorship somewhere in the world, but it is a reflection of attitudes Americans hold toward their public institutions. And in the present climate of nationalist population, trust in international institutions stand roughly on par with participation rates in Congressional elections, that is, a trend tending in the 30 percent rate at the lower end and in the 40 percent range in the higher end.[203]

What, then, should be considered to improve public trust and public participation in elections in which key economic functions of government require critical decisions? At the outset, it is worth emphasizing some basic underpinnings that shape attitudes toward governance.

One is that individuals are driven by two basic instincts: greed and fear. Elected officials are prone to take advantage of any perk they can once in office, and only under duress are the promises that they make to serve the public wind up being addressed. Fear also drives elected officials, both in whether they can avoid being voted or thrown out of office and through intimidation of others, seeking to make the opposition fearful of them.

This rather Hobbesian view of human nature stands in contrast to the nobler goals one might look to in terms of public service. It also is part of the genius of the U.S. Constitution in which power is shared between the Federal and State governments, and across the executive, legislative, and judicial branches. Checks and balances are cornerstones of looking to decisions that may wind up serving the interests of the population as a whole rather than a narrow group of self-interested individuals.

Against this is the broader significance of risk in the degree of public intervention in the economy. As we have noted earlier, how we process information generally is biased by the proximity and severity of events that shape our decisions. When economic performance looks positive in terms of an economy's unemployment, inflation, and growth rates, there is a tendency to call for reducing government intervention in the economy by invoking a notion that free markets provide the best way to allocate scarce resources.

This optimistic view of matters is periodically punctuated by crises of various sorts, be they are Great Depression, an asset speculative bubble crash, or a health crisis such as the current coronavirus pandemic. When they are, all of a sudden, notions of free markets are cast aside in an urgent call for public intervention to guide the economy through the crisis.

Figure 10.3 Trust in U.S. Public Institutions.

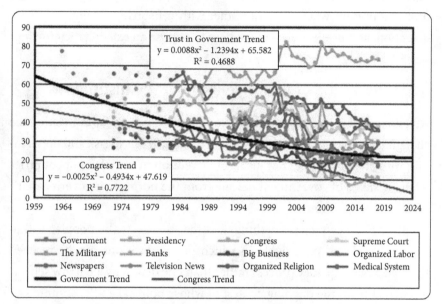

What lies behind this is broad-scale perceptions of risk and whether market institutions can provide a better solution than relying on government intervention. In the short-run, there is a tendency to look to government while in the longer run, it is the inevitable costs of greater government intervention that bear greater weight. When the U.S. Congress passes a $3 trillion stimulus package to mitigate the impact of the coronavirus pandemic, members of Congress are looking to whether double digit unemployment rates will come to haunt them in the next election. Accordingly, they tend to discount the longer-term increase in debt that such a stimulus package involves, if for no other reason than when all of that debt must be paid, they may either retired from public office, or are no longer around.

Competition, whether economic or political, is generally healthy for a society as long as it does not lead to a monopoly in which choice has been reduced or eliminated. In observing the seemingly endless debating in the English Parliament, Winston Churchill once quipped, "It has been said that democracy is the worst form of government except all the others that have been tried." It resonates in comparison to authoritarian governments of the past and present where dissent is met with censorship, arbitrary arrests, detention, and death to those who dare to oppose an existing dictatorship.

The Virtue of Inclusive Democratic Institutions

All of this said, democracy and a mixed economy can go far in meeting the changing aspirations of a society as events shape levels of risk and opportunity. This statement does not justify intervention in the affairs of countries whose systems of government deviate from the norms that govern a democratic mixed economy.

If democracy means anything, it is that is reflects the popular will to have political and civil rights in which public decisions can be reached through a participatory process rather than one driven by a narrow self-interested elite. In the ongoing contest of whose political and economic system provides a leadership model for world governance, the likelihood that an inclusive and more democratic system is greater than when power lies in the hands of the few. And the explanation for this state of affairs is simple: corruption can best be reduced when an open society provides a mechanism of accountability for those who otherwise might simply pursue the path of narrow material self-interest to the exclusion of the greater interests of the population as a whole.

Are greed and fear the only drivers of behavior? Certainly not. In fact, there is some truth in political statements that improving the level of general welfare is sincerely declared beyond election cycle sloganeering. Looking to having government perform its basic functions in an inclusive manner can be understood as a form of patriotism. And there are more than a few Presidents whose leadership demonstrated a genuine effort to guide the country through difficult times such as wars, depressions, and pandemics. What can be said is that while such sentiments may be selfless and genuine, the Constitution embodies the spirit of arms treaty negotiations along the lines once expressed by Ronald Reagan in the context of nuclear arms negotiations: Trust but verify.

And from this characterization of human nature, what kinds of institutions and reforms might improve public trust in the pursuit of the common interests? To answer this question, we provide a framework of reforms for economic and political governance which reflect the underlying assumptions about human nature we already have noted.

The Political Legitimacy of Economic Institutions

The idea of competition in markets has dominated economic thinking for generations. Its appeal lies in the freedom of choice that such markets provide in which the consumer exerts as much influence on outcomes as any limited or single firm might choose. Public incentives should be structured in such a way as to invite innovation and to reduce barriers to entry and exit from markets.

Innovation depends on a well-defined system of property rights that are upheld by an independent judicial system that is as immune from private bias as possible. The United States has done remarkably well in promoting innovations that have transformed industries and markets over time and in which real per capita incomes have increased. Patent, trademark, and copyright protections are essential instruments of enabling individuals and institutions to take on the risks of innovation. At the same time, they should have finite lives to ensure that they do not provide economic rents above and beyond the risks individuals and firms undertake in their innovations in the first place.

Distributive justice remains an eternal question of to what extent government should intervene in the economy. Given how perceptions and attitudes toward risk shape the resulting distribution of income, at a minimum, government's function should emphasize fairness in how economic opportunities can be realized, and in the second instance, look to redress rising inequality through judicious forms of redistributive actions. Such actions take the form of both taxation and fiscal transfers to affect a desired level of equality.

Perfect equality undermines incentives to create wealth, just as perfect inequality can reduce the overall level of social welfare. In between lies a degree of equality that redresses a level of both absolute and relative poverty in a way that an economy can still look to increases, through saving and investment, in real per capita income over time in an environmentally sustainable fashion.

Correcting for both deficiencies and excesses in the composition of goods and services through market forces requires that government engage in corrective taxes and subsidies. These positive and negative external benefits and costs require a measure of government intervention, whose ultimate degree depends on the extent to which transactions cost reduce increases in real levels of per capita income by a measurable degree.

Just how much corrective action should be undertaken depends on prevailing attitudes toward risk. If one discounts substantially the future, then ignoring these external effects will prevail over the longer-term consequences of leaving to market forces alone what best constitutes the optimal composition of production in the mix of goods and services. As Yogi Berra has quipped, "it's hard to make predictions, especially about the future". That becomes particularly relevant in terms of the extent to which individuals choose a high or low rate of social discount of future consequences. It is nearly impossible for government to know what that rate of discount should be, but it is most certainly lower than purely market rates of interest, and about which political positions will be framed in both democratic and authoritarian societies. Years ago, Frank P. Ramsey (1903–1930) advocated a zero rate of interest as the appropriate level in the case of natural resource extraction.[204] No one has embraced that position today, even though sustainable environmental growth advocates come close to its equivalent.

An Agenda of Institutional Reforms

In terms of fiscal stabilization and growth, while state and local governments are required to comply with some degree of capital budgeting, it is an essential reform to be undertaken at the central government level. As in past cases of major stabilization initiatives such as in the New Deal, Great

Recession, and now the coronavirus pandemic responses, the U.S. federal government engages in substantial increases in the level of public debt with little regard to the distinction between capital and recurrent expenditures.

As noted previously, John Maynard Keynes was known for advocating deliberate government deficit spending to combat the Great Depression in the 1930's, but he was less well known for advocating government surpluses in periods of full employment. His recommendation was that governments combine deficit spending in downturns with government surpluses in upturns such that over the long term, the ratio of government debt not exceed a sustainable, or solvency equivalent, level.

The principle of a fiscal deficit rule has been adopted approximately in the EU membership governance rule. Though also not always adhered to, EU country government deficits should not exceed 3 percent of a given country's GDP. Any such thinking is wholly unacknowledged in any form in U.S. policy circles save those known as "fiscal hawks", whose positions go so far as to have a constitutional amendment for a balanced budget. Stopping short of any balanced budget amendment on government borrowing, one key component of any capital budgeting requirement is that each legislative proposal is to contain a project of the impact of any bill on future levels of Per capita real GDP and on the government's net position prior to submission to the White House for action.

Fiscal prudence does not require a constitutional amendment, but it does require adoption of a system of budget accounting now largely absent in any discussion of government legislative proposals. In our view, while capital budgeting is no panacea for how to decide on government tax and spending levels, it would serve as a preliminary step in creating greater rationality in fiscal policy decisions. It just might be taxing for members of Congress to have to draw a distinction between recurrent and capital expenditures, even if it would address such issues as spending on infrastructure renewal and development.

A corollary reform to capital budgeting is the adoption of a government budget within a prescribed and predictable time frame. When government partisan divisions have become too great to achieve consensus, Congress has turned to continuing resolutions as a way of enacting tax and spending legislation. This is a forfeiture of its responsibilities to engage in a reasoned review of budget priorities in an open and transparent fashion As a continuing resolution is an abdication of responsibility by elected members of Congress, within one month of the scheduled beginning of a fiscal year, in this case October 1, a new election shall be called to take place no later than two months of the date of lapse. In such elections, no sitting member of Congress is authorized to run for Congress. Following the election, a new budget deadline of October 1 would apply. If that also fails to be upheld in the following October, the same dissolution of Congress and a new election would then also apply.

What should be done when Congress refuses to authorize and appropriate government spending or the President refuses to execute Congressionally approved appropriations? Ordinary Presidential veto and Congressional override rules no longer apply, and government essentially begins a process of shutting down operations, as it has done in recent years. First, during a shutdown, all active federal payroll payments shall cease for the duration of a shutdown and Congress will be barred from authorizing a restitution of lost pay once government operations are resumed.

To this provision, one should add the same election consequences as in the failure to adopt a timely budget. If a government shutdown lasts longer than one month, a new election shall take place within two months of a shutdown, and no sitting member of Congress may run for re-election. More fundamentally, if the shutdown is caused by a refusal of the President to implement appropriations approved by Congress, then the election shall also be for the President as well as members of Congress.

Government legislation often is complex and difficult to understand not just by the voting public but also by some elected members who have either voted for or against a particular resolution. To reduce the level and perceptions of risk, a few simplifications could facilitate a more transparent legislative process. First, although amendments often lead to logrolling in which the outcome may not reflect the wishes of a majority, some amendments may be useful. Toward this end, limit the number of amendments in any piece of legislation to five. The author of each amendment should be required to list for public inspection all sources of political contributions to that elected official at the time before an amendment is voted on. This information is to be available to the general public at least five days before any vote on an amendment takes place.

In addition, the Federal Government budget now comprises some 2,648 pages, a figure that suggests the complexity of the mix of tax, spending, and borrowing measures that Congress and the President debate in formulating an approved version to be submitted to the President before signature and implementation on October 1.[205] While members of Congress have staff to help in the formulation of legislation, they also are assigned responsibility for analyzing the implications of legislative proposals in terms of various criteria they may wish to apply: efficiency, effectiveness, fairness, and simplicity. Unfortunately, none of these criteria are transparent nor readily understood in light of the complexity of budget proposals. To remedy this condition, set a limit of no more than 200 pages for the federal budget, with each version made available online to all citizens at least 10 days before a vote is to take place. All Representatives and Senators must inform their constituents either electronically or in writing prior to the ten-way countdown of any version of the budget.

Each of these proposed reforms provides no panacea for improving the performance of government in the execution of its economic responsibilities. At the same time, through simplification and greater transparency, the implementation of consequences on the decisions by Congress and the Executive represent steps that could enhance the significance of fiscal policy in the greater responsibility of managing the economy in a more inclusive manner. It also would improve coordination with the other major instrument of economic management, namely, monetary policy.

As noted earlier, monetary policy plays an important role in the stabilization of the economy. At the same time, the Federal Reserve, the central bank of the United States, play both a national and international role in coordinating with other countries how stabilization and economic growth are pursued. From our discussion, we know that the Federal Reserve has not always been correct in its decisions regarding contractionary or expansionary moves, as we have learned from the Great Depression of the 1930s.

At the same time, the Federal Reserve has learned from past experience and while it still is chartered to be independent of political pressures, it generally adopts and communicates policies on the economic outlook and the choice of interest rates that provide important guidance to all sectors of the economy. As in the case of fiscal policy not bound by any particular rule, monetary policy also has not adopted a specific rule for the framing and implementation of its decisions. The closest that it has come is to consider what is known as the Taylor Rule, in which the rate of expansion of money and credit would evolve in proportion to a weighted mix of recent inflation and unemployment rates.[206]

As in the case of using financial derivatives to manage risk, there is no simple formula that could guarantee that the economy can expand along a smooth trajectory over time. Thus, the Fed should be able to continue in its present mode without further constraints on the boundaries of its operations. By its obligation to provide periodic reports to Congress, the Fed remains an indispensable instrument for the allocation of credit in the economy, and thus, it is important to keep the Fed as an independent institution that can best serve the greater needs of the economy without passing through the political filters that guide so much of fiscal policy.

Reforming Political Governance

As we have discussed throughout, there are many types of regimes that may satisfy some definition of political legitimacy. What we have done is to examine how economic foundations and insights from neuroscience inform how political legitimacy can be seen. What remains are some considerations on how it could be improved in terms of political governance.

Taking as our point of departure that government leaders may be guided by a mix of both altruistic and self-interested motivation, we look at ways in which greater public trust could be achieved in terms of how governments choose their leaders. We put aside authoritarian regimes in that they may or may not reflect the preferences of a population when coercive measures may be used in making political decisions. Our emphasis, then is on democratic accountability.

Part of the distrust many citizens have of government is the assignment of benefits that are unique to elected officials, but which are not applicable to the general public. Examples include health care insurance and pensions that are different from the prevailing standards that apply to the rest of the citizenry. And elected officials often carry significant conflicts of interest in terms of the legislation on which they are voting when viewed in terms of their own personal self-interest. With this in mind, then, here are some suggestions on how to increase the level of trust in elected officials, each of which is bound by the principle of greater transparency and accountability.

We already have pointed out the contradiction between the Electoral College and the popular voting majority. It has not always been a contradiction, nor will it necessarily be the case in any upcoming election. Yet the contradiction is that as long as the United States has a system in which one person one vote does not count, trust in government is diminished.

Since a constitutional amendment would be required to formally eliminate the Electoral College, a simpler solution would be to have states pledge their Electoral College vote in proportion to the nationwide popular vote. It does not have to require that Electoral College state votes be cast on a winner-take-all basis, and can allow for votes to reflect the outcome in each individual state. If as a result of this proportional voting system the Electoral College fails to come up with a 51 percent majority, or the 270 votes needed to confirm a winner, one can simply rely on the plurality of the winner over other candidates. Even with third-party candidates, the likelihood that a 51 percent majority outcome will be realized is still quite likely.

Another reform is to change the incentives to increase voter turnout. Voter participation should always be discretionary. At the same time, ease of voting should be a consideration in an election. For national and presidential elections, the Constitution mandates that they take place the first Tuesday in November. Tuesday is a working day, and this discourages voter turnout. One way around this constraint is to declare voting Tuesday a national holiday. Alternatively, one could change the voting date to a weekend just prior to the traditional first Tuesday in November.

Additionally, voting in person, even if not constrained by a working day, also faces challenges when weather or health conditions are unfavorable. In light of the recent coronavirus pandemic, many states are shifting from in-person November voting to mail-in ballots open the Thursday before the official election day. This already takes place when absentee ballots are issued, as in the case of overseas voting by U.S. citizens.

No evidence has been found that invalidates mail-in votes in previous elections, and shifting to a mail-in system could solve two problems: 1. Increasing voter turnout by avoiding an in-person Tuesday requirement; 2. Avoiding a constitutional issue as to whether Tuesday voting could be changed by something other than a constitutional amendment.

Another reform is term limits for various branches of government. Following the adoption of the 22nd amendment to the Constitution in 1951, no President can serve for more than two terms, that is, eight years. A similar principle should apply to both houses of Congress and to the Supreme Court, even though tenure limits may logically differ. For the Senate, setting a two-term, or twelve-year limit, would enable to Senate to transcend an eight-year potential presidential administration, and dilute the vested interests that accumulate through prevailing seniority rules. As to the House, in setting a four-term, or eight-year limit, would help guarantee suitable input for new voices to be heard in their district.

In terms of the Supreme Court, deeply divisive, and increasingly partisan, battles are fought every time a vacancy opens up. Right now appointees to the Supreme Court can serve life terms unless a justice chooses to retire, as was the case with Justices Sandra Day O'Connor, Anthony Kennedy, and David Souter. Instead of setting an age limit of service, one way to address the problem is to select nominees who have attained a certain minimum age, say 55, and then leave to the discretion of a Justice when he or she may choose to retire. It is not a perfect solution, nor is the choice of 55 years beyond an arbitrary number, but it may help to reduce the partisan nature of the selection process now in place.

Funding Presidential and Congressional elections has long been fraught with conflicts of interest wrought by the reliance on private donors to gain a candidate exposure to voters through television, radio, and print advertising. For some time, efforts to reform campaign finance laws have been driven by debates over the McCain-Feingold Act of 2002.[207] That legislation banned unrestricted donations directly to political parties by individuals, unions, and corporations.

McCain-Feingold also set limits on the advertising that unions, corporations, and non-profit organizations can spend on political parties' use of funds for advertising on behalf of candidates in the form of "issue ads", that is around issues such as abortion rights, gun control legislation, school prayer, among others. McCain-Feingold did not stem spending on political campaigns in part because it did not address the role of Super PAC's, that is, fund raising agencies that can spend unlimited amounts for or against political figures even though they are barred from contributing directly to a politician or a political party. All of this stands in comparison to a position put forth by Common Cause and others years ago, namely, to limit campaign expenditures to funds raised through tax withholding contributions only. Even though we still have discretionary withholding, private funding dwarfs all levels of publicly supported election campaigns.

A key problem with campaign finance is not just the cost of elections. It also is that in a democratic society, one person one vote rules do not reflect the intensity of voter preferences. Were Congress to adopt legislation that would severely restrict the flow of money, even to Super PAC's, the intensity preference would find a way around any constraint to allow financial voting to supplant individual voting.

In 1987, the FCC dropped what was known as the Fairness Doctrine, in which network television and radio stations were required to provide equal time to opposing candidates in an election cycle. This meant that candidates could not rely on essentially network funded campaign time to get their message across to voters. Then, in 2010, the Supreme Court issued a ruling in Citizens United v. FEC in which corporations, unions, and nonprofit organizations could henceforth spend funds on political advertising as an exercise in free speech, in effect, treating corporations as "persons", whose function originally served simply as a way of sharing risk in economic decisions rather than in occupying a space in political election contests.

Given the intensity of voter preferences, one way of addressing the issue of campaign finance is to declare that anyone can give as much as he or she wishes on an individual basis in support or in opposition to a candidate for public office. A corollary condition is that campaign contributions cannot hide behind a corporate, union or otherwise veil. All contributions must be registered through the Federal Elections Commission and be accessible via the internet or other means within ten days of a contribution by such individuals.

Failure to list the individual source of funding from corporate or other group entities shall be considered a felony, with fines and imprisonment to be levied on chief executives of the organization to which such contributions have been made. This applies to both domestic as well as to foreign contributions by governments, firms, entities or individuals, and shall be accessible to voters in the same manner as domestic contributions. While this proposal does not resolve the shadow nature of "fake" advertising, to the extent that tracing can be done goes some distance in creating election transparency and providing voters with a clearer picture of where a candidate's campaign funding has come from.

Another proposal is a requirement that all candidates for public office disclosure their tax returns for at least the past ten years prior to assuming office.

A tradition of so doing dates back to the Teapot Dome scandal in 1924, but was recently rejected by Donald Trump when he was elected President in 2016. Not only should all candidates be required to have their tax returns available for public inspection, it should be done in the same way as contributions to candidates via the Federal Elections Commission, or FEC.

Disclosure of tax returns does not guarantee minimizing conflicts of interest between an elected individual's private interest and the public. Blind trusts have been the usual method of treating such conflicts of interest, and typically have required that the candidate sell private holdings that are then entrusted to the blind trust. The shortcoming here is that blind trusts may not be that blind, especially if left in the hands of a family member, or with close friends who may provide critical information on which an elected official's decision may be made. This issue has arisen not just in the case of President Trump, but also in the case of other elected officials. Recusal from decisions is one way of avoiding such decisions, but to the extent that an elected official's private interests are pervasive, then he or she may be limited in the ability to exercise the public duties to which that person has been elected. Crafting rules for more independent blind trusts may be the best way to go forward.

Another issue already mentioned is gerrymandering, that is, the crafting of Congressional and other legislative districts by the majority party after the decennial census. Independent bipartisan commissions have failed to displace the role of partisan gerrymandering, and even though court challenges been largely unsuccessful, there is a simpler way to respond to the issue. After each election, the largest losing party is authorized to re-draw districts for the next election. After a few such election cycles, it is likely that partisan gerrymandering may give way to genuinely bipartisan independent election districting rules.

Finally, a series of benefits that now accrue to elected officials should be brought to a halt. One is that members of Congress should be required to participate in the same pension and insurance programs for which they have passed legislation involving the voting public. This means no separate pension from Social Security, and health insurance standards follow the same as those in the private sector, that is, Medicare and private insurance programs for as long as such programs are the standard for coverage. At present, members of Congress are entitled to pension at full-time pay after one term in office. This should be terminated. Elected officials should be required to develop their own pension plan from which contributions can be made while in office, but with no benefits beyond the term of office beyond what has been accumulated.

Pay increases for elected officials should be set at no more than the change in the current consumer price index. Allowing elected officials to vote increases in their compensation with no approval by voters constitutes a basic conflict of interest.

To round this out, once out of public office, many formerly elected officials often become consultants hired by various organizations seeking the value of connections to pursue a particular legislative agenda while individually pursuing financial gain. Former elected officials should be banned for ten years from work for any lobbying organization, and failure to comply should result in fines or jail terms for periods up to ten years for so doing.

None of these reforms may see the light of day any time soon. Congress and the Executive Branch have acquired long-standing traditions of benefits that reward tenure in office, even if the result is a failure to conduct the nation's business through the pursuit of private self-interest. As long as this prevails, skepticism and a lack of trust in government will persist. In the end, critical economic functions of the public sector may fail to be realized in a timely fashion, and the well-being of the country will suffer as a result.

NOTES

1. Based on UN and World Bank data, in 1950, average global life expectancy was 30 years. In 2018 it stood at 72 years. In 1950, global real per capita GDP stood at $2,957, rising to $6,410 by 1980. In 2018 it stood at $11,365. Globalization of trade and investment through multilateral agreements have been major contributors to this economic transformation.

2. https://winstonchurchill.org/resources/speeches/1946–1963-elder-statesman/the-sinews-of-peace/ Churchill always was concerned over Soviet expansion into Eastern Europe during the Second World War and was convinced that the wartime alliance between Josef Stalin and the western powers was not tenable.

3. Kennan was Deputy Chief of Mission of the United States to the USSR from 1944 to 1946. Kennan saw the Soviet Union as an expansionist Russian power that should be contained through a combination of economic aid and military force where necessary, and in which he anticipated that it would eventually succumb to the forces of economic growth in a more prosperous West. https://en.wikipedia.org/wiki/X_Article

4. One can ask the question, "Cui bono", or whose interests are being served. Political stability does not mean that the interests of the population at large are served. Self-preservation is the first priority of rulers, whether dictators, monarchs, or democratically elected individuals. The appeal of democracy is that it forestalls dynastic rule better than other forms of government.

5. In *Capitalism and Freedom* (1962), Nobel economist Milton Friedman (1912–2006) once broke this down into three primary functions when he said: "Government has three primary functions. It should provide for military defense of

the nation. It should enforce contracts between individuals. It should protect citizens from crimes against themselves or their property. When government – in pursuit of good intentions tries to rearrange the economy, legislate morality, or help special interest, the cost in inefficiency, lack of motivation, and loss of freedom. Government should be a referee, not an active player."

6. British Conservative MP Enoch Powell (1912–1998), was a critic of Asian immigration that was increasing from Kenya and Uganda as these newly independent countries set limits on citizenship. The result was a surge in Asians into England, and which resulted in rising racial tensions that eventually erupted when under Prime Minister David Cameron a referendum on Great Britain's membership in the UK would be put to a vote. A slight majority of 51.9 percent chose to leave, with 48.1 choosing to remain. Failure to reach an orderly exit agreement led to the defeat of Prime Minister Theresa May's government (2016–2019), and from which Conservative Boris Johnson has promised a speedy withdrawal.

7. In a January 11, 2018 Oval Office talk with several U.S. Senators, Trump asked "Why are we having all these people from shithole countries (meaning Haiti, El Salvador, and African countries) come here?" Earlier he had complained that Nigerian immigrants would never "go back to their huts", and Haitians "all having AIDS". He asked, "Why do we need more Haïtians?" "Take them out." See: https://www.theatlantic.com/politics/archive/2019/01/shithole-countries/580054/

8. https://www.npr.org/sections/thetwo-way/2018/03/11/592694991/china-removes-presidential-term-limits-enabling-xi-jinping-to-rule-indefinitely

9. https://www.wsj.com/articles/russias-parliament-passes-putins-constitutional-plans-on-first-reading-11579775327

10. http://www.nbcnews.com/id/7632057/ns/world_news/t/putin-soviet-collapse-genuine-tragedy/

11. https://www.reuters.com/article/us-russia-election-putin/putin-before-vote-says-hed-reverse-soviet-collapse-if-he-could-agencies-idUSKCN1GE2TF

12. https://searchworks.stanford.edu/view/12087384 for Gertrude Bell. T.E. Lawrence wrote a memoir, *Seven Pillars of Wisdom,* in 1922 in which he recounted

his efforts to negotiate a settlement between the Saudis and the Ottoman empire. It was not published until 1926, but has been a benchmark illustration of how European powers have intervened in Middle Eastern affairs over several decades. https://en.wikipedia.org/wiki/Seven_Pillars_of_Wisdom

13. The Sykes-Picot agreement also reflected the 1917 Balfour Declaration, when British Lord Balfour interpreted the Palestinian mandate as one that would provide a homeland for Jews. It was viewed less important when first drafted than in the aftermath of the Holocaust of World War II when millions of European Jews had perished in Nazi concentration camps and which resulted in the declaration of the State of Israel in 1948. For an account that links the Balfour Declaration to the Sykes-Picot Agreement see: http://theconversation.com/the-sykes-picot-agreement-and-the-making-of-the-modern-middle-east-58780

14. Hong Kong protests against Beijing began when Beijing began to implement a law that would allow for the extradition of Hong Kong residents to the mainland for court cases. Protestors took to the streets, based on the "One Country Two Systems" policy that had governed Hong Kong and Mainland China relations since the retrocession of Hong Kong to the Government in Beijing in 1997. https://www.bbc.com/news/world-asia-china-49317695

15. Falun Gong is a spiritual movement that is seen as subversive to Beijing's official policy of atheism. https://en.wikipedia.org/wiki/Persecution_of_Falun_Gong

16. When Mao Tse Tung's Communist forces defeated the Nationalists under Chiang Kai Shek in 1949, they also occupied Tibet. Tibetans have a long-standing independent culture and the spiritual leader, the Dali Lama, has been viewed as a peaceful opponent of Chinese treatment of Tibetans as second-class citizens. https://newint.org/features/web-exclusive/2016/02/04/chinas-oppression-of-tibetans-has-dramatically-increased

17. Moslem Uighurs living in Xinjiang province in China has increased in recent years, though China has remained immune to criticism thus far in their treatment. https://www.cfr.org/backgrounder/chinas-repression-uighurs-xinjiang

18. Charges of genocide are being brought before the UN International Criminal Court, and other international agencies. https://en.wikipedia.org/wiki/

Rohingya_genocide. Action at the UN to provide protection to the Rohingya are hampered by China's own policy toward its Moslem Uighur population, along with a general tendency to ignore human rights abuses in the presence of nationalist sentiments in several countries. This is an echo of what happened in Nazi Germany when Adolf Hitler became Chancellor in 1933 and began a systematic repression of rights of Jews, Gypsies, and other minorities long before the adoption of genocidal practices in extermination camps during the Second World War.

19. Moslems in India are now waging large-scale protests against restrictions imposed by Modi's government. https://www.nytimes.com/2020/01/04/world/asia/india-protests-modi-citizenship.html

20. Based on UN and World Bank data, in 1950, average global life expectancy was 30 years. In 2018 it stood at 72 years. In 1950, global real per capita GDP stood at $2,957, rising to $6,410 by 1980. In 2018 it stood at $11,365.

21. The share of income in China going to the top 1 percent has risen from 6 percent in 1978 to approximately 14 percent in 2015. https://qz.com/1591961/thomas-pikettys-new-research-shows-rising-inequality-in-china/

22. Based on WID data, In the mid-1970's the mean one percent share world level stood at 20 percent, and which by 2016 had increased to 25 percent.

23. Among other provisions, the Sykes-Picot Agreement was used in the selection of an Alawite minority administration in Damascus that would broker relations between the Sunni and Shi'a communities within its borders.

24. https://www.reuters.com/article/us-warcrimes-afghanistan-trump-eu-idUSKBN23N2GJ

25. A country's central government debt to GDP ratio is another metric often cited in the context of political and economic sustainability. When a country such as Greece, or Italy, or Ireland reached unprecedented levels where the ratio was in excess of 100 percent, as they did during the 2007–2012 period, bond rating agencies and currency managers began to downgrade debt quality, forcing a de facto increase in interest rates beyond the levels targeted by central banks. But this does alone not explain why some countries faced currency runs and sovereign default risks since a country such as Japan has had a ratio central

government debt to GDP well over 100 percent for over a decade, and has even reached the 200 percent level as of 2012. What counts in all of this is whether there underlying assets that can be liquidated if needed to satisfy debt service requirements. Since Japan has considerable assets, it thus has not faced the kind of debt quality downgrades that smaller countries such as Greece, Italy, Spain, Portugal and Ireland.

26. This estimate comes from a working paper by University of Michigan economist Mark J. Perry, whose comparison is based on the extent of government regulation that prevailed in 1949 with those for the U.S. in 2011. http://www.aei-ideas. org/2013/06/federal-regulations-have-lowered-gdp-growth-by-2-per-year/

27. The current crisis in the Ukraine suggests that the Russian Federation also has a large population in the military. The .77 million armed service personnel in the Russian Federation belies the nuclear military capability that had been built back in the days of the Soviet Union, giving the Russian Federation more leverage than its armed services personnel alone would suggest.

28. Together Russian and U.S. missile stockpiles account for 72 percent of the world total of 22,600.

29. https://www.heritage.org/index/

30. See, for example, Leo Strauss and Joseph Cropsey, editors (1987, 1972, 1963). *History of Political Philosophy*, 3rd edition. (Chicago, Illinois: University of Chicago Press), for a critical view of the state. For a sympathetic view of the state, see, for example, John Rawls (1971), *A Theory of Justice.* (Cambridge, Mass: Harvard University Press).

31. A useful source is Eric Roll (1992, 1942). *A History of Economic Thought*, 5th revised edition. (London: Faber and Faber).

32. Although Keynes cited Malthus as a constructive figure in the great debate over England's use of protectionism during the Napoleonic wars, it was David Ricardo's model of comparative advantage that led to the repeal of tariffs in the 1834 Corn Law legislation.

33. Friedrich Hayek (1975, 1944). *The Road to Serfdom.* (Chicago, Illinois: The University of Chicago Press, published originally by Routledge and Kegan Paul, London in 1944). One useful source of Hayek's views on the role of

information in pricing can be found in F.A. Hayek (1980, 1948). *Individualism and Economic Order*. (Chicago, Illinois: The University of Chicago Press).

34. Friedman's 1991 book, *Free to Choose*, expands on the themes in Capitalism and Freedom to argue that markets represent a global solution to poverty.

35. Milton Friedman and Anna Jacobson Schwartz (1963). *A Monetary History of the United States, 1867–1960*. (Princeton, New Jersey: Princeton University Press for the National Bureau of Economic Research).

36. John Kenneth Galbraith's *The Great Crash of 1929* (Boston, Mass.: Houghton Mifflin, 1988, 1954) exemplified how widespread was the Keynesian notion that the stock market crash and Great Depression were due largely to financial speculation rather than monetary policy. Nowhere in Galbraith's treatment does monetary policy get mention as a possible cause of the crash or the Depression.

37. For accounts of East Asia's financial crisis, see, for example: Noland, Markus, Li-gang Liu, Sherman Robinson, and Zhi Wang (1998). *Global Economic Effects of the Asian Currency Devaluations*. Policy Analyses in International Economics, No. 56. (Washington, D.C.: Institutional for International Economics); Kaufman, G.G., Krueger, Th., and Hunter, W.C. (1999). *The Asian Financial Crisis: Origins, Implications, and Solutions*: (New York: Springer Publications); and Michael Pettis (2001). *The Volatility Machine: Emerging Economies and the Threat of Financial Collapse*. (New York: Oxford University Press).

38. In an Op-Ed article published in the September 23, 1997 issue of the Wall Street Journal, Mohammed Mahathir called currency traders in general and George Soros in particular "Highwaymen of the Global Economy", a view that he later moderated in his 1999 book, *A New Deal for Asia* (Selangor Darul Ehsan, Malasia: Pelanduk Publications). Stephen J. Brown, William N. Goetzmann, and James Park tested the proposition that hedge fund currency speculators were behind the East Asia financial crisis of 1997 and found no compelling evidence. See their "Hedge Funds and the Asian Currency Crisis of 1997," NBER Working Paper 6247 (Cambridge, Mass.: NBER).

39. Roger Lowenstein (2000). *When Genius Failed: The Rise and Fall of Long-Term Capital Management*. (New York: Random House). LTCM's returns

after partners' fees and expenses were 20 percent in 1994, 43 percent in 1995, 41 percent in 1996 and 17 percent in 1997.

40. Quantitative Easing, or QE, went through various phases of expansion from 2010 through 2013. As the economy showed signs of recovery, and as then Federal Reserve incoming Chair Janet Yellen replaced outgoing chair Ben Bernanke on February 14, 2014. The challenge to the Fed is to decide when to wind down its purchases of U.S. Treasury securities, which will generate an increase in interest rates, and thus affect the rate of growth of the economy.

41. Daniel Bernoulli (1954, 1738) "Exposition of a New Theory on the Measurement of Risk", *Econometrica* 22:1 (January), pp. 23–36. Bernouilli's original essay was written in Latin and remained largely unnoticed until John von Neumann and Oscar Morgenstern came across it when preparing their book, *Theory of Games and Economic Behavior* that was published originally in 1944 and which established game theory as a field of research.

42. Daniel Kahneman and Amos Tversky (1979), "Prospect Theory: An Analysis of Decision Under Risk", *Econometrica* 47:2 (March), pp. 263–292. A more accessible source is Daniel Kahneman's 2011 book, *Thinking Fast and Slow* (New York: Farrar, Strauss and Giroux), which summarizes much of the research on behavioral science and which resulted in his being awarded a Nobel Memorial Prize in Economic Science in 2002.

43. Mohammed AlKhars, Nicholas Evangelopoulos, Robert Pavur, and Shailesh Kulkam (2019) "Cognitive Biases resulting from the representativeness heuristic in operations management: An experimental investigation" *Psychology Research and Behavior Management*, 12 (April), pp. 263–276.

44. In his 2010 book *The Hidden Brain: How Our Unconscious Minds Elect Presidents, Control Markets, Wage Wars, and Save Our Lives* (New York: Spiegel and Grau), Shankar Vedantam provides an accessible treatment of advances in neuroscience that affect a range of decisions. Sebastian Seung traces the brain down to the wiring level in *Connectome* (New York: Houghton Mifflin Harcourt, 2010). These are but two publications of a rapidly expanding literature on neuroscience and which is re-shaping our understanding of decision-making.

45. Daniel Kahneman, and Amos Tversky (1979), "Prospect Theory: An Analysis of Decision under Risk", *Econometrica* 47:2, pp. 263–291.

46. William Jennings Bryan argued for the prosecution, while Clarence Darrow defended Scopes. Stanley Kramer directed a 1960 film, *Inherit the Wind*, an adaptation of a 1955 play by the same name, to portray the Scopes Trial as a mirror to McCarthyism, which still echoed the anti-Communist hysteria pursued by Wisconsin Senator Joseph McCarthy.

47. The Smithsonian Museum of Natural History contains a wealth of evidence and displays on human evolution. See, for example, http://humanorigins. si.edu/evidence. The point here is not to review this literature but to indicate the contradiction between scientific evidence and many religious teachings.

48. Among Johanson's publications, see *Lucy: The Beginning of Humankind* (Touchstone Simon & Schuster, 1990).

49. See, for example, Dean Falk (2017), *The Fossil Chronicles* (Berkeley, California: University of California Press).

50. Ham has published several books to argue in behalf of creationism, most recently in 2019, with Bodie Hodge, *Glass house: Shattering the Myth of Evolution* (Green Forest, Arkansas: Master Books).

51. The late Stephen Jay Gould wrote extensively on evolution during a teaching and research career at Harvard University. He reframed Darwin's theory to account for random events such as meteor strikes that wiped out the dinosaurs, to formulate a theory of contingent evolution. Contingent evolution allows for throwback changes as well as advances in human evolution in the context of other species. His 1996 book, first published in 1981, *The Mismeasure of Man*, took direct aim at racially framed theories of evolution, notably Richard J. Herrnstein and Charles Murray's 1994 book, *The Bell Curve—Intelligence and Class Structure in American Life* (New York: The Free Press).

52. Richard Dawkins (2006) *The God Delusion* (London: Bantam Press).

53. Stephen Jay Gould (1999), *Rocks of ages: Science and Religion in the Fullness of Life* (New York: Ballantine Publishing Group). Francis S. Collins (2006), *The Language of God: A Scientist Presents Evidence for Belief* (New York: The Free Press).

54. A good summary of this research can be found in Elinor Ostrom's 1997 address to the American Political Science Association. "A Behavioral Approach to the Rational Choice Theory of Collection Action", *American Political Science Review* 92:1 (March 1998), 2–23.

55. Malcolm Gladwell, *Blink: The Power of Thinking Without Thinking* (Boston: Little, Brown Publishing, 2005); Daniel Kahneman, *Thinking, Fast and Slow* (New York: Farrar, Straus, and Giroux, 2011).

56. Thomas S. Kuhn, *The Structure of Scientific Revolutions* (Chicago: University of Chicago Press, 2012, 1996, 1970, 1962).

57. Svante Arrhenius, "On the Influence of Carbonic Acid in the Air upon the Temperature of the Ground", *Philosophical Magazine and Journal of Science* 5:41 (April 1896), pp. 237–276.

58. Documentation on the Paris Agreement can be found at: https://unfccc.int/process-and-meetings/the-paris-agreement/the-paris-agreement

59. https://sealevelrise.org/forecast/

60. https://www.nationalgeographic.com/magazine/2013/09/rising-seas-ice-melt-new-shoreline-maps/

61. https://www.ucsusa.org/resources/science-under-trump

62. Riley E. Dunlap (2013) "Climate Change Skepticism and Denial: An Introduction" *American Behavioral Scientist* 57:6, pp. 691–698; Riley E. Dunlap, Aaron M. McCright (2011) *Climate Change Denial: Sources, actors, and strategies* (New York: Taylor and Francis); Pascal Diethelm and Martin McKee (January 2009), "Denialism: What is it and How Should Scientists Respond?" *European Journal of Public Health* 19:1, pp. 2–4.

63. https://www.businessinsider.com/hillary-clinton-biggest-campaign-mistake-2017-9.

64. Schumpeter's position reflected concern over speculation in the stock market and neglect of the role of long-term innovation. In *Joseph Alois Schumpeter: The Public Life of a Private* Man (Princeton University Press, 1994), Wolfgang F. Stolper characterized Schumpeter's stance on the Great Depression as better to do nothing than to do something that might result in central bank monetary control. Cf. page 344.

65. John Maynard Keynes (1965, 1953, 1936). *The General Theory of Employment, Interest, and Money* (New York: Harcourt Brace and World Publishing).

66. John Maynard Keynes (1923). *A Tract on Monetary Reform* (London: Macmillan Publishers), p. 80.

67. Milton Friedman and Anna J. Schwartz, *A Monetary History of the United States, 1867–1960*. (Cambridge, Mass.: National Bureau of Economic Research, and Princeton University Press).

68. Bernanke noted Friedman's contribution to monetary policy in a speech delivered in 2002, and which he would later apply to the events of 2008–2009 in adopting quantitative easing as a tool of monetary policy. https://www.federalreserve.gov/BOARDDOCS/SPEECHES/2002/20021108/

69. One notable critic of the Federal Reserve has been the libertarian politician Ron Paul. *His End the Fed* (New York: Grand Central Publishing for the Hachette Book Group, 2009) illustrates the libertarian opposition to government intervention in the economy. His views were translated in his serving in the U.S. House of Representatives from Texas and in three failed U.S. presidential bids in 1968, 2008, and 2012. As a U.S. Senator from Kentucky, his son Rand Paul has advocated similar critical views of government intervention.

70. There are numerous sources for data on public finance in the U.S. Our comparisons here draw on Historical US Federal Expenditures by Function, 1902–1970; the Bicentennial Edition of Historical Statistics of the United States, Colonial times to 1970. Recent analyses of the size of the U.S. government include: Tamim Bayoumi and Fernando M. Gonçalves, "'Government for the People: On the Determinants of the Size of U.S. Government," IMF Working Paper number 289 (Washington, D.C.: International Monetary Fund), and William A. Niskanen (2003), *Autocratic, Democratic, and Optimal Government: Fiscal Choices and Economic Outcomes* (Northampton, Mass.: Edward Elgar Publishing for the Locke Institute).

71. In David Nasaw's 2006 compelling biography of Andrew Carnegie, he notes Carnegie's efforts to secure world peace were driven in part by recognition that the U.S. did not yet have a global military presence on a scale that could match those of England and Germany. Carnegie was disturbed by Theodore

McKinley's efforts to out Spain in Cuba and the Philippines, going so far as to openly criticize interventionists as not being true Americans in an 1899 essay, "Americanism versus Imperialism" in the *North American Review*. *Andrew Carnegie* (New York: Penguin Books), p. 544. By 1913, Theodore Roosevelt had sent his Great White fleet around the world, a harbinger of the First World War that would break out in August 1914. Yet the U.S. only entered the war in April 1917, which delayed the expansion of the federal government even with the a standardized income tax under the newly adopted sixteenth amendment of 1913.

72. Up until the adoption of the sixteenth amendment, Congress did have the authority to impose income taxes, but only in proportion to each state's population. This is one factor that lay behind the relatively high tariffs that were adopted in the late 19th century, but not for subsequently higher tariffs such as the Smoot-Hawley tariff of 1931.

73. Interestingly, one of those who supported payroll withholding was conservative economist Milton Friedman (1912–2006). For insights on the origins of withholding, see Charlotte Twight (Winter 1995), "Evolution of Federal Income Tax Withholding: The Machinery of Institutional Change, *The Cato Journal*, 14:3, pp. 359–395.

74. One argument in favor of such transfers is that federal taxation is viewed as economically more efficient to administer than many state and local taxes. Yet, as we will argue, transfer payments are a means of managing risk, though not necessarily the most efficient method of doing so.

75. These programs have operated under various names, as periodic reforms have been adopted. The most notable recent reform that led to the creation of the TANF (temporary assistance to needy families) program was the welfare reform act of 1996, also known as the Personal Responsibility and Work Opportunity Reconciliation Act, or PWWORA (PL 104–193). This legislation eliminated the Aid to Families with Dependent Children legislation that dated from the 1960s with a greater emphasis on temporary assistance and incentives for job placement.

76. The standard used by economists is whether markets can achieve a Pareto-optimal allocation of resources. Pareto efficiency, by which any further change

to the benefit of at least one individual must by definition result in a reduction in welfare of someone else, helps economic theorizing avoid the pitfall of interpersonal subjective value judgments. Rigorous statements regarding the equivalence of pareto efficiency with a competitive market structure have been developed by Kenneth Arrow and Gerard Debreu, in such works as their 1954 essay, "Existence of an equilibrium for a competitive economy" *Econometrica* 22, pp. 265–290. They have been challenged more recently when imperfect information and transactions costs are taken into consideration, a summary of which can be found in Joseph Stiglitz' (1994) *Whither Socialism?* (Cambridge, Mass.: MIT) from which the quote at the beginning of this chapter is taken.

77. Thomas Aquinas' most famous work was his Summa Theologica, written during his lifetime (1225–1274), but a full text was not issued until Michael Wenssler of Basel had one published in 1485. A pdf version is can be found at: http://www.documentacatholicaomnia.eu/03d/1225–1274,_Thomas_Aquinas,_Summa_Theologiae_%5B1%5D,_EN.pdf

78. There are several books on Islamic finance. See, for example, Mohammed Ayub (2007), Understanding Islamic Finance (New York: John Wiley and Sons). Islamic finance does not eliminate the existence of the time value of money, nor of risk. What it does provide is a risk-sharing contractual arrangement between buyer and seller.

79. There are numerous accounts of the rise of the Dutch Republic. See, for example, Jonathan Israel (1998, 1995) *The Dutch Republic: Its Rise, Greatness, and Fall 1477–1806* (New York: Oxford University Press), and Simon Schama (1997, 1987), *The Embarrassment of Riches: An Interpretation of Dutch Culture in the Golden Age.* (New York: Alfred A. Knopf and Vintage paper editions).

80. Four Anglo-Dutch wars were fought during the seventeenth and eighteenth centuries. Dates of these conflicts were: 1. 1652–1654; 2. 1665–1667; 3. 1672–1674; and 4. 1780–1784. The English won a decisive victory during the last conflict, thereby helping them to establish naval supremacy in the north Atlantic, and to continue their imperial expansion in Asia.

81. Holland became a refuge for populations seeking to escape the ravages of European wars and religious persecution. Jews, French Huguenot Protestants,

and other minorities were welcome to live and work in the country, and helped create a flourishing and tolerant culture that survives to this day. Baruch Spinoza (1632–1677), Pierre Bayle (1647–1706), and René Descartes (1596–1650) were among those who lived and worked in Holland. Though nominally Catholic, Descartes joined the Dutch army of Maurice of Nassau in the struggle of the United Provinces to become independent, and thereafter chose to live in Holland.

82. In 1841, English writer Charles Mackay took note of the tulip bubble in his book, *Extraordinary Popular Delusions and the Madness of Crowds* (London: Richard Bentley), reprinted more recently by Three Rivers Press in 1980. More recently, Charles Kindleberger wrote, *Manias, Panics, and Crashes: A History of Financial Crises* (New York: John Wiley and Sons, 1996, 1989, and 1978). Mike Dash's, *Tulipomania: The Story of the World's Most Coveted Flower and the Extraordinary Passions It Aroused* (1999), provides a dramatic account of the Dutch tulip bubble.

83. Andrew Ross Sorkin (2009). *Too Big to Fail: The Inside Story of How Wall Street and Washington Fought to Save the Financial System –and Themselves* (New York: Viking Penguin Publishing).

84. After a crisis, or failure of a firm, reporters often produce informative accounts of how markets fail and how management fails. For the LCTM story, see Roger Lowenstein (2000). *When Genius Failed: The Rise and Fall of Long-Term Capital Management.* (New York: Random House Inc.); For an account of the failure of Lehman Brothers, see Lawrence M. Ball (2018). *The Fed and Lehman Brothers: Setting the Record Straight.* (New York: Cambridge University Press).

85. Named the Wiley act after is sponsor, the FDA's authority was directed not just at meatpacking, but any number of food and drug products. It is one of the most powerful regulatory agencies operating in the U.S. today, and whose effectiveness is subject to rising skepticism over the unintended anticompetitive consequences of its actions, let alone the extent to which its actions have created prudential decisions in the face of risk.

86. For a specific chronology of events in Enron's downfall, see "Timeline of Enron's Collapse", Washingtonpost.com.

87. Alma Cohen and Liran Einav (2003) provide evidence of the effectiveness of seat belt laws in "The Effects of Mandatory Seat Belt Laws on Driving Behavior and Traffic Fatalities", *Review of Economics and Statistics* 85:4 (November), pp. 838–843.

88. EPA standards on aftermarket converters can be found in "Sale and Use of Aftermarket Catalytic Converters", US Federal Register, Volume 51. https:// www.epa.gov/compliance/resources/policies/civil/caa/mobile/amccpolicy.pdf

89. President Trump targeted California emissions standards and said that the federal government would move to relax them to support greater sales of vehicles. https://www.nytimes.com/2019/09/17/climate/trump-california-emissions-waiver.html

90. https://www.ncbi.nlm.nih.gov/pubmed/16378050

91. We use a simple index of inequality here based on a formula by David Champernowne (1912–2000): $I = 1-g/x$, where g is the geometric mean of a series and x is the arithmetic mean. The geometric mean is the nth root of the product of n terms.

92. https://givingusa.org/giving-usa-2019-americans-gave-427–71-billion-to-charity-in-2018-amid-complex-year-for-charitable-giving/

93. Comparative data on estate taxation can be found at: https://files.taxfoundation.org/legacy/docs/TaxFoundation_FF458.pdf

94. A larger index would also include the ratio of public debt to GDP, but our augmented index serve to illustrate the comparison we are making. All U.S. data used in this comparison include both federal and state and local government taxes and spending.

95. Abram Bergson (Burk), "A Reformulation of Certain Aspects of Welfare Economics", *Quarterly Journal of Economics* 52, (1938), pp. 310–334. Samuelson incorporated Bergson's framework in his 1947 publication, *Foundations of Economic Analysis* (Cambridge, Mass.: Harvard University Press).

96. Vilfredo Pareto, *Manuel d'économie politique* (Paris: V. Viard & E. Brière, 1909), translated into English and incorporated in *The Economics of Welfare* (London: Macmillan & Co., 1932).

97. Nicholas Kaldor (1939), "Welfare Propositions in Economics and Interpersonal Comparisons of Utility", *The Economic Journal* 49:195, pp. 549–552.

98. Kenneth J. Arrow (1951), *Social Choice and Individual Values* (New Haven, Connecticut: John Wiley and Sons). Gérard Debreu (1959), *The Theory of Value: An Axiomatic Analysis of Economic Equilibrium* (New York: John Wiley and Sons).

99. John Rawls (1971), A *Theory of Justice*. (Cambridge, Mass.: Harvard University Press). Robert Nozick (1974). *Anarchy, State and Utopia* (New York: Basic Books).

100. Ron Paul (2009). *End the Fed*. (New York: Grand Central Publishing).

101. Ayn Rand, an immigrant from Russia, witnessed the confiscation of property at the time of the Russian Revolution. Arriving in the United States in 1926, she became well known through two novels, *The Fountainhead* (1943), and *Atlas Shrugged* (1957). From these books she espoused a philosophy of objectivism, based on the notion of rational behavior built on ethical egoism. She opposed altruism, collectivism as well as anarchy, and viewed self-interested private markets as the only morally ethical form of social institutions.

102. https://freedomhouse.org/. Freedom House scores and ranking cannot avoid a measure of subjectivity, nor do they lend themselves to ready comparisons across countries. This said, they do offer a first-order approximation of political liberties and civil rights.

103. In a 1997, Fareed Zakaria pointed out that counting elections does not provide an adequate indication of democracy. Instead, he noted that without underlying institutions such as an independent judiciary and well-established property rights, elections may provide only an illiberal form of democracy. "The rise of Illiberal Democracy", *Foreign Affairs* (November/December1997), pp. 1–22. We thus use a variant of his definition here.

104. In the *Wealth of Nations* (1776), Adam Smith wrote of the ability of firms to raise prices without limits. Today we know that this is not so, given how demand for a good becomes price elastic as prices are raised. In the elastic range of demand, a monopolist would produce a price-decreasing strategy to maximize revenues and profits, even though the profit-maximizing level of output and price would still be higher than for a competitive market as a whole.

105. Adam Smith, *The Wealth of Nations*, Book IV, Chapter VIII, vii., p. 660, paragraph 49. An online pdf version can be obtained at: http://files.libertyfund.org/files/220/0141-02_Bk.pdf

106. Technical efficiency received particular attention by Harvey Leibenstein (1922–1994), in his 1966 article on evaluating firm and industry performance: "Allocative Efficiency vs. 'X-Efficiency'", *American Economic Review* 56:3 (June, 1966), pp. 392–415. Leibenstein was responding to the question of where reported profits and profitability of firms provided evidence of economic profit in concentrated industries, notably an article by Arnold Harberger: "Monopoly and Resource Allocation" *American Economic Review* 44:2 (Papers and Proceedings, May, 1954), pp. 77–87. Harberger had found little evidence of excess profitability, but Leibenstein argued that firms may not be technically efficient, and that the social welfare losses from imperfect competition could be much greater than the relatively low estimates provided by Harberger.

107. Albert Hirschman (1915–2012) characterized this decision framework in his book, *Exit, Voice, and Loyalty* (Cambridge, Mass.: Harvard University Press, 1970), in reference to consumer choices regarding products, memberships, and emigration. His book highlights the role of informational transparency in guiding such decisions.

108. Another key figure in the question of transactions costs is Ronald Coase (1910–2013), whose 1960 article, "The Problem of Social Cost", *Journal of Law and Economics* 3 (October), pp. 1–44, helped to set the stage for the question of whether external costs are best managed by private individuals or by a public agency. Coase argued that in many cases, private firms and consumers can develop satisfactory agreements without the cost of public agency.

109. Antoine Augustin Cournot wrote *Recherches sur les principes mathématiques de la théorie des richesses* in 1838. It was not well known at the time to economists, largely because it was a mathematical treatment far advanced at a time when most writings on economics were in a literary or simple tabular form. A French paper edition was issued by Calmann-Lévy publishers in 1974, while the first English translation was undertaken in 1897 by Nathaniel T.

Bacon for Macmillan Publishers. A 2008 paper edition is available through BiblioLife publishers. Cournot today is seen as a pioneer in mathematical economics that helped lay the foundations of contemporary game theory.

110. Without going through a technical exposition here, social welfare can be measured as the sum or producer and consumer surplus. Producer surplus is the value area of production between the equilibrium market price and the supply curve, while consumer surplus is the area below the demand curve and the equilibrium price. Together these form a measure of total social welfare, from which deviations from a perfectly competitive level of output can be used to estimate what economists refer to as deadweight social welfare loss, and its remaining complement, the existing level of total social welfare.

111. British journalist Anthony Sampson wrote a detailed account of the international petroleum industry in his book, *The Seven Sisters: The Great Oil Companies and the World They Shaped.* (New York: Viking Press, 1975). Another popular account of international oil can be found in Daniel Yergin, *The Prize: The Epic Quest for Oil, Money, and Power* (New York: Simon and Schuster, 2008, 1991).

112. Vaseline was first introduced in 1872 by Robert Chesebrough. With a petroleum jelly base, it contains a eucalyptus derived camphor-injected compound and serves as a topical decongestant cream.

113. Forbes magazine publishes an annual list of the estimated wealth of the top 400 richest individuals in the world. https://www.forbes.com/billionaires/ For the 2018 list, Donald Trump is listed as having net worth of $2.1 billion, placing him as 766th in the world, and 248th in the United States.

114. From Bernie Sanders' 2020 campaign website: https://berniesanders.com/issues/real-wall-street-reform/ Sanders comes from a long line of Leftist activists going back to Eugene Debs (1855–1926), who ran unsuccessfully five times for President of the United States. What typically has happened with such campaigns is that some of their ideas wind up being co-opted by a majoritarian party, which in Sanders' case is the Democratic Party.

115. Several biographies of John D. Rockefeller and his descendants have been published in recent years. Notable is Ron Chernow's *Titan: The Life of*

John D. Rockefeller (New York: Random House, 1998), which won a National Book Award and was a best seller for some time.

116. Tarbell's book is available in a variety of formats. The following link provides open access options: https://openlibrary.org/books/OL7196550M/ The_history_of_the_Standard_Oil_Company

117. Senator John Sherman (1823–1900) was the brother of noted Civil War Union General William Tecumseh Sherman (1820–1891), who along with Ulysses S. Grant were the primary leaders of the Union army that brought the Confederacy to defeat. One of General Sherman's quotes, "War is Hell", might have applied equally to the Sherman Act, once the 1911 Supreme Court decision was delivered.

118. The Cobb-Douglas production function equation is: $Y = AL^{\beta}K^{\alpha}$, where Y is the level of output, A is a constant reflecting the state of technology, and alpha and beta reflect the respective marginal contributions to total output. If α and ß add to 1, there are constant returns to scale. If greater than 1, then increasing returns to scale, and conversely, if less than one decreasing returns to scale. Using a logarithmic transformation of the formula and applying it to time series data for a series of industries, one could determine which industries displayed decreasing returns to scale, in which case a justification could be made for a restructuring the industry. Despite the elegance of the function, George Stigler argued that the best way to determine economies of scale would be to rely on the survivorship principle, implying that the petroleum industry's structure justified a measure of concentration, and thus economies of scale. George J. Stigler (1958), "The Economies of Scale", *The Journal of Law and Economies* 1 (October), pp. 54–71.

119. Walter Isaacson, *Steve Jobs* (New York: Simon and Schuster, 2011).

120. Joseph Schumpeter (1934, 1911). *The Theory of Economic Development* (Cambridge, Mass.: Harvard University Press). Schumpeter's book is as a clear statement of the role of the entrepreneur as has been written. Many who look to understanding the entrepreneur are drawn to Russian émigré writer Ayn Rand's *Atlas Shrugged* (1957, Random House) and *The Fountainhead* (1943, Bobbs-Merrill), both of which provide a romantic portrayal through these novels of the entrepreneur.

121. https://www.nytimes.com/1982/01/09/business/why-baxter-dropped-the-ibm-suit.html

122. Getting a fix on a company's value can be done in purely accounting terms, that is, the net worth, or sales of a firm. But beyond this is the value of a brand, which includes the reputation of a firm. In 2018, the following brands were ranked, in $U.S. billions, in the following order: Google ($302), Apple ($300), Amazon (207), and Microsoft ($200). https://ww.fashionnetwork.com/news/Which-are-the-most-valuable-global-brands-in-2018-,982294.html

123. The act called for Congressional appropriations of $26 billion dollars to create a network of 41,000 modern highways. The rationale for its creation was national security, that is, the need to be able to transport military equipment and personnel in times of a national emergency. A background link can be found at: https://en.wikipedia.org/wiki/Federal_Aid_Highway_Act_of_1956

124. Space exploration resulted in many commercial innovations now taken for granted. One was the development of polymer materials that could be used in space equipment such as space suits. Dupont Corporation's Teflon came out of this initiative and now is used in many applications from cooking equipment to bio-hazard suits and bullet-proof vests. In addition, the need to perform orbital trajectory calculations aboard spacecraft resulted in the development of hand-held computing equipment, which began with battery-powered calculators such as Texas Instruments and Hewlett-Packard's models. Before the launch of desktop computing by innovators such as Steve Jobs hand-held calculators were able to perform sophisticated operations with machine-readable programs on plastic strips. Desktop computing was thus already able to build on existing technological innovations.

125. U.S. opposition has been based on privacy and security concerns that also reflects the fact that the U.S. has been slow to roll out 5G technology. U.S. efforts to discourage other countries from adopting Huawei's 5G technology have not thus far succeeded: https://www.census.gov/econ/concentration.html

126. William Baumol, John C. Panzar, and Robert D. Willig (1982). *Contestable Markets and the Theory of Industry Structure.* (New York: Harcourt, Brace,

and Jovanovich). Their research was supported by AT&T and they served as expert witnesses during the trial phase of the case. At the time, it seemed that this could serve as a middle way between radical restructuring as applied in the Standard Oil Case, and continued regulation, or the use of taxes and subsidies. The consent decree of 1984 illustrated the continuing influence of antitrust even though it did not require a guilty verdict to restructure.

127. Apart from his writing on the entrepreneur, Schumpeter noted how innovation provides a flow of positive rates of economic return, and thus how they could justify varying degrees of industrial concentration over time. Were innovation a purely static configuration in which no technological change were to occur, then one might have a clearer case in which to look more favorably as instruments to correct for imperfect competition. Ironically, Schumpeter did not see innovative capitalism being replaced by a socialist system because of its faults, but rather of its success in eliminating poverty and creating wealth. All of this can be found in his 1942 treatise, *Capitalism, Socialism, and Democracy* (New York: Harper & Brothers, 1950, 1947, and 1942 editions).

128. Sources for these comparisons have been taken from the U.S. Trade Administration and the U.S. Transportation Administration. https://www.trade.gov/; https://www.transportation.gov/

129. Elon Musk, whose net worth is estimated at $U.S. 39 billion in 2020, has invested in high density battery storage systems, and launched Tesla in 2003.

130. The U.S. Department of Commerce has been a source of concentration ratios in U.S. manufacturing for some time. Looking at breakfast cereal, glass, metal can, household vacuum cleaner and underwear manufacturing, the average concentration ratio for these 5 industries rose from 85 percent in 1963 to 95.5 percent in 2007, yet major attention almost always has focused on industries with larger market value. These data now are compiled through surveys by the U.S. Census Bureau: https://www.census.gov/econ/concentration.html

131. In 1960, passenger vehicles made up 85 percent of domestic vehicle sales in the U.S. By 2017, their share had fallen to 29.5 percent. U.S. vehicle manufacturers General Motors, Ford, and Fiat-Chrysler now emphasize SUV and

truck sales over passenger vehicles, even as they race to reconfigure vehicles to operate on hybrid and all-electric systems.

132. These statements are not meant to evaluate the profitability to private defense contractors once a level of government spending on national security has been determined. If defense contractors are seen as enjoying economic rates of return, they become the focus of those who would reduce defense spending, as opposed to diagnosing whether a defense sector is competitive. This question has been raised most acutely in the context of government contracts for private firms that may be producing both military and civilian clients. The rivalry between Boeing and Airbus has gone on for decades in which charges and countercharges have been made as to whether government military equipment expenditures provide an edge to firms producing civilian products, in this case Boeing's B747, B757, B777, and B787 commercial airliners, and Airbus' A380, A350, A340 and A330 commercial airliners. For an account of this competition, see John Newhouse (2007), *Boeing versus Airbus: The Inside Story of the Greatest International Competition in Business* (New York Alfred A. Knopf, Random House).

133. U.S. Department of Defense Statistics, as reported in: https://en.wikipedia.org/wiki/United_States_military_deployments

134. James Fallows, *National Defense* (New York: Random House Publishers, 1981).

135. The original price when introduced in the early 1960's was U.S. $2.1 million.

136. Costs of these different fighter planes are not comparable in that the F-22 has far greater capabilities than the F-5 once did. And since initial production, 195 have been built. https://en.wikipedia.org/wiki/Lockheed_Martin_F-22_Raptor. Similar comparisons could be drawn in terms of aircraft carriers such as the 2017 launch of the nuclear-powered USS Gerald R. Ford, which carries 75+ fighter planes for a total cost of U.S. $12.5 billion.

137. During World War II, the U.S. needed to expand production of landing ships. Henry J. Kaiser started building standardized 10-ton Liberty Ship landing craft at a plant in California. The first unit took several months to complete. By 1944, Kaiser was completing 3 Liberty ships every 2 days, for a total of 2,710 units, in today's dollars, each unit cost $36 million.

138. Rankings vary by agency and time. The UN Office on Drugs and Crime compiles estimates of homicide rates that is a common course. For 2017, it ranks the United States 55th, based on the list of countries it tracks, while the list I used had a smaller number of countries. https://www.indexmundi.com/facts/indicators/VC.IHR.PSRC.P5/rankings

139. The Joyce Foundation is but one of many advocating stronger gun rights. www.joycefdn.org/programs/gun-violence?gclid=EAIaIQobChMInJyeiar86 AIViZ6fCh0AcQRdEAAYASAAEgK-4vD_BwE

140. For years, the World Bank has tracked estimates of the rate of return to education, and which are largely positive in comparison to the opportunity cost. What the Bank's research shows, however, is that the private rate of return is less than the social rate of return, in which case public support for education is justified. https://blogs.worldbank.org/education/50-years-returns-education-studies George Psacharopoulos, formerly at the World Bank, authored a number of studies of the rate of return to education, and which helped to guide Bank lending to this sector. A 2018 update provides recent evidence. https://openknowledge.worldbank.org/handle/10986/29672

141. Milton Friedman (1962) *Capitalism and Freedom* (Chicago, Illinois: University of Chicago Press).

142. In the 2015–16 academic year, there were 6,855 charter schools in the U.S. 3,854 were elementary schools, 1,576 were combined elementary and secondary schools. The first charter school was opened in 1992. In terms of regions, 23 percent of traditional public schools are found in the western states in the U.S. while 37 percent of charter schools are found in those states. Some data can be found at: http://www.in-perspective.org/pages/introduction#sub5

143. https://www.edweek.org/ew/articles/2019/02/27/in-many-charter-high-schools-graduation-odds.html

144. The Pew Research Center tracks results from the Programme for International Student Assessment (PISA) and the Trends in International Mathematics and Science (TIMSS) tests. PISA results from 2015 revealed that the U.S. placed 38th out of 71 countries in math, and 24th in science.

See: https://www.edweek.org/ew/articles/2019/02/27/in-many-charter-high-schools-graduation-odds.html

145. Although the United States has won more prizes than any other country (383 as of 2019), on a per million population basis, it ranks 12th in the top groupings. Switzerland is number 1 at 3.23, followed by Sweden at 3.17, Austria at 2.44, all the way to the U.S. at 1.16. See: https://en.wikipedia.org/wiki/List_of_Nobel_laureates_by_country

146. Documentation of health care legislation can be found at: https://www.cms.gov/About-CMS/Agency-Information/History

147. Gary Akerlof (1970). "The Market for 'Lemons': Quality Uncertainty and the Market Mechanism" *Quarterly Journal of Economics* 84:3, pp. 488–500.

148. https://www.federalregister.gov/agencies/consumer-financial-protection-bureau Elizabeth Warren, then a Professor of Law at Harvard Law School, helped to craft legislation for the Consumer Financial Protection Bureau and was named as its first Commissioner. This legislation served as part of her candidacy for President in 2020.

149. Installation of catalytic converters on new vehicles in the United States was adopted in the 1980 Clean Air Act, and amended in 1990. https://www.federalregister.gov/agencies/consumer-financial-protection-bureau

150. Gasoline taxes have been adopted in the U.S. at the federal and state levels. Taxes on gasoline and diesel are mostly in the form of excise rather than sales, although some states use both. California has the highest excise tax, at $.612 per gallon, and a 2.25 percent sales tax, in addition to a federal excise tax of $.184 per gallon. In California, diesel fuel is taxes at $.869 a gallon, in addition to a 9.25 percent sales tax, and a federal excise tax of $.184 per gallon. Alaska has the lowest tax rates on fuel: $.147 per gallon on gasoline and $.144 for diesel, in addition to the same federal taxes as applied in California and other states. https://en.wikipedia.org/wiki/Fuel_taxes_in_the_United_States

151. The first law of thermodynamics states that the quantity of mass and energy in the universe is constant for a closed system. The second law was formulated by, among others, Sadi Carnot (1796–1832), A French engineer who wrote a

treatise, *Reflections on the Motive Power of Heat*, published in 1832, and which served as a foundation for the second law. Carnot's formulation is straightforward: The efficiency of an energy transformation is a function of the ratio of combustion and the ambient temperature and which is subtracted from 1. A pdf translation of 1890 can be found at: https://www3.nd.edu/~powers/ ame.20231/carnot1897.pdf

152. Edward O. Wilson (1993, 1992). *The Diversity of Life.* (New York: W.W. Norton & Company), p. 351.

153. This illustration is taken from a paper "Optimal Pricing of Biodiverse Natural Resources", *Journal of Development Alternatives* 24:1–2 (March-June, 2005), pp. 5–38.

154. Several agencies track wildlife endangered species. The World Wildlife Fund is one, and whose website is: https://www.worldwildlife.org/species/directory?direction=desc&sort=extinction_statusAnother is the International Union for Conservation of Nature: https://www.iucn.org/.

155. Estimates of the 1918 pandemic have been compiled by the Center for Disease Control (CDC), in Atlanta, Georgia, and which serves as a principal source of national health information. https://www.cdc.gov/flu/pandemic-resources/1918-pandemic-h1n1.html

156. Nicholas Nassim Taleb, *The Black Swan: The Impact of the Highly Improbable* (New York: Random House, 2007). The Roman writer Juvenal noted that a good person is as rare as a black swan, and the term has come down through the ages to express extremely rare events.

157. https://www.washingtonpost.com/news/to-your-health/wp/2017/12/29/ trump-administration-fires-all-members-of-hivaids-advisory-council/. Trump's firing of the HIV-AIDS Advisory Council had nothing to do with the coronavirus pandemic, though critics have said that were it to have remained in place it could have anticipated several of the precautionary measures now being implemented.

158. U.S. states in the southern confederacy opposed the creation of a central bank. They relied instead on a series of loans through local banks, in addition to printing money, which created high rates of inflation in the south relative

to Union northern states. For an account: https://eh.net/encyclopedia/money-and-finance-in-the-confederate-states-of-america/

159. Several panics ensued in the United States following the end of the Civil War. For an account, see: https://www.federalreservehistory.org/essays/banking_panics_of_the_gilded_age

160. Historian Ron Chernow provides an up to date account of how J.P. Morgan came to wield considerable power at a time when the United States was undergoing rapid industrialization at the end of the 19th century. See, *The House of Morgan: An American Banking Dynasty and the Rise of Modern Finance*. (New York: Grove Press, 2010, 2001, 1990).

161. Milton Friedman and Anna Schwartz (1963). *A Monetary History of the United States, 1857–1960*. (Princeton, New Jersey: Princeton University Press for the National Bureau of Economic Research).

162. "Fisher Sees Stocks Permanently High: Yale Economist Tells Purchasing Agents", *The New York Times,* October 16, 1929, P. 8. By 1932, stocks had lost almost 90 percent of their value, and it would take decades to recover to the September 1929 peak. Fisher's judgment was the opposite of Roger Babson, who on September 5, 1929, told attendees at the 16th National Business conference that stocks were overvalued and that a downturn would soon happen. Babson's prediction was correct, though stock forecasters have yet to discern when pivots in the market can be predicted with accuracy.

163. Arthur Okun first proposed the misery index as a simple gauge of well-being while a resident scholar at the Brookings Institution in the 1970s. The index places an equal weight on each of the component inflation and unemployment rates, and has since been applied in various forms to states and countries around the world.

164. John Maynard Keynes (1936). *The General Theory of Employment, Interest, and Money* (New York: Harcourt World Publishing).

165. Friedrich Hayek (1944). *The Road to Serfdom* (London: Routledge Press, and in the United States by the University of Chicago Press).

166. Milton Friedman (1948), "A Monetary and Fiscal Framework for Economic Stability", *American Economic Review* 38:3, (June), pp. 246–264; (1956),

"The Quantity Theory of Money: A Restatement", *Studies in Quantity Theory* (Chicago: University of Chicago Press); (1959) "The Demand for Money: Some Theoretical and Empirical Results," Journal of Political Economy 67:4 (August), pp. 327–351.

167. https://clintonwhitehouse5.archives.gov/pcscb/wt_eisner.html Robert Eisner, then on leave from the Council of Economic Advisors, testified before Congress to propose the adoption of capital budgeting principles at all levels of government. The U.S. Federal government budget acknowledges no formal separation of recurrent from capital expenditures, while at the state and local levels, capital projects require voter approval for each specific project. As a result, U.S. states do not have the same flexibility to engage in discretionary fiscal policy actions as the Federal government, as indicated by the call by State governors for Federal assistance in addressing shortfalls in coronavirus testing equipment. This said, U.S. States tend to be more fiscally responsible, and not just to voters but to investors, in terms of deficit spending.

168. https://en.wikipedia.org/wiki/List_of_sovereign_debt_crises

169. The significance of the dollar became evident in the tangled financial transactions that emerged from the settlements agreed by the Versailles Peace Treaty. The reparations burden on Germany was so severe that the then Weimar Republic wound up printing money that generated a hyperinflation in 1923, and by severely eroding the assets of its middle class, laid the foundations for the rise of Adolf Hitler. Various re-negotiations, the Dawes Plan of 1924, the Young Plan of 1928, each looked to ways to ease the burden of reparations, but all failed eventually, and right at the time when the U.S. experienced the stock market crash of October 1929 that precipitated the onset of the Great Depression. At the time, no single country was able to avoid the financial crises of the 1920's, and it would be only at the end of Second World War that the International Monetary Fund was created to avoid sovereign debt crises. For an account of the challenges that Hjalmar Schacht of Germany, Montagu Norman of England, Émile Moreau of France, and Benjamin Strong of the United States, faced, Liaquat Ahamed provides an arresting account in *Lords of Finance - The Bankers Who Broke the World* (New York: Penguin Books,

2009). Ahamed's account was preceded by others such as John Maynard Keynes, who in 1919 wrote *The Economic Consequences of the Peace* (London: Macmillan, re-published by Skyhorse Publishing in paperback in 2007.

170. https://www.thebalance.com/world-currency-3305931

171. Through the ECB, the European Central Bank, European member states are to conform to policies such that government deficits do not exceed 3 percent of GDP, that overall government debt not exceed 60 percent of GDP, and that inflation rates are not to exceed 2 percent over the medium term. These have been more difficult to achieve as the number of member states has expanded to its current 27. https://www.ecb.europa.eu/mopo/html/index.en.html

172. When the United States became independent from Great Britain in 1783, raising funds to operate government depended largely on tariffs on international trade. By the end of the 19th century, dependence on tariff revenues went into decline as governments found alternative ways of raising funds, notably through excise and sales taxes. Then, in the 20th century, Congress adopted legislation to enact income taxes and which became law with the passage of the 16th amendment on February 3, 1913.

173. China was one of the five countries to be granted a permanent seat on the UN Security Council when it was created in 1945. At the time, China was governed by the nationalist group under Chiang Kai Shek (1887–1975), but whose government was overthrown following a civil war with Communists led by Mao Tse Tung (1893–1976) in 1949. For years thereafter, the United States refused to recognize the government in Beijing, and maintained that the nationalist government, then exiled to Taiwan, was the legitimate government of China. This also changed when Richard Nixon made an historic trip to China in 1971, resulting in an agreement that recognized the Communist regime in Beijing as the legitimate government of China. In turn, the Chinese government adopted a one-country two-system model of governance in which it claimed that Taiwan and Hong Kong were part of China but that they could provide their own system of governance. This changed further with the retrocession of Hong Kong to mainland China in 1997, and which since

then has been a point of contention as to whether Hong Kong's constitutional government would be recognized by Beijing.

174. Daniel Chiquiar, Jesus Cañas, Armando Aguirre, and Alfonso Cebreros, "Mexico's higher Costs Under USMCA May Potentially Offset Gains from China-Related Trade Spurt with U.S." Federal Reserve Bank of Dallas, *Southwest Economy*, First Quarter 2020, pp. 3–6.

175. Trump's efforts to create jobs in coal-producing states have not offset the shift from coal to alternative sources of energy, especially in electric utilities, the major consumer of coal. https://www.cnbc.com/2019/10/08/trumps-pledge-to-save-us-coal-is-failing-leaving-wyoming-in-crisis.html

176. These comparisons are based on the World Bank's Development Indicators database.

177. Arnold Harberger (1924–), offered an assessment of the U.S. economy years ago, based on the underlying elasticities of demand for goods and services. His conclusion was that the U.S. is quite competitive and that the losses from monopoly amounted to no more than .1 percent of GDP. Arnold C. Harberger (1954), "Monopoly and Resource Allocation", *The American Economic Review*, 44:2 (May), pp. 77–87. Harberger's article provoked a debate over technical and allocative efficiency, a key response was given by Harvey Leibenstein (1966), in "Allocative Efficiency vs. 'X-Efficiency'", *The American Economic Review* 56:3 (June), pp. 392–415.

178. One of the oldest asset valuation measures is the Sharpe ratio. It defines the additional return to an asset in proportion to an increase in the level of risk. It is calculated by subtracting the rate of return of a risk-free asset (as in U.S. Treasury bills) from the average rate of return of a fund's portfolio. This is then divided by the standard deviation of the fund's returns. The higher the Sharpe ratio, the better the portfolio is delivering lower-risk returns. As with the Fame and French models, it operates independently of an investor's tolerance for risk. To adjust for this difference in attitude, Pension manager Frank Sortino came up with a ratio that subtracts the rate of return of a risk-free asset from the risker asset, but divided the resulting amount by the riskier asset's downside deviation, thus accounting for an investor's rate of return

goal. Susanne McGee, "4 Different Ways to Think About Risk", *The Wall Street Journal*, May 4, 2020, P.R1.

179. Paul Cootner, Editor (1969, 1967, 1964). *The Random Character of Stock Market Prices* (Cambridge, Massachusetts: MIT Press).

180. The Black-Sholes model for the price of a call option, that is, the right to buy an asset at a future price, can be expressed as:

$$C = S_t N(d_1) - Ke^{-rt} N(d_2)$$

where:

$$d_1 = \frac{ln\dfrac{S_t}{K} + \left(r + \dfrac{\sigma_v^2}{2}\right)t}{\sigma_s \sqrt{t}}$$

and

$$d_2 = d_1 - \sigma_s \sqrt{t}$$

where:

C = Call option price

S = Current stock (or other underlying)

K = Strike price

r = Risk-free interest rate

t = Time to maturity

N = A normal distribution

181. The banks included: Bankers Trust, Barclays, Chase Manhattan Bank, Crédit Agricole, Credit Suisse First Boston, Deutsche Bank, Goldman Sachs, JP Morgan, Merrill Lynch, Morgan Stanley, Paribas, Salomon Smith Barney, Société Générale, and UBS. Roger Lowenstein, a writer for the Wall Street Journal wrote an account, *When Genius Failed: The Rise and Fall of Long-Term Capital Management* (New York: Random House, 2000). The story of option price contracts and LTCM was the subject of an early 2000 NOVA PBS documentary, The Trillion Dollar Bet, the title being extracted from the fact that when LTCM approached bankruptcy, if all contracts were cashed in at once, the losses would amount to a trillion dollars, the size of the U.S. federal

government budget at the time, and which led many to conclude that when firms are too big to fail, government will bail them out.

182. Peter Wallison, of the American Enterprise Institute, has argued regularly that Fannie Mae and Freddie Mac should be phased out of the housing market for the excess risk they impose on taxpayers. As an example, see Peter J. Allison (2009), "The Price for Fannie and Freddie Keeps Going Up", *The Wall Street Journal*, December 29, 2009, and "Moving Beyond Fannie and Freddie", *The Wall Street Journal*, January 3, 2011.

183. Andrew Ross Sorkin (2009). *Too Big to Fail – The inside story of how Wall Street and Washington fought to save the financial system and themselves.* (New York: Viking Penguin Books).

184. David A. Moss (2002). *When All Else Fails: Government as the Ultimate Risk Manager* (Cambridge, Massachusetts: Harvard University Press).

185. Dodd-Frank also included the creation of the Consumer Financial Protection Bureau, whose principal function has to been to impose clarity in credit contracts in order to avoid hidden costs and risks faced by consumers. https://www.govinfo.gov/content/pkg/PLAW-111publ203/pdf/PLAW-111publ203.pdf. Massachusetts Senator Elizabeth Warren led the effort to create the CFPB.

186. So named after former Federal Reserve Board Chair Paul Volcker, the rule was established in response to the financial reforms of the late 1990s and early 2000's that essentially removed the distinction between commercial and investment banks. Unlike commercial banks, investment banks always have been authorized to hold stocks while lending to firms. When the financial crisis of 2008 unfolded, many investment banks merged with commercial banks so that they could qualify for credit services such as the discount rate and the federal funds rate, thus enlarging the scope of risk exposure from the enlarged scope of financial institutions. The Volcker rule was designed to restore some of the distinctions that had operated in the former Glass-Steagall Act of 1933. Glass-Steagall was created to reduce taxpayer responsibility to banking risk and remained in force until passage of the Gramm-Leach-Bliley Act of 1999.

187. Alan Rappeport and Emily Flitter, "Congress Approves First Big Dodd-Frank Rollback", *The New York Times*, May 18, 2018.

188. Calculations based on a simulation model that can be downloaded: https://msuweb.montclair.edu/%7elebelp/ApplicationModules.html/Pension Systems.xls

189. Robert Shiller, who wrote a telling account on how markets can become speculative and inefficient in his 2000 book, *Irrational Exuberance*, has argued that derivative contracts should be used to hedge against not just individual stocks, but stock indices as well as the GDP itself, among other possibilities. The point is that with more hedging contracts, we wind up with greater transparency, and thus less risk overall. Robert Shiller (2000). *Irrational Exuberance* (Princeton, New Jersey: Princeton University Press). In 1993, Shiller had written *Macro Markets: Creating Institutions for Managing Society's Largest Economic Risks* (New York: Oxford University Press, 2003, 1999, 1998, 1993) in which he recommended creating derivative based insurance markets for macro institutions all the way up to the GDP and global climate. These recommendations were updated in *The New Financial Order: Risk in the 21st* Century (Princeton, New Jersey: Princeton University Press, 2003).

190. Baruch Fischoff, et al., (1981), *Acceptable Risk* (Cambridge, U.K.: Cambridge University Press).

191. https://www.livescience.com/65304-smallpox.html

192. The Center for Disease Control, or CDC, maintains survey data by the National Center for Health Statistics, from which these comparisons have been drawn. https://www.cdc.gov/nchs/

193. China's number of cases per million population as of May 5, 2020 stood at 115.28, in comparison to a world average of 480.49, and 3,740.4 in the United States. Chinese authorities have argued that their low infection and fatality rates are due to the timely adoption of quarantine measures in the country, and although the country has experienced a significant loss in economic output, they have used the low figures as justification for the measures and of the success they have achieved as a result. What is clear is that threats to impose sanctions on China are not likely to lead to greater information as to the epidemiology of the coronavirus in the country.

194. There are any number of works on political legitimacy, often with an emphasis on political philosophy rather than through the lens of economic and neuroscience insights we put forth here. Examples include: Jack Knights and Melissa Schwartzberg, Editors (2019), *Political Legitimacy: NOMOS LXI (NOMOS – American Society for Political and Legal Philosophy.* (New York: New York University Press); Rodney Barker (1990). *Political Legitimacy and the State* (New York: Oxford University Press); Muthiah Alagappa, editor (1995) *Political Legitimacy in Southeast Asia.* (Stanford, California: Stanford University Press); Lanxin Xiang (2019). *The Quest for Legitimacy in Chinese Politics: A New Interpretation* (London: Routledge); Seymour Martin Lipset (1983) *Political Man: The Social Bases of Politics*, 2nd ed. (London: Heinemann Publishing)

195. The importance of institutions that support electoral democracy was emphasized by Fareed Zakaria in a 1997 essay in Foreign Affairs, and later issued in a book, *The Future of Freedom: Illiberal Democracy at Home and Abroad* (New York: W.W. Norton Publishing, 2007, 2003).

196. The Apportionment Act of August 8, 1911, and as amended on March 4, 1913, set the number of seats in the House of Representatives at 435.

197. These simulations can be derived from a spreadsheet file posted on my website: https://msuweb.montclair.edu/~lebelp/PointVotingSystems.xlsx

198. One we do not take up here is the expand the size of Congress to bring the ratio of citizens to elected members of the House something closer to what it was in 1910. Another is to end the two Senate seats per state standard to something closer to proportional representation in the House. Neither has been a subject of major public debate in recent elections, which means that proportionality aside, there is a continuing dilution of representation based on the 1910 rule.

199. Since 1945, voter participation rates have averaged 63.42 percent in the United States, in comparison to 66.2 percent in Africa, 69.9 percent in Central and Latin America, 72.7 percent in the U.K., and 80.64 percent in the core states that would make up the European Union. Source data from which

these mean values have been compiled can be found at: https://www.idea.int/data-tools/vt-advanced-search?region=&question=

200. Voter participation rates in Presidential and Congressional primary elections are even lower than for general elections, ranging from a low around 10 percent in Congressional elections, to 30 percent in Presidential primaries.

201. Max Weber (1918), "Politics as a Vocation", in H.H. Gerth and C. Wright Mills, editors, *From Max Weber: Essays in Sociology* (London: Routledge, 1991).

202. https://news.gallup.com/poll/5392/trust-government.aspx;https://www.pewresearch.org/chart/public-trust-in-government-near-historic-lows/

203. Gallup polls undertaken between 1958 and 2019 of Americans who think the United Nations is doing a good job display an average of 39.4 percent.

204. Frank P. Ramsey (1928). "A Mathematical Theory of Saving," *Economic Journal* 38:4, pp. 543–559.

205. https://www.govinfo.gov/app/collection/budget/2021

206. https://web.stanford.edu/~johntayl/Onlinepaperscombinedbyyear/1993/Discretion_versus_Policy_Rules_in_Practice.pdf

207. Pub.L.107–155, 116 Stat.81, March 27, 2002.

REFERENCES

Economics

Aaron, Henry, and Martin McGuire (1970). "Public Goods and Income Distribution" *Econometrica* 38:6 (November), pp. 907–920.

Abreu, Dilip, and Markus K. Brunnermeier (2003). "Bubbles and Crashes", *Econometrica* 71:1 (January), pp. 173–204.

Acemoglu, Daron, and James A. Robinson (2012). *Why Nations Fail – The Origins of Power, Prosperity, and Poverty.* (New York: Crown Publishing Group for Random House, Inc.)

Adelegan, O. Janet, and Bozena Radzewics-Bak (2009). "What Determines Bond Market Development in Sub-Saharan Africa?", WP/09/213. (Washington, D.C.: International Monetary Fund Working Paper, September), pp. 1–32.

Agbeyegbe, Terence, Janet G. Stotsky, and Asegedech WoldeMariam (2004). "Trade Liberalization, Exchange Rate Changes, and Tax Revenue in Sub-Saharan Africa". WP/04/178 (Washington, D.C.: International Monetary Fund), pp. 1–31.

Aghion, Philippe and Peter Howitt (2005). "Appropriate Growth Policy: A Unifying Framework" EEA 20th Annual Congress (August 25), pp. 2–47.

Agur, Itai, Anil Ari, Giovanni Del'Ariccia (2019). "Designing Central Bank Digital Currencies", WP/19/252. (Washington, D.C.: International Monetary Fund Working Paper).

Akerlof, George A. (1970). "The Market for Lemons" *Quarterly Journal of Economics* 84:3 (August), pp. 388–500.

Alichi, Ali (2008). "A Model of Sovereign Debt in Democracies", WP/08/152. (Washington D.C.: International Monetary Fund, June).

Allen, Franklin, and Douglas Gale (2004). "Financial Intermediaries and Markets", *Econometrica 72:4 (July)*, pp. 1023–1061.

Allen, Franklin, and Douglas Gale (2000). "Financial Contagion", *Journal of Political Economy* 108:1 (February), pp. 1–33.

Allen, Franklin, and Douglas Gale (1998). "Bubbles and Crises", *The Economic Journal* 110 (January), pp. 236–255.

Amin, Samir (1974). *Accumulation on a World Scale – A Critique of the Theory of Underdevelopment.* (New York: Monthly Review Press).

Arcand, Jean-Louis (2015). "Weak Governments and Preferential Trade Agreements", WP Graduate Institute of International and Development Studies.

Arrow, Kenneth J. and Robert C. Lind (1970). "Uncertainty and the Evaluation of Public Investment Decisions", *American Economic Review* 60:3 (June), pp. 364–378.

Arrow, Kenneth J. (1972, 1963, 1951). *Social Choice and Individual Values.* (New Haven, Connecticut: The Cowles Foundation, Yale University Press).

Arthur, Brian (1989). "Competing Technologies, Increasing Returns, and Lock-In by Historical Events", *Economic Journal* 99:394 (March), pp. 116–131.

Atkinson, Anthony B. (1987). "On the Measurement of Poverty", *Econometrica* 55:4 (July), pp. 749–764.

Atkinson, Anthony B. (1970). "On the Measurement of Inequality", *Journal of Economic Theory* 2, pp. 244–263.

Avery, Christopher and Peter Zemsky (1998). "Multidimensional Uncertainty and Herd Behavior in Financial Markets", *American Economic Review* 88:4 (September), pp. 724–748.

Bagwhati, Jagdish (2005, 2004). *In Defense of Globalization.* (New York: Council on Foreign Relations, Oxford University Press).

Baldacci, Emanuele, Sanjeev Gupta, and Amine Mati (2008). "Is it (Still) Mostly Fiscal? Determinants of Sovereign Spreads in Emerging Markets". WP/08/259. (Washington, D.C.: International Monetary Fund Working Paper, November).

Baltussen, Guido, Thierry Post, and Pim van Vliet (2006). "Violations of Cumulative Prospect Theory in Mixed Gambles with Moderate Probabilities", *Management Science* 52:8 (August), pp. 1288–1290.

Banerjee, Abhijit V. (1992). "A Simple Model of Herd Behavior", *Quarterly Journal of Economics* 101:3 (August), pp. 797–817.

Barberis, Nicholas, Ming Huang, Tano Santos (2001). "Prospect Theory and Asset Prices", The *Quarterly Journal of Economics* 116:1 (February), pp. 1–53.

Barro, Robert J. (1998). *Getting It Right – Markets and Choices in a Free Society.* (Cambridge, Massachusetts: MIT Press).

Barro, Robert J. (1998, 1997). *Determinants of Economic Growth – A Cross-Country Empirical Study.* (Cambridge, Massachusetts: MIT Press).

Barsky, Robert B., and J. Bradford De Long (1993). "Why Does the Stock Market Fluctuate? *Quarterly Journal of Economics* 108:2 (May), pp. 291–311.

Barth, James R., Gerard Caprio, Jr., and Ross Levine (2001). "Banking Systems Around the Globe Do Regulation and Ownership Affect Performance and Stability?" (Cambridge, Mass.: NBER), pp. 1–67.

Barzel, Yoram (1997, 1989) *Economic Analysis of Property Rights.* (New York: Cambridge University Press).

Bator, Francis M. (19580. "The Anatomy of Market Failure", *Quarterly Journal of Economics* 72:3 (August), pp. 351–379.

Baumol, William, John C. Panzar, and Robert D. Willig (1982). *Contestable Markets and the Theory of Industry Structure* (New York: Harcourt, Brace, and Jovanovich).

Baumol, William (1969, 1965). *Welfare Economics and the Theory of the State.* (Cambridge, Massachusetts: Harvard University Press).

Bayoumi, Tamim, and Fernando M. Gonçalves (2007). "Government for the People: On the Determinants of the Size of U.S. Government", *IMF WP/07/289* (Washington, D.C.: IMF, December)

Bell, Daniel and Irving Kristol, editors (1981). *The Crisis in Economic Theory.* (New York: Harper Colophon Books for Basic Books).

Bergemann, Dirk and Juuso Välimäki (2019). "Dynamic Mechanism Design: An Introduction", *Journal of Economic Literature* 57:2, pp. 235–274.

Birkeland, Kathryn, and Edward C. Prescott (2006). "On the Needed Quantity of Government Debt", Working Paper 648 (Minneapolis: Federal Reserve Bank of Minneapolis, December).

Bernanke, Ben S., Timothy F. Geithner, and Henry M. Paulson, Jr. (2019). *Firefighting: The Financial Crisis and Its Lessons* (New York: Penguin Books).

Bernouilli, Daniel (1954, 1738). "Exposition of a New Theory on the Measurement of Risk", *Econometrica* 22:1 (January), pp. 23–36.

Bikhchandani, Sushil, David Hirshleifer, and Ivo Welch (1992). "A Theory of Fads, Fashion, Custom, and Cultural Change in Informational Cascades", *The Journal of Political Economy* 100:5 (October), pp. 992–1026.

Binici, Mahir, Michael Hutchison, and Martin Schindler (2009). "Controlling Capital? Legal Restrictions and the Asset Composition of International Financial Flows". WP/09/208. (Washington, D.C.: International Monetary Fund).

Bleichrodt, Han, Jose Luis Pinto, and Peter P. Wakker (2001), "Making Descriptive Ue of Prospect Theory to Improve the Prescriptive Use of Expected Utility", *Management Science* 47:11 (November), pp. 1498–1514.

Bluhm, Christian, and Ludger Overbeck (2004). "Semi-analytic Approaches to Collateralized Debt Obligation Modelling", Banca Monte dei Paschi di Siena, Economic Notes 33:2, pp. 233–255.

Board of Governors, Federal Reserve System (2010). Proposed Rules for Consumer Protection. (Washington, D.C.: Board of Governors, Federal Reserve System)

Bolton, Patrick, and Howard Rosenthal (2002). "Political Intervention in Debt Contracts", *Journal of Political Economy* 110:5 (October), pp. 1103–1134.

Borensztein Eduardo, Olivier Jeanne, and Damiano Sandri (2009). "Macro-Hedging for Commodity Exporters" WP/09/229. (Washington, D.C.: International Monetary Fund Working Paper, October), pp. 1–29.

Bowles, Samuel (2012). "Economic Incentives and Social Preferences: Substitutes or Complements?" *Journal of Economic Literature* 50:2, pp. 368–425.

Bowles, Samuel (1998). "Endogenous Preferences: The Cultural Consequences of Markets and Other Economic Institutions", *Journal of Economic Literature*, XXXVI (March), pp. 75–111.

Breton, Albert (1974). *The Economic Theory of Representative Government.* (Chicago: Aldine Publishing Company).

Brown, Jeffrey R., and Austan Goolsbee (2002). "Does the Internet Make Markets More Competitive? Evidence from the Life Insurance Industry", *Journal of Political Economy* 110:3 (June), pp. 481–507.

Bulow, Jeremy, and Paul Klemperer (1994). "Rational Frenzies and Crashes" *The Journal of Political Economy* 102:1 (February), pp. 1–23.

Business Roundtable (2019). "Statement on the Purpose of a Corporation", The Wall Street Journal (August 19), pp. A6-A7.

Camerer, Colin (1989). "Bubbles and Fads in Asset Prices", *Journal of Economic Surveys* 3:3.

Campbell, John Y., Peter A. Diamond, and John B. Shoven (2001). "Estimating the Real Rate of Return on Stocks Over the Long Term". (Washington, D.C.: Social Security Advisory Board), pp. 1–46.

Campbell, John Y. and Albert S. Kyle (1993). "Smart Money Noise Trading and Stock Price Behaviour" *Review of Economic Studies* 60 (May), pp. 1–33.

Cantor, Richard, and Frank Packer (1996). "Determinants and Impact of Sovereign Credit Ratings", *FRBNY Economic Policy Review* (October), pp. 37–53.

Caouette, John B., Edward I. Altman, Paul Narayanan, and Robert Nimmo (2008). *Managing Credit Risk: The Great Challenge for the Global Financial Markets,* 2nd edition. (New York: John Wiley and Sons).

Caplin, Andres and John Leahy (2004). "The Social Discount Rate", *Journal of Political Economy* 112:6, pp. 1257–1268.

Cartwright, Edward (2011). *Behavioral Economics.* (New York: Routledge, Taylor and Francis Group).

Cassidy, John (2010, 2009). *How Markets Fail – The Logic of Economic Calamities.* (New York: Picador Books for Farrar, Straus, and Giroux).

Cecchetti, Stephen, Hans Genberg, and Sushil Wadhwani (2002). "Asset Prices in a Flexible Inflation Targeting Framework", NBER Working Paper 8970 (Cambridge, Massachusetts: NBER, June).

Çelen, Bogaçhan, and Shachar Kariv (2004). "Distinguishing Informational Cascades from Herd Behavior in the Laboratory", *American Economic Review* 91:3 (June), pp. 484–498.

Chan-Lau, Jorge A, and Amadou N.R. Sy (2006). "Distance-to-Default in Banking: A Bridge Too Far?" WP/06/215. (Washington, D.C.: International Monetary Fund Working Paper, September), pp. 1–19.

Chan-Lau, Jorge A, (2006). "Market-Based Estimation of Default Probabilities and Its Application to Financial market Surveillance", *IMF Working Paper 06/104* (International Monetary Fund: April), pp. 1–17).

Chan-Lau, Jorge A. (2004). "Equity Prices, Credit Default Swaps, and Bond Spreads in Emerging Markets WP/04/27 (Washington, D.C.: International Monetary Fund Working Paper, February), pp. 1–30.

Chiappori, Pierre-André and Bernard Salanié (2000). "Testing for Asymmetric Information in Insurance Markets", *Journal of Political Economy* 108:1 (February), pp. 56–78.

Cho, Man (1996). "House Price Dynamics: A Survey of Theoretical and Empirical Issues", *Journal of Housing Research* 7:2, pp. 145–172.

Cipriani, Marco, and Antonio Guarino (2005). "Herd Behavior in a Laboratory Financial Market", *American Economic Review* 95:5 (December), pp. 1427–1443.

Coase, R. H. (1937). "The Nature of the Firm", *Economica*, New Series 4:16 (November), pp. 386–405.

Cochrane, John H. (1999). "New Facts in Finance", NBER WP7169. (Cambridge, Massachusetts: NBER (June), pp. 1–42.

Cozzi, Guido (1998). "Culture as a Bubble", *The Journal of Political Economy* 106:2 (April), pp. 376–394.

Cuevas, Alfredo, Maria Gonzalez, Davide Lombardo, and Arnoldo Lopez-Marmolejo (2008). "Pension Privatization and Country Risk", WP/08/195. (Washington, D.C.: International Monetary Fund).

Das, Udaibir S., Marc Quintyn, and Kina Chenard (2004). WP/04/89 (Washington, D.C.: International Monetary Fund Working Paper, May).

Debotari, Aliona (2009). "Fiscal Risks: Sources, Disclosure, and Management" (Washington, D.C.: International Monetary Fund Fiscal Affairs Department).

Debotari, Aliona (2008). "Contingent Liabilities: Issues and Practice". WP/08/245. (Washington, D.C.: International Monetary Fund Working Paper, October).

De Grauwe, Paul (2017). *The Limits of the Market – The Pendulum Between Government and the Market.* (New York: Oxford University Press).

De Meza, David, and David Webb (2000). "Does credit rationing imply insufficient lending?" *Journal of Public Economics* 78, pp. 215–234.

Dercon, Stefan, and Pramila Krishnan (2000). "In Sickness and in Health: Risk Sharing within Households in rural Ethiopia". *Journal of Political Economy* 108:4 (August), pp. 688–727.

De Soto, Hernando (2000). *The Mystery of Capital – Why Capitalism Triumphs in the West and Fails Everywhere Else.* (New York: Basic Books).

Detken, Carsten, and Frank Smets (2004). "Asset Price Booms and Monetary Policy", WP 364, European Central Bank (May),

Dhami, Sanjit and Ali al-Nowaihi (2007). "Why do People Pay Taxes? Prospect Theory vs. Expected Utility Theory", *Journal Economic Behavior and Organization* 64.

Dodd-Frank Wall Street Reform and Consumer Protection Act, PL 111–203 (2018-05-24) Washington, D.C.: U.S. Government Printing Office.

Doherty, Neil and Kent Smetters (2005). "Moral Hazard in Reinsurance Markets", *Journal of Risk and Insurance* (September 1).

Downs Anthony (1957). "An Economic Theory of Political Action in a Democracy", *The Journal of Political Economy* 65:2 (April), 135–150.

Dufwenberg, Martin, Tobias Lindqvist, and Evan Moore (2005). "Bubbles and Experience: An Experiment" *American Economic Review* 95:5 (December), pp. 1731–1737.

Duttagupta, Rupa, and Paul Cashing (2008). "The Anatomy of Banking Crises", *IMF Working Paper 08/93* (International Monetary Fund: April), pp. 1–37.

Easterly, William (2002, 2001). *The Elusive Quest for Growth – Economists' Adventures and Misadventures in the Tropics.* (Cambridge, Massachusetts: MIT Press).

Edison, Hali J., Pongsak Luangaram, and Marcus Miller (1998). "Asset Bubbles, Domino Effects and 'Lifeboats': Elements of the East Asian Crisis", CSGR WP No 05/98 (Coventry, U.K.: Center for the Study of Globalisation and Regionalisation, February), pp. 1–31.

Eichengreen, Barry (2008). "Anatomy of the financial crisis", VOX (September).

Ellman, Michael (1979). *Socialist Planning.* (New York: Cambridge University Press).

Emmanuel, Arghiri (1972, 1969). *Unequal Exchange – A Study of the Imperialism of Trade.* (New York: Monthly Review Press).

Emmons, William R., Ana H. Kent, and Lowell R. Ricketts (2019). "Is College Still Worth It? The New Calculus of Falling Returns". (St. Louis: Federal Reserve Bank of St. Louis Review, Q4), pp. 297–329.

Engel, Charles (2009). "Exchange Rate Policies". *Federal Reserve Bank of Dallas Working Paper Number 8* (Dallas: Federal Reserve Bank, November), pp. 1–27.

Flood, Robert P., Nancy P. Marion, and Akito Matsumoto (2009). "International Risk Sharing During the Globalization Era". WP/09/209. (Washington, D.C.: International Monetary Fund).

Flood, Robert P., and Robert J. Hodrick (1990). "On Testing for Speculative Bubbles", *Journal of Economic Perspectives*, 4:2, pp. 85–101.

Frederick, Shane, George Loewenstein Ted O'Donoghue (2002). "Time Discounting and Time Preference: A Critical Review" *Journal of Economic Literature* (40:2, June), 351–401.

Friedman, Milton and Rose (1980, 1979). *Free to Choose – A Personal Statement.* (New York: Avon Books)

Friedman, Milton (1970, 1962). *Capitalism and Freedom.* (Chicago: University of Chicago Press).

Friedman, Milton, and Leonard J. Savage (1948). "The Utility Analysis of Choices Involving Risk", *The Journal of Political Economy* 56:4 (August), pp. 279–304.

Fukui, Toshihiko (1997). "The Measurement of Aggregate Market Risk", (Basle, Switzerland: Bank for International Settlements, November).

Garber, Peter M. (1990). "Famous First Bubbles", *Journal of Economic Perspectives*, 4:2, pp. 35–54.

Gasha, J. Ciancarlo and R. Armando Morales (2004). *Identifying Threshold Effects in credit Risk Stress Testing,* IMF Working Paper WP/04/150. (Washington, D.C.: International Monetary Fund, August).

Glen, Jack, and Ajit Singh (2004). "Corporate Governance, Competition and Finance: Re-Thinking Lessons from the Asian Crisis" (Cambridge, U.K.: University of Cambridge Center for Business Research, Working Paper No. 288).

Godelier, Maurice (1972, 1966). *Rationality and Irrationality in Economics* (New York: Monthly Review Press).

González-Hermosillo, Brenda and Heiko Hesse (2009). "Global Market Conditions and Systemic Risk", WP/09/230. (Washington, D.C.: International Monetary Fund Working Paper, October), pp. 1–22.

Greenspan, Alan (2007). "The Roots of the Mortgage Crisis", *The Wall Street Journal.*

Groves, Theodore, and John Ledyard (1977). "Optimal Allocation of Public Goods: A Solution to the 'Free Rider' Problem" *Econometrica* 45:4 (May), pp. 783–809.

Gunther, Jeffery (2007). "Hedge Fund Investors More Rational Than Rash", *Economic Letter,* 2:8 (Federal Reserve Bank of Dallas, August).

Gürkaynak, Refet S. (2005). "Econometric Tests of Asset Price Bubbles: Taking Stock", Board of Governors, Federal Reserve System Staff Working Paper (January).

Harris, Milton, and Robert M. Townsend (1981). "Resource Allocation Under Asymmetric Information", *Econometrica* 49:1 (January), pp. 33–64.

Hauner, David and Annette Kyobe (1998). "Determinants of Government Efficiency", Working Paper 2008-228 (Washington, D.C.: IMF).

Hayek, Friedrich A. (1980, 1948). *Individualism and Economic Order.* (Chicago: University of Chicago Press).

Hayek, Friedrich A. (1975, 1944). *The Road to Serfdom.* (Chicago: University of Chicago Press).

Hayek, Friedrich A. (1937). "Economics and Knowledge" *Economica,* New Series 4:13 (February), pp. 33–54.

Hellmann, Thomas F., Kevin C. Murdock, and Joseph E. Stiglitz (2000). "Liberalization, Moral Hazard in Banking, and Prudential Regulation: Are Capital Requirements Enough?" *American Economic Review* 90:1 (March), pp. 147–165.

Honda, Jiro (2008). "Do IMF Programs Improve Economic Governance?" WP/08/114 (Washington, D.C.: International Monetary Fund).

Hoshi, Takeo and Anil K. Kashyap (2004). "Japan's Financial Crisis and Economic Stagnation", *Journal of Economic Perspectives* 18:4, pp. 3–26.

Houben, Aerdt, Jan Kakes, and Garry Schinasi (2004). "Toward a Framework for Safeguarding Financial Stability". *IMF Working Paper WP/04/101* (Washington, D.C.: International Monetary Fund, June), pp. 1–47.

Houthakker, H. S. (1957). "An International Comparison of Household Expenditure Patterns, Commemorating the Centenary of Engel's Law", *Econometrica*, 25:4 (October), pp. 532–551.

Iida, Akira (2000). "What Happened in Japan When the Bubble Crashed in the 1990s?, (Tokyo: Ministry of Finance International Seminar, April 21).

Imbs, Jean, and Paolo Mauro (2007). "Pooling Risk Among Countries", WP/07/132 (Washington, D.C.: International Monetary Fund, June).

Impavido, Gregorio, Yu-Wei Hu, and Ziaohong Li (2009). "Governance and Fund Management in the Chinese Pension System", WP/09/246. (Washington, D.C.: International Monetary Fund Working Paper, November).

Jaeger, Albert, and Ludger Schuknecht (2004). "Boom-Bust Phases in Asset Prices and Fiscal Policy Behavior", Working Paper WP2004/04/54 (Washington, D.C.: International Monetary Fund, April).

James, Christopher (1996). "RAROC Based Capital Budgeting and Performance Evaluation: A Case Study of Bank Capital Allocation", WP96–40 (Philadelphia: University of Pennsylvania, The Wharton School), pp. 1–31.

Jarrow, Robert A., Philip Protter, and Kazuhiro Shimbo (2007). "Asset Price Bubbles in Incomplete Markets", (Ithaca, New York: Cornell University, March 19), pp. 1–42.

Kahneman, Daniel and Amos Tversky (1979). "Prospect Theory: An Analysis of Decision under Risk", *Econometrica* 47:2 (March), pp. 263–292.

Kambhu, John, Scott Weidman, and Neel Krishnan (2007). "New Directions for Understanding Systemic Risk", *Economic Policy Review*, Federal Reserve Bank of New York 13:2 (November),

Kamien, Morton I. and Nancy L. Schwartz (1982). *Market Structure and* Innovation. (New York: Cambridge University Press).

Kamin, Steven H. (2002). "Identifying the Role of Moral Hazard in International Financial Markets", *International Finance Discussion Paper Number 736* (Washington, D.C.: Board of Governors, Federal Reserve System, September), 1–46.

Kaul, Inge, Isabelle Grunberg, and Marc A. Stern (1999). *Global Public Goods – International Cooperation in the 21st Century.* (New York: UNDP for Oxford University Press).

Kawai, Masahiro (2004). "Reform of the Japanese Banking System", Paper presentation, University of Michigan and Hitotsubashi University (Ann Arbor, Michigan: October 21, 2004).

Kelly, Morgan and Cormac O Gráda (2000). "Market Contagion: Evidence from the Panics of 1854 and 1857" *American Economic Review* 90:5 (December), pp. 1110–1124.

Keynes, John Maynard (1936). *The General Theory of Employment, Interest, and Money.* (New York: Harcourt, Brace, and World).

Kiff, John, Jennifer Elliott, Elias Kazarian, Jodi Scarlata, and Carolyne Spackman (2009). "Credit Derivatives: Systemic Risks and Policy Options", WP/09/254 (Washington, D.C.: International Monetary Fund).

Kiyotaki, Nobuhiro and John Moore (1997). "Credit Cycles", *Journal of Political Economy* 195:2 (April), pp. 211–248.

Kornai, János (1990). *The Road to a Free Economy – Shifting from a Socialist System, The Example of Hungary.* (New York: W.W. Norton and Company).

Kozack, Julie (2005). "Considerations in the Choice of the Appropriate Discount Rate for Evaluating Sovereign Debt Restructurings" PDP/05/9 (Washington, D.C.: International Monetary Fund, December).

Kozul-Wright, Richard, and Paul Rayment (2007). *The Resistible Rise of Market Fundamentalism.* (New York: Zed Books, for Palgrave Macmillan and St. Martin's Press).

Kruger, Mark, and Miguel Messmacher (2004). "Sovereign Debt Defaults and Financing Needs." *IMF Working Paper WP/05/53.* (Washington, D.C.: International Monetary Fund, March), 1–32.

Krugman, Paul (1998). *Development, Geography, and Economic Theory.* (Cambridge, Massachusetts: MIT Press).

Laeven, Luc, and Fabian Valencia (2008). "The Use of Blanket Guarantees in Banking Crises" WP/08/250. (Washington, D.C.: International Monetary Fund Working Paper, October).

Laffont, Jean-Jacques (1985). "On the Welfare Analysis of Rational Expectations Equilibria with Asymmetric Information." *Econometrica* 53:1 (January), pp. 1–30.

LaPerriere, Andy (2007), "No Bailout for Borrowers", *Wall Street Journal*, (December 4), p.A21.

Lavoie, Don (1985). *National Economic Planning – What is Left?* (Cambridge, Massachusetts: Ballinger Publishing Company for Harper and Row Publishers and the Cato Institute).

LeBel, Phillip (2008). "Managing Risk in Africa through Institutional Reform", *Atlantic Economic Journal* 36:2 (June), pp. 165–181.

LeBel, Phillip (2008). "The Role of Creative Innovation in Economic Growth: Some International Comparisons", *Journal of Asian Economics* (August), pp. 334–347.

LeBel, Phillip (2005). "Optimal Choices for Risk Management: The Economic Value of Institutional Reform in Globalizing Economies" Presentation at the Ninth International Conference on Global Business and Economic Development, Seoul, Korea, May 25–28, 2005)

LeBel, Phillip (2005). "Optimal Pricing of Biodiverse Natural Resources", *Journal of Development Alternatives* 24:1–2 (March-June), pp. 5–38.

LeBel, Phillip (1998). "Asset Bubbles and Moral Hazard: Evidence from Japan", Working Paper, School of Business, Montclair State University.

LeBel, Phillip (1998). "Understanding East Asia's Financial Crisis: Insights from Agency Theory" in C. Jayachandran, et al. editors, Managing Economic Liberalisation in South Asia – Directions for the 21st Century (Delhi: Macmillan India Publishers), pp. 210–231.

Leibenstein, Harvey (1966). "Allocative Efficiency vs. "X-Inefficiency". *American Economic Review*, 56:3 (June), pp. 392–415.

Leibenstein, Harvey (1950). "Bandwagon, Snob, and Veblen Effects in the Theory of Consumers' Demand", *Quarterly Journal of Economics* 64:2 (May), 183–207.

Lei, Vivian, Charles N. Noussair, Charles R. Plott (2001). "Non-speculative Bubbles in Experimental Asset Markets: Lack of Common Knowledge of Rationality vs. Actual Irrationality". *Econometrica* 69:4 (July), pp. 831–859.

Leland, Hayne E. (1978). "Optimal Risk Sharing and the Leasing of Natural Resources, with Application to Oil and Gas Leasing on the OCS", *Quarterly Journal of Economics* 92:3 (August), pp. 413–438.

Lerner, Abba (1944). *The Economics of Control – Principles of Welfare Economics.* (New York: The Macmillan Company).

LeRoy, Stephen F. (1989). "Efficient Capital Markets and Martingales", *Journal of Economic Literature* 27:4 (December), pp. 1583–1621.

Lipset, Seymour Martin (1994). "The Social Requisites of Democracy Revisited", 1993 Presidential Address, *American Sociological Review* 59 (February), pp. 1–33.

Loko, Boileau, and Mame Astou Diouf (2009). "Revisiting the Determinants of Prouctivity Growth: What's New?" WP/09/225. (Washington, D.C.: International Monetary Fund Working Paper, October), pp. 1–29.

Lopez, José A. (1997). "Regulatory Evaluation of Value-at-Risk Models", Staff Report, *Federal Reserve Bank of New York* (November), pp. 1–31.

Lu, Yinqiu and Salih Neftci (2008). "Financial Instruments to Hedge Commodity Price Risk for Developing Countries, *IMF Working Paper WP/08/6* (International Monetary Fund: January), 1–20.

Lucas, Robert E., Jr. (1990). "Why Doesn't Capital Flow from Rich to Poor Countries?" *American Economic Review* 80:2 (May), pp. 92–96.

MacLeod, W. Bentley (2007). "Can Contract Theory Explain Social Preferences?" (Department of Economics, Columbia University).

Magdoff, Harry (1969, 1966). *The Age of Imperialism – The Economics of U.S. Foreign Policy.* (New York: Monthly Review Press).

Makin, John H. (2008). "Risk and Systemic Risk", (Washington, D.C.: American Enterprise Institute for Public Policy Research).

Manski, Charles F. (2004), "Measuring Expectations", *Econometrica* 72:5, pp. 1329–1376.

McCarthy, Nancy, with Celine Dutilly-Diane, Boureima Drabo, Abdul Kamara, and Jean-Paul Vanderlinden (2004). "Managing Resources in Erratic Environments – An Analysis of Pastoralist Systems in Ethiopia, Niger, and Burkina Faso" Research Report 135. (Washington, D.C.: International Food Policy Research Institute), pp. 1–89.

Mellor, John W., and Bruce F. Johnston (1984). "The World Food Equation: Inter-relations Among Development, Employment, and Food Consumption". *Journal of Economic Literature* XXII (June), pp. 531–574.

Merton, Robert C. (1996). "Applications of Option Pricing Theory: Twenty-Five Years Later", *American Economic Review* 88:3 (June), pp. 323–349.

Michalopoulos, Stelios, and Elias Papaioannou (2016). "The Long-Run Effects of the Scramble for Africa", *American Economic* Review 106:7 (July), pp. 1802–1848.

Mirestean, Alin, and Charalambos Tsangarides (2009). "Growth Determinants Revisited" WP/09/268 (Washington, D.C.: International Monetary Fund Working Paper, December).

Monge-Naranjo, Alexander, Juan M.Sánchez, Raül Santaeulàtia-Llopis and Faisal Sohail (2019). "Should Capital Flow from Rich to Poor Countries", FRB St. Louis Review (Q4), pp. 277–297).

Moore, Frederick T. (1959). "Economies of Scale: Some Statistical Evidence", *Quarterly Journal of Economics* 73:2, pp. 232–245.

Mora, Nada (2005). "The Effect of Bank Credit on Asset Prices: Evidence from the Japanese Real Estate Boom during the 1980s", Working Paper (Beirut: American University of Beirut, July 25).

Morgan, Donald P. Benjamin Iverson, and Matthew Botsch (2008). "Seismic Effects of the Bankruptcy Reform", FRBNY Staff Report No. 358. (New York: Federal Reserve Bank of New York, November), pp. 1–30.

Morgan, Donald P. (2002). "Rating Banks: Risk and Uncertainty in an Opaque Industry", *American Economic Review* 92:4 (September), pp. 874–888.

Moss, David A. (2002). *When All Else Fails – Government as the Ultimate Risk Manager.* (Cambridge, Massachusetts: Harvard University Press).

Myrdal, Gunnar (1969, 1954, 1929). *The Political Element in the Development of Economic Theory*. (New York: Clarion Books for Simon and Schuster).

Niskanen, William A. (2003). *Autocratic, Democratic, and Optimal Government – Fiscal Choices and Economic Outcomes*. (Northampton, Massachusetts: The Locke Institute for Edward Elgar Publishing).

Nkurunziza, Janvier D., and Robert H. Bates (2003). "Political Institutions and Economic Growth in Africa" (Cambridge, Massachusetts; Harvard University Center for International Development Working Paper No. 098, March).

Olson, Mancur (1977, 1965). *The Logic of Collective Action – Public Goods and the Theory of Groups*. (Cambridge, Massachusetts: Harvard University Press).

Nash, John F., Jr. (1950). "The Bargaining Problem". *Econometrica* 18:2 (April), pp. 155–162.

Nier, Erlend W. (2009). "Financial Stability Frameworks and the Role of Central Banks: Lessons From the Crisis" WP/09/70 (Washington, D.C.: International Monetary Fund Working Paper, April), 1–66.

Ostrom, Elinor (1998). "A Behavioral Approach to the Rational Choice Theory of Collective Action: Presidential Address, American Political Science Association, 1997" *American Political Science Review* 92:1 (March), pp. 1–22.

Page, William H., and John E. Lopatka (1997). "Network Externalities", in the *Encyclopedia of Law and Economics*.

Pattanaik, Prasanta K., and Bezalel Peleg (1986). "Distribution of Power under Stochastic Social Choice Rules". *Econometrica* 54:4 (July), pp. 909–922.

Pew Research Center for the People and the Press (2009). *America's Place in the World, 2009*. (Washington, D.C.: Council on Foreign Relations and the Pew Research Center).

Phlips, Louis (1988). *The Economics of Imperfect Information*. (New York: Cambridge University Press).

Piketty, Thomas (2014). *Inequality in the Twenty-First Century*. (Cambridge, Massachusetts: Harvard University Press).

Pindyck, Robert S., and Julio J. Rotemberg (1993). "The Comovement of Stock Prices", *Quarterly Journal of Economics* 108:4 (November), pp. 1073–1104.

Plott, Charles R. (1973). "Path Independence, Rationality, and Social Choice", *Econometrica* 41:6 (November), pp. 1075–1091.

Pollock, Alex J. (2011). "On Housing, There Will Be More Lean Years Ahead", WSJ Opinion (May 12),

Pollock, Alex J. (2008). "The Human Foundations of Financial Risk", AEI paper (May).

Pollock, Alex J. (2007). "The Subprime Bust and the One-Page Mortgage Disclosure", AEI paper (November 28)

Pollock, Alex J. (2005). "End the Government-Sponsored Cartel in Credit Ratings", AEI paper (January).

Porter, Michael E. (2004). "Competition in Japan", 18:1, *Journal of Economic Perspectives* 18:1 (Winter), pp. 27–50.

Posen, Adam (2006). "Why Central Banks Should Not Burst Bubbles", WP06–1 (Washington, D.C.: Institute of International Economics).

Posen, Adam (2003). "It Takes More than a Bubble to Become Japan". (Washington, D.C.: Institute of International Economics, October).

Posner, Richard A. (1983, 1981). *The Economics of Justice.* (Cambridge, Massachusetts: Harvard University Press)

Powell, Andrew (1991). "Commodity and Developing Country Terms of Trade: What Does the Long Run Show?" *The Economic Journal* 101:409 (November), pp. 1485–1496.

Pratt, John W. (1964). "Risk Aversion in the Small and in the Large", *Econometrica* 32:1 (April), pp. 122–136.

Rabin, Matthew, and Richard H. Thaler (2001). "Anomalies – Risk Aversion", *Journal of Economic Perspectives* 15:1 (Winter), pp. 219–232.

Reynolds Lloyd G. (1983). "The Spread of Economic Growth to the Third World: 1850–1980" *Journal of Economic Literature* XXI (September), pp. 941–980.

Ricardo, David (1965, 1817). *The Principles of Political Economy and Taxation.* (London: Everyman's Library for J.A. Dent & Sons, Ltd).

Rigotti, Luca, and Chris Shannon (2005). "Uncertainty and Risk in Financial Markets", Econometrica 73:1 (January), pp. 203–243.

Roach, Shaun K. (2008). "Commodities and the Market Price of Risk", WP/08/221 (Washington, D.C.: International Monetary Fund, September), pp. 1–23.

Robson, Arthur J. (1992). "Status, the Distribution of Wealth, Private and Social Attitudes to Risk, *Econometrica* 60:4 (July), pp. 837–857.

Roemer, John E. (1996). *Theories of Distributive Justice.* (Cambridge, Massachusetts: Harvard University Press).

Romer, Paul M. (1990). "Endogenous Technological Change" *Journal of Political Economy* 98:5, (October), pp. S71–S102.

Ronci, Marcio (2004). "Trade Finance and Trade Flows: Panel Data Evidence from 10 Crises", *IMF Working Paper 04/225* (International Monetary Fund, December), pp. 1–19.

Ross, Don (2005). *Economic Theory and Cognitive Science – Microexplanation.* (Cambridge, Mass.: MIT Press).

Rostow, W. W. (1964). *The Stages of Economic Growth – A Non-Communist Manifesto.* (Cambridge, U.K.: Cambridge University Press).

Roubini, Nouriel (2006, 2005). "Why Central Banks Should Burst Bubbles", *International Finance* 9:1.

Ruiz-Arranz, Marta, and Milan Zavadjil (2008). "Are Emerging Asia's Reserves Really Too High?" WP/08/192 (Washington, D.C.: International Monetary Fund Working Paper, August).

Sahm, Claudia R. (2007). "Stability of Risk Preference", *Finance and Economics Discussion Series Staff Working Paper,* (Washington, D.C.: Federal Reserve Board, October 26), pp. 1–43.

Salin, Pascal (2000). *Libéralisme.* (Paris: Éditions Odile Jacob.)

Samuelson, Paul A. (1977). "St. Petersburg Paradoxes: Defanged, Dissected, and Historically Described", *Journal of Economic Literature* 15:1 (March), pp. 24–55.

Santos, Manuel S., and Michael Woodford (1997). "Rational Asset Pricing Bubbles", *Econometrica* 65:1 (January), pp. 19–57.

Sarbanes-Oxley Act of 2002, Washington, D.C.: U.S. Congress, U.S. Government Printing Office.

Scheinkman, José A., and Wei Xiong (2005). "Overconfidence and Speculative Bubbles", *Journal of Political* Economy 11:6, pp. 1183–1219.

Schinasi, Garry J. (2004). "Defining Financial Stability", WP/04/187. (Washington, D.C.: Internaitonal Monetary Fund Working Paper, October).

Schmidt, Ulrich, and Horst Zank (2008). "Risk Aversion in Cumulative Prospect Theory", *Management Science* 54:1 (January), pp. 208–216.

Schularick, Moritz (2006). "Financial Globalization and Emerging Market Bond Price Bubbles: Some Historical Lessons", working paper (May), pp. 27.

Schulders, Guy (2016). *Les Dynamiques D'Émergence dans un Monde en Perpétuelle Mutation.* (Paris: L'Harmattan).

Schumpeter, Joseph A. (1967, 1961 1934). *The Theory of Economic Development.* (Cambridge, Massachusetts: Harvard University Press).

Schumpeter, Joseph A. (1968, 19551, 1951, 1927). *Imperialism and Social Classes.* (New York: Meridian Books of The World Publishing Company).

Schumpeter, Joseph A. (1962, 1947, 1942). *Capitalism, Socialism, and Democracy.* (New York: Harper and Row Publishers).

Schwarcz, Steven L. (2007). "Systemic Risk", testimony before the U.S. House of Representatives Committee on Financial Services (Washington, D.C.: AEI-Brookings Joint Center for Regulatory Studies, October), pp. 1–70.

Segoviano, Miguel A., and Manmohan Singh (2008) "Counterparty Risk in the Over-The-Counter Derivatives Market" WP/08/258. (Washington, D.C.: International Monetary Fund working Paper, November), pp. 1–19.

Sen, Amartya (1997, 1973). *On Economic Inequality.* (Oxford, U.K.: Clarendon Books, for Oxford University Press).

Sen, Amartya (1994). "The Formulation of Rational Choice", *American Economic Review*, Paper and Proceedings 84:2 (May), pp. 385–390.

Sen, Amartya (1997, 1984). *Resources Values, and Development.* (Cambridge, Massachusetts: Harvard University Press).

Shane, Frederick, George Loewenstein and Ted O'Donoghue (2002). "Time Discounting and Time Preference: A Critical Review, *Journal of Economic Literature* (June), pp. 351–401.

Shiller, Robert J. (2003). *The New Financial Order – Risk in the 21st Century.* (Princeton, New Jersey: Princeton University Press).

Shiller, Robert J. (2000). *Irrational Exuberance.* (Princeton, New Jersey: Princeton University Press).

Shiller, Robert J. (1990). "Speculative Prices and Popular Models", *Journal of Economic Perspectives* 4:2, pp. 55–63.

Shleifer, Andrei, and Lawrence H. Summers (1990). "the Noise Trader Approach to Finance", *Journal of Economic Perspectives* 4–2, pp. 19–33.

Shin, Hyun Song (2003). "Disclosures and Asset Returns", *Econometrica* 71:1 (January), pp. 105–133.

Shoven, John B. (2001). "What Are Reasonable Long-Run Rates of Return to Expect on Equities? (Stanford University Department of Economics).

Singh, Ajit and Jack Glen (2005). "Shareholder Value Maximisation, Stock Market and New Technology: Should the US Corporate Model be the Universal Standard?" (Cambridge, UK: University of Cambridge Center For Business Research Working Paper No. 315).

Singh, Raju Jan, Markus Haacker, and Kyung-woo Lee (2009). "Determinants and Macroeocnomic Impact of Remittances in Sub-Saharan Africa", WP/09/216 (Washington, D.C.: International Monetary Fund Working Paper, October), pp. 1–26.

Smith, Adam (2018, 2014, 1776). *An Inquiry into the Nature and Causes of Wealth Among Nations.* (New York: Shine Classics)

Smith, Vernon L. (2008). *Rationality in Economics – Constructivist and Ecological Forms.* (New York: Cambridge University Press).

Smith, Vernon L., Gerry L. Suchanek, and Arlington W. Williams (1988). "Bubbles, Crashes, and Endogenous Expectations in Experimental Spot Asset Markets", *Econometrica* 56:5 (September), pp. 1119–1151.

Spatafora, Nikola, and Irina Tytell (2009). "Commodity Terms of Trade: The History of Booms and Busts," WP/09/205. (Washington, D.C.: International Monetary Fund).

Sraffa, Piero (1960). *Production of Commodities by Means of Commodities – Prelude to a Critique of Economic Theory.* (New York: Cambridge University Press).

Starmer, Chris (2000). "Developments in Non-Expected Utility Theory: The Hunt for a Descriptive Theory of Choice under Risk", *Journal of Economic Literature* XXXVIII (June), pp. 332–382.

Stigler, George J. (1957). "Perfect Competition, Historically Contemplated". *Journal of Political Economy*, 65:1 (February), pp. 1–17.

Stiglitz, Joseph E. (1994). *Whither Socialism?* (Cambridge, Massachusetts: MIT Press).

Stiglitz, Joseph E. (1990). "Symposium on Bubbles", *Journal of Economic Perspectives* 4:2, pp. 13–18.

Stiglitz, Joseph E. (1987). "The Causes and Consequences of The Dependence of Quality on Price", *Journal of Economic Literature*, 25:1 (March), pp. 1–48.

Stone Mark R., and Ashok J. Bhundia (2004). "A New Taxonomy of Monetary Regimes" WP/04/191. (Washington, D.C.: International Monetary Fund Working Paper, October), pp. 1–43.

Summers, Lawrence H. (2000). "International Financial Crises: Causes, Prevention, and Cures", *American Economic Review* 90:2 (May), pp. 1–16.

Temin, Peter, and Hans-Joachim Voth (2004). "Riding the South Sea Bubble", *American Economic Review* 94:5 (December), pp. 1654–1668.

Thaler, Richard H. and Cass R. Sunstein (2009). *Nudge – Improving Decisions About Health, Wealth, and Happiness.* New York: Penguin Paperback Books)

Thorbecke, Willem (2005). "Monetary Policy and Asset Prices Bubbles", Working Paper (George Mason University).

Tieman, Alexander F., and Andrea M. Maechler (2009). "The Real Effects of Financial Sector Risk", Working Paper WP/09/198 (Washington, D.C.: International Monetary Fund, September).

Tirole, Jean (2017). *Economics for the Common Good.* (Princeton, New Jersey: Princeton University Press).

Tirole, Jean (1999). "Incomplete Contracts: Where Do We Stand?" *Econometrica* 67:4 (July), pp. 741–781.

Tirole, Jean (1985). "Asset Bubbles and Overlapping Generations", *Econometrica* 53:5 (September), pp. 1071–1100.

Tversky, Amos, and Daniel Kahneman (1992). "Advances in Prospect Theory: Cumulative Representation of Uncertainty", *Journal of Risk and Uncertainty* 5, pp. 297–323.

Tversky, Amos, and Daniel Kahneman (1986). "Rational Choice and the Framing of Decisions", *The Journal of Business* 56:4 (October), pp. S251-S278.

Tversky, Amos, and Daniel Kahneman (1981). "The Framing of Decisions and the Psychology of Choice", *Science* 211 (January 30).

Valderrama, Laura (2009). "Political Risk Aversion", WP/09/194. (Washington, D.C.: International Monetary Fund).

Von Mises, Ludwig (2013, 1912). *The Theory of Money and Credit.* (New York: Skyhorse Publishing).

Wachter, Susan M. (2005). "The Role of the GSEs in the Mortgage Market: Supporting Homeownership and Financial Stability", Testimony to the Committee on Banking, Housing, and Urban Affairs, U.S. Senate (February 10).

Wallison, Peter J. (2009). "The Price for Fannie and Freddie Keeps Going Up", The Wall Street Journal (December 29).

Wallison, Peter J. (2008). "The Last Trillion-Dollar Commitment: The Destruction of Fannie Mae and Freddie Mac", (Washington, D.C.: American Enterprise Institute, September), pp. 1–10.

Wallison, Peter J. (2007). "Don't Bail Out Fannie and Freddie", Opinion, *The Wall Street Journal* (November 29), P. A19.

Wallison, Peter J. (2005). "Regulating Fannie Mae and Freddie Mac – now Its Gets Serious", (Washington, D.C.: American Enterprise Institute).

Wang, Jiang (1993). "A Model of Intertemporal Asset Prices Under Asymmetric Information" *Review of Economic Studies* 60 (September), pp. 249–281.

Watkins, Thayer (2009). "Long-Term Capital Management", Application. (San José, California: San José State University).

Welch, Finis (1999). "In Defense of Inequality" *American Economic Review*, Papers and Proceedings, (May), pp. 1–17.

Wen, Yi, and George E. Fortier (2016). "The Visible Hand: The Role of Government in China's Long-Awaited Industrial Revolution", (St. Louis: Federal Reserve Bank of St. Louis Review, Third Quarter), pp. 189–226.

White, Eugene N. (1990). "The Stock Market Boom and Crash of 1929 Revisited", *Journal of Economic Perspectives,* 4:2, pp. 67–83.

White, Lawrence J. (2004). "Fannie Mae, Freddie Mac, and Housing Finance: Why True Privatization Is Good Public Policy". Policy Analysis, No. 528 (October 7). pp. 1–41.

Wilkinson, Nick (2008). *An Introduction to Behavioral Economics*. (New York: Palgrave Macmillan Publishing).

Williamson, Oliver E. (2004, 1996). *The Mechanisms of Governance*. (New York: Oxford University Press).

Woodford, Michael (1990). "Learning to Believe in Sunspots", *Econometrica* 55:2 (March), pp. 277–307.

History, Politics, and Social Affairs

Ahamed, Liaquat (2009). *Lords of Finance – The Bankers Who Broke the World*. (New York: Penguin Books)

Ajami, Fouad (1998). *The Dream Palace of the Arabs – A Generation's Odyssey*. (New York: Pantheon Books).

Ashburn, Percy Moreau (1980, 1947). *The Ranks of Death – A Medical History of the Conquest of America*. (Philadelphia, Pennsylvania: The Porcupine Press for Coward-McCann, Inc.).

Baer, Robert (2004, 2003). *Sleeping with the Devil – How Washington Sold Our Soul for Saudi Crude*. (New York: Three Rivers Press).

Bailyn, Bernard (2012). *The Barbarous Years – The People of British North America: The Conflict of Civilizations,1600–1675*. (New York Alfred A. Knopf)

Barry, John M. (2005, 2004). *The Great Influenza – The Epic Story of the Deadliest Plague in History*. (New York: Penguin Books)

Bartlett, Bruce (1994). "How Excessive Government Killed Ancient Rome", *Cato Journal* 14:2 (Fall), pp. 287–303.

Beard, Mary (2015). *SPQR – A History of Ancient Rome*. (Liverlight Publishing Corporation, Division of W.W. Norton and Company).

Berman, Paul (2003). *Terror and Liberalism*. (New York: W.W. Norton and Company).

Bernanke, Ben S., Timothy Geithner, and Henry M. Paulson, Jr. (2019). *Firefighting – The Financial Crisis and Its Lessons*. (New York: Penguin Books for Random House).

Bernstein, Peter L. (2005). *Capital Ideas – The Improbable Origins of Modern Wall Street*. (New York: W.W. Norton and Company)

Bernstein, Peter L. (1998, 1996). *Against the Gods – The Remarkable Story of Risk*. (New York: W.W. Norton and Company)

Booth, William James (1994). "On the Idea of the Moral Economy", *American Political Science Review* 88:3 (September), pp. 653–667.

Bradley, James (2009). *The Imperial Cruise – A Secret History of Empire and War*. (Boston: Back Bay Books for Little Brown and Company).

Byers, Michael (2005). *War Law – Understanding International Law and Armed Conflict*. (New York: Grove Press).

Caro, Robert A. (2002). *The Years of Lyndon Johnson – Master of the Senate*. (New York: Alfred A. Knopf).

Caro, Robert A. (1990). *The Years of Lyndon Johnson – Means of Ascent*. (New York: Vintage Books for Random House Publishers).

Caro, Robet A. (1982, 1981). *The Years of Lyndon Johnson – The Path to Power*. (New York: Vintage Books for Random House Publishers).

Chomsky, Noam (2000). *Rogue States The Rule of Force in World Affairs*. (Cambridge, Mass.: South End Press).

Croston, Glenn (2012). *The Real Story of Risk – Adventures in a Hazardous World*. (Amherst, New York: Prometheus Books).

Dash, Mike (1999). *Tulipomania – The Story of the World' Most Coveted Flower and the Extraordinary Passions It Aroused*. (New York: Three Rivers Press).

Djilas, Milovan (1969, 1957). *The New Class – An Analysis of the Communist System*. (New York: Praeger Publishers).

Fisk, Robert (2006). *The Great War for Civilisation – The Conquest of the Middle East*. (New York: Alfred A. Knopf).

Foucault, Michel (1973, 1965). *Madness and Civilization – A History of Insanity in the Age of Reason* (New York: Vintage Books).

Fox, Justin (2009). *The Myth of the Rational Market – A History of Risk, Reward, and Delusion on Wall Street*. (New York: HarperCollins Publishing).

Gaibulloev, Khusrav, and Todd Sandler (2019). "What We Have Learned About Terrorism since 9/11", *Journal of Economic Literature* 57:2, pp. 275–328.

Gates, Henry Louis, Jr. (2012, 1987). *The Classic Slave Narratives – The Life of Olaudah Equiano, The History of Mary Prince, Narrative of the Life of Frederick Douglass, Incidents in the Life of a Slave Girl.* (New York: Signet Classics for the New American Library division of Random House).

Garrett, Laurie (1994). *The Coming Plague – Newly Emerging Diseases in a World Out of Balance.* (New York: Penguin Books).

Genovese, Eugene D. (1965, 1961). *The Political Economy of Slavery.* (New York: Vintage Books for Random House).

Gerges, Fawaz A. (2017, 2016). *A History of ISIS.* (Princeton, N.J.: Princeton University Press).

Goldsworthy, Adrian (2016). Pax Romana – *War, Peace and Conquest in the Roman World.* (New Haven, Connecticut: Yale University Press).

Goldsworthy, Adrian (2004, 2003). *In the Name of Rome – The Men Who Won the Roman Empire.* (London: Phoenix Books for Orion Books and Weidenfeld and Nicholson).

Gibbon, Edward (1985, 1952, 1788). *The Decline and Fall of the Roman Empire.* (New York: Penguins Books).

Harari, Yuval Noah (2018, 2017). *Homo Deus - A Brief History of Tomorrow.* (New York: Harper Perennial Paper editions).

Hourani, Albert (1991). *A History of The Arab Peoples.* (New York: MJF Books).

Huillery, Elise (2009). "History Matters: The Long-Term Impact of Colonial Public Investments in French West Africa" *American Economics Journal* 1:2, pp. 170–215.

Huntington, Samuel P. (2003, 1996). *The Clash of Civilizations and the Remaking of World Order.* (New York: Simon and Schuster Paper editions).

Kagan, Robert (2012). *The World America Made.* (New York: Alfred A. Knopf)

Karnow, Stanley (1983). *Vietnam – A History – The First Complete Account of Vietnam at War.* (New York: Viking Press).

Kennedy, Paul (1989, 1987). *The Rise and Fall of the Great Powers*. (New York: Vintage Books for Random House).

Kershaw, Stephen P. (2013). *A Brief History of the Roman Empire – Rise and Fall*. (New York: Little Brown Publishers).

Khalili, Jim Al (2011). *The House of Wisdom – How Arabic Science Saved Ancient Knowledge and Gave Us the Renaissance* (New York: The Penguin Press).

Kindleberger, Charles P. (1996, 1989, 1978). *Manias, Panics, and Crashes – A History of Financial Crises*. (New York: John Wiley and Sons).

Larson, Kate Clifford (2003). *Harriet Tubman – Portrait of an American Hero – Bound for the Promised Land*. (New York: One World Books for Random Housing Publishing).

Lewis, Bernard (2003). *The Crisis of Islam – Holy War and Unholy Terror*. (New York: Modern Library).

Lewis, Bernard (2002). *What Went Wrong? – Western Impact and Middle Eastern Response*. (New York: Oxford University Press).

Lyons, Jonathan (2009). *The House of Wisdom – How the Arabs Transformed Western Civilization*. (New York: Bloomsbury Press).

Mackay, Charles (1980, 1841). *Extraordinary Popular Delusions, and the Madness of Crowds*. (New York: Three Rivers Press).

Macmillan, Margaret (2002, 2001). *Paris 1919 – Six Months That Changed the World*. (New York: Random House).

Malvazzi, Aldobrandino (1927). "Italian Colonies and Colonial Policy" *Journal of the royal Institute of International Affairs* 6:4 (July), pp. 233–245.

Markoe, Glenn E. (2000). *The Phoenicians*. (Berkeley, California: University of California Press).

McDermott, Rose, James H. Fowler, and Oleg Smirnov (2008). "On the Evolutionary Origin of Prospect Theory Preferences", *The Journal of Politics* 70:2 (April), 335–350.

Miles, Richard (2011). *Carthage Must Be Destroyed – The Rise and Fall of an Ancient Civilization*. (New York: Penguin Group for Viking Press).

Morgan, David (2007, 1990, 1986). *The Mongols*. (Malden, Massachusetts: Blackwell Publishing).

Muller, Jerry Z. (2002). *The Mind and the Market – Capitalism in Western Thought.* (New York: Anchor Books for Random House Publishers).

Nau, Henry R. (1992, 1990). *The Myth of America's Decline – Leading the World Economy into the 1990s.* (New York: Oxford University Press).

Newhouse, John (2003). *Imperial America – The Bush Assault on the World Order.* (New York: Alfred A. Knopf).

Rai, Milan (2002). *War Plan – Ten Reasons Against War on Iraq.* (New York: Verso Books).

Raspail, Jean (1995, 1987, 1975). *The Camp of the Saints.* (Petoskey, Michigan: The Social Contract Press).

Riley, Dylan, and Rebecca Jean Emigh (2002). "Post-Colonial Journeys: Historical Roots of Immigration and Integration ", *Comparative Sociology* 1:2, pp. 169–190.

Saïd, Edward (2007, 1992, 1978). *Orientalism.* (New York: Vintage Books, A Division of Random House).

Scheidel, Walter (2017). The Great Leveler – *Violence and the History of Inequality from the Stone Age to the Twenty-First Century.* (Princeton, New Jersey: Princeton University Press).

Schlesinger, Arthur Jr. (1962, 1945). *The Age of Jackson.* (New York: Mentor Books for the New American Library).

Shinn, David H. (2009). "The Intensity, Spread and Economics of Somali Piracy", Presentation at the Harvard Kennedy School on Controlling Maritime Piracy (December 10–12).

Silber, William L. (2019). *The Story of Silver – How the White Metal Shaped America and the Modern World.* (Princeton, New Jersey: Princeton University Press).

Soloway, Richard A. (1995, 1990). *Demography and Degeneration – Eugenics and the Declining Birthrate in Twentieth Century Britain.* (Chapel Hill, North Carolina: University of North Carolina Press).

Unger, Craig (2004). *House of Bush, House of Saud – The Secret Relationship Between the World' Two Most Powerful Dynasties.* (New York: Scribner for Simon and Schuster).

Wallerstein, Immanuel (2003). *The Decline of American Power* (New York: The New Press for W.W. Norton and Company).

White, Trumbull (1898). *Pictorial History of Our War with Spain for Cuba's Freedom.* (New York: Freedom Publishing Company)

Yoo, John (2006). *War by Other Means – An Insider's Account of the War on Terror.* (New York: Atlantic Monthly Press).

Zinn, Howard (2005, 2001, 1999). *A People's History of the United States.* (New York: Harper Perennial for Harper Collins).

Neuro, Social, and Natural Science

Ariely, Dan (2010). *The Upside of Irrationality – The Unexpected Benefits of Defying Logic.* (New York: Harper Perennial for HarperCollins Publishing).

Bargh, John (2017). *Before You Know It – The Unconscious Reasons We Do What We do.* (New York: Touchstone Books for Simon and Schuster).

Brooks, David (2011). *The Social Animal – The Hidden Sources of Love, Character, and Achievement.* (New York: Random House).

Buchanan, James M., and Gordon Tullock (1971, 1965, 1962). *The Calculus of Consent – Logical Foundations of Constitutional Democracy.* (Ann Arbor, Michigan: University of Michigan Press).

Caplan, Bryan (2007). *The Myth of the Rational Voter – Why Democracies Choose Bad Policies.* (Princeton, N.J.: Princeton University Press).

Carson, Rachel (1962). *Silent Spring.* (New York: Crest Books for Houghton Mifflin Publishers).

Collins, James P. and Martha L. Crump (2009). *Extinction In Our Times – Global Amphibian Decline.* (New York: Oxford University Press).

Gladwell, Malcolm (2005). *Blink – The Power of Thinking Without Thinking.* (Boston: Back Bay Books for Little Brown and Company).

Gladwell, Malcolm (2002, 2000). *The Tipping Point – How Little Things Can Make a Big Difference.* (Boston: Back Bay Books for Little Brown and Company).

IPCC (various authors). Global Warming of 1.5 Degrees Celsius – An IPCC Special Report on the Impacts of Global Warming of 1.5 Degrees Celsius. https://www.ipcc.ch/sr15/

Judis, John B. (2007). "How Political Psychology Explains Bush's Ghastly Success", *The New Republic* (August 17).

Kahneman, Daniel (2011). *Thinking, Fast and Slow.* (New York: Farrar, Straus, and Giroux).

Kahneman, Daniel, Paul Slovic, and Amos Tversky (1988, 1985, 1984, 1982). *Judgment Under Uncertainty – Heuristics and Biases.* (New York: Cambridge University Press).

Kourilsky, Philippe et Geneviève Viney (2000, 1999). *Le Principe de Précaution.* (Paris: La Documentation française, Édtions Odile Jacob).

Lakoff, George (2006) *Moral Politics – How Liberals and Conservatives Think.* (Chicago: University of Chicago Press).

McKibben, Bill (2006, 1989). *The End of Nature.* (New York: Random House Trade Paperback Editions).

Perrings, Charles, Karl-Göran Mäle, Carl Folke, C.S. Holling, Bengt-Owe Jansson (1997, 1995). *Biodiversity Loss – Economic and Ecological Issues.* (New York: Cambridge University Press).

Pinker, Steven (2018). *Enlightenment Now – The Case for Reason, Science, Humanism, and Progress.* (New York: Penguin Books).

Rayner, John N. (2001). *Dynamic Climatology – Basis in Mathematics and Physics.* (New York: Blackwell Publishers).

Rieger, Marc Oliver (2010, 2007). "Too Risk-Averse for Prospect Theory", University of Trier (June 21, 2007).

Sapolsky, Robert M. (2017). *Behave – The Biology of Humans at Our Best and Worst.* (New York: Penguin Press).

Seung, Sebastian (2012). *Connectome – How the Brain's Wiring Makes Us Who We Are.* (New York: Houghton Mifflin Harcourt).

Shermer, Michael (2008). *The Mind of the Market – Compassionate Apes, Competitive Humans, and Other Tales from Evolutionary Economics.* (New York: Times Books for Henry Holt and Company).

Smiley, Gene (2009). "The U.S. Economy in the 1920s" (Economic History Net).

Thaler, Richard H. (2015). *Misbehaving – The Making of Behavioral Economics.* (New York: W.W. Norton and Company).

Tirole, Jean (1999). "Incomplete Contracts: Where Do We Stand?" *Econometrica* 67:4 (July), pp. 741–781.

Vedantam, Shankar (2010). *The Hidden Brain – How Our Unconscious Minds Elect Presidents, Control Markets, Wage Wars, and Save our Lives.* (New York: Spiegel and Grau).

Whybrow, Peter C. (2015). *The Well-Tuned Brain – Neuroscience and the Life Well Lived* (New York: W.W. Norton and Company).

Wilson, Edward O. (2012). *The Social Conquest of Earth.* (New York: Liverlight Publishing Corporation for W.W. Norton And Company)

Politics and Political Philosophy

Anderson, Perry (2007, 2005). *Spectrum – From Right to Left in the World of Ideas.* (New York: Verso Books).

Arendt, Hannah (1968, 1951). *Imperialism – Part Two of The Origins of Totalitarianism.* (New York: Harvest Books for Harcourt, Brace and World, Inc).

Audard, Catherine (2009). *Qu'est-ce que le libéralisme – Éthique, politique, société.* (Paris: Éditions Gallimard).

Bentham, Jeremy (1987, 1789, 1780). *Utilitarianism and Other Essays.* (New York: Penguin Paperback Books).

Bernstein, Carl, and Bob Woodward (2014, 1974). *All the President's Men.* (New York: Simon and Schuster Paperbacks).

Bourdieu, Pierre (2000). *Les Structures Sociales de l'Économie.* (Paris: Editions du Seuil).

Brambrough, Renford (2011). *The Philosophy of Aristotle.* (New York: Signet Classics).

Brennan, Stephen (2011). *The U.S. Constitution and Related Documents.* (New York: Skyhorse Publishing).

Burgogue-Larsen, Laurence, Anne Levade, et Fabrice Picod. (2005). *La Constitution européenne expliquée au citoyen.* (Paris: Hachette Littéraires).

Chomsky, Noam (2007, 2006). Failed States – *The Abuse of Power and the Assault on Democracy.* (New York: Henry Holt and Company).

Cicero, Marcus Tullius (1998, 54BCE). *The Republic and the Laws,* translated by Niall Rudd. (New York: Oxford University Press).

Clark, Ian (2005). *Legitimacy in International Society.* (New York: Oxford University Press).

Cochrane, Feargal, Rosaleen Duffy and Jan Selby, editors (2003). *Global Governance, Conflict and Resistance.* (New York: Palgrave Macmillan)

Conn, Steven (2012). *To Promote the General Welfare – The Case for Big Government.* (New York: Oxford University Press).

De Tocqueville, Alexis (2000, 1835). *Democracy in America.* (New York: Bantam Books).

Everitt, Anthony (2003). *Cicero – The Life and Times of Rome's Greatest Politician.* (New York: Random House).

Fanon, Frantz (2005, 1961). *The Wretched of the Earth.* (New York: Amazon Books).

Ferguson, Niall (2002). *Empire – The Rise and Demise of the British World Order and the Lessons for Global Power.* (New York: Basic Books).

Fukuyama, Francis (2018). Identity – *The Demand for Dignity and the Politics of Resentment.* (New York: Farrar, Straus, and Giroux).

Fukuyama, Francis (2014). *Political Order and Political Decay – From the Industrial Revolution to the Globalization of Democracy* (New York: Farrar, Straus, and Giroux).

Fukuyama, Francis (2011). *The Origins of Political Order – From Prehuman Times to the French Revolution.* (New York: Farrar, Straus, and Giroux).

Gilder, George (2012, 1981). *Wealth and Poverty.* (Washington, D.C.: Regnery Publishing)

Goldwater, Barry (1960). *The Conscience of a Conservative.* (Princeton, New Jersey: Princeton University Press).

Goldsmith, Jack L. and Eric A. Posner (2005). *The Limits of International Law.* (New York: Oxford University Press).

Grotius, Hugo (1625). On the Rights of War and Peace, in Which are Explained The Laws and Claims of Nature and Nations, and the Principal Points that Relate Either to Publick Government, or the Conduct of Private Life, vols. 1–3.

https://play.google.com/store/books/details/H_Grotius_Of_the_Rights_of_War_and_Peace_In_which_?id=Ohk2AQAAMAAJ&hl=sw

Habermas, Jürgen (1975, 1973). *Legitimation Crisis.* (Boston, Massachusetts: Beacon Books).

Hacker, Jacob S. (2006). *The Great Risk Shift – The Assault on American Jobs, Families, Health Care, and Retirement and How You Can Fight Back.* New York: Oxford University Press).

Hardt, Michael and Antonio Negri (2004). *Multitude – War and Democracy in the Age of Empire.* (New York: Penguin Books).

Hazony, Yoram (2018). *The Virtue of Nationalism.* (New York: Basic Books).

Held, David, editor (1993, 1992). *Prospects for Democracy.* (Palo Alto, California: Stanford University Press).

Hiskes, Richard P. (1998). *Democracy, Risk, and Community – Technological Hazards and the Evolution of Liberalism.* (New York: Oxford University Press).

Hobbes, Thomas (2017, 1651). *Leviathan.* (New York: Penguin Classics Paper edition).

Hodgson, Godfrey (2009). *The Myth of American Exceptionalism.* (New Haven, Connecticut: Yale University Press).

Ignatieff, Michael (1985, 1984). *The Needs of Strangers – An essay on privacy, solidarity, and the politics of being human.* (New York: Penguin Paperback Books).

Kagan, Robert (2003). *Of Paradise and Power – America and Europe in the New World Order.* (New York: Alfred A. Knopf).

Kauffman, Bill (2016). *America First! – Its History, Culture, and Politics.* (New York: Prometheus Books).

Kaufmann, Karen M., John R. Petrocik, and Daron R. Shaw (2008). *Unconventional Wisdom – Facts and Myths About American Voters.* (New York: Oxford University Press).

Kinzer, Stephen (2006). *Overthrow – America's Century of Regime Change from Hawaii to Iraq*. (New York: Times Books for Henry Holt and Company).

Kissinger, Henry (2014). *World Order*. (New York: Penguin Press).

Krugman, Paul (2009, 2007). *The Conscience of a Liberal*. (New York: W.W. Norton and Company).

Lakoff, George (2006). *Whose Freedom – The Battle Over America's Most Important Idea*. (New York: Picador Books for Farrar, Straus, and Giroux).

Lenin, Vladimir (2008, 1916). *Imperialism, the Highest Stage of Capitalism*. (Delhi, India: Leopard Books).

Lenin, Vladimir (1943, 1932). *State and Revolution*. (New York: International Publishers).

Levin, Mark R. (2019). *Unfreedom of the Press*. (New York: Threshold Editions for Simon and Schuster).

Levin, Mark R. (2015). *Plunder and Deceit – Big Government's Exploitation of Young People and the Future*. (New York: Threshold Editions for Simon and Schuster).

Lofgren, Mike. (2016). *The Deep State – The Fall of the Constitution and the Rise of a Shadow Government*. (New York: Viking, an Imprint of Penguin Random House).

Machiavelli, Niccolo (2014, 1513). *The Prince*. (New York: Amazon Books).

Manicas, Peter T. (1974). *The Death of the State*. (New York: Capricorn Books for G.P. Putnam's Sons).

Marx, Karl and Friedrich Engels (2015, 1848). *The Communist Manifesto*. (New York: Soho Books)

Meegan, Dan (2019). *America the Fair: Using Brain Science to Create a More Just Nation*. (Ithaca, New York: Cornell University Press).

Mill, John Stuart (2015, 1859). *On Liberty*. (New York: Oxford University Press).

Montesquieu, Baron (1989, 1748). *The Spirit of the Laws*. (New York: Oxford University Press Paperback edition).

Mooney, Chris (2006, 2005). *The Republican War on Science*, revised edition. (New York: Perseus Books for Basic Books).

Muller, Robert (2019). *The Mueller Report*. (New York: Scribner, an imprint of Simon and Schuster).

Niemi, Richard, and William F. Riker (1976). "The Choice of Voting Systems". *Scientific American* 234:6 (June), pp. 21–27.

Nozick, Robert (1974). *Anarchy, State, and Utopia*. (New York: Basic Books).

Ofuatey-Kodjoe, Wentworth (1977). *The Principle of Self-Determination in International Law*. (New York: Nellen Publishing Company).

Orwell, George (1977, 1961, 1950). *1984*. (New York: Signet Classics, New American Library, for the Penguin Group).

Paxton, Robert O. (2004). *The Anatomy of Fascism* (New York: Alfred A. Knopf).

Poulantzas, Nicos (1978, 1974). *Classes in Contemporary Capitalism*. (London, U.K.: Verso Books)

Plutarch, Lucius Mestrius (1960, ca. 60 CE). *The Rise and Fall of Athens – Nine Greek Lives*, translated by Ian Scott-Kivert. (New York: Penguin Books).

Przeworski, Adam (2019). *Crises of Democracy*. (London: Cambridge University Press).

Quattrone, George A., and Amos Tversky (1988). "Contrasting Rational and Psychological Analyses of Political Choice", *American Political Science Review* 82:3 (September), pp. 719–736.

Rawls, John (1971). *A Theory of Justice*. (Cambridge, Massachusetts: Harvard University Press).

Renmin Ribau (People's Daily) (1965). *The Leaders of the CPSU Are Betrayers of the Declaration and The Statement*. (Peking: Foreign Languages Press).

Rousseau, Jean-Jacques (2014, 1762). *The Social Contract*. (New York: First Rate Publishers).

Ruse, Austin (2017). *Fake Science – Exposing the Left's Skewed Statistics, Fuzzy Facts, and Dodgy Data*. (New York: Regnery Publishing)

Sheehan, Neil, E. W. Kenworthy, Fox Butterfield, and Hedrick Smith (2017, 1971). *The Pentagon Papers – The Secret History of the Vietnam War*. (New York: Racehorse Publishing)

Smith, Adam (2010, 1759). *The Theory of Moral Sentiments*. (New York: Amazon Books).

Stiglitz, Joseph E. (2003, 2002). *Globalization and Its Discontents.* (New York: W.W. Norton and Company).

Strauss, Leo, and Joseph Cropsey (1987, 1972, 1963). *History of Political Philosophy*, Third edition. (Chicago: University of Chicago Press)

Suetonius (2007, 1957, 121CE). *The Twelve Caesars*, translated by Robert Graves. (New York: Penguin Books)

Tacitus (1964, 105 CE). *The Histories*, translation by Kenneth Wellesley. (New York: Penguin Classics).

Thompson, J. A. K. (1963). *Aristotle – The Nichomachaen Ethics*. (London, U.K.: Penguin Publishers).

Trento, Joseph J. (2001). *The Secret History of the CIA*. (Roseville, California: Forum Books, for Prima Publishing, member of Crown Publishing, a division of Random House, Inc.)

Trotsky, Leon (1972, 1937). *The Revolution Betrayed – What is The Soviet Union and Where Is It Going?* (New York: Pathfinder Press).

Van Rooy, Alison (2004). *The Global Legitimacy Game – Civil Society, Globalization, and Protest*. (New York: Palgrave Macmillan).

Walzer, Michael (2006, 1977). *Just and Unjust Wars – A Moral Argument with Historical Illustrations*. (New York: Basic Books).

Wolf, Michael (2018). *Fire and Fury – Inside the Trump White House*. (Henry Holt and Company).

Woodward, Bob (2018). *Fear – Trump in the White House*. (New York: Simon and Schuster Publishers).

Zakaria, Fareed (2003). *The Future of Freedom – Illiberal Democracy at Home and Abroad*. (New York: W.W. Norton and Company)

INDEX